Wittgenstein's Ladder

Wittgenstein's Ladder

Poetic Language and the Strangeness of the Ordinary

Marjorie Perloff

The University of Chicago Press   *Chicago and London*

Marjorie Perloff is the Sadie Dernham Patek Professor of Humanities at Stanford University. She is the author of *The Futurist Moment* and *Radical Artifice* and the coeditor of *John Cage: Composed in America*, all published by the University of Chicago Press.

The University of Chicago Press, Chicago 60637
The University of Chicago Press, Ltd., London
© 1996 by The University of Chicago
All rights reserved. Published 1996
Printed in the United States of America
05 04 03 02 01 00 99 98 97 96   1 2 3 4 5

ISBN: 0-226-66058-3 (cloth)

Perloff, Marjorie.
    Wittgenstein's ladder : poetic language and the strangeness of
the ordinary / Marjorie Perloff.
        p.   cm.
    Includes bibliographical references and index.
        1. Wittgenstein, Ludwig, 1889–1951—Contributions in
criticism.   2. Literature—Philosophy.   3. Criticism.   I. Title.
PN49.P413   1996
809'.04—dc20   95-47873
                                                        CIP

Portions of chapter 1 appeared in *Common Knowledge* 2, no. 1 (Spring 1993): 15–34, and in *Intimate Enemies: English and German Literary Reactions to the Great War 1914–1918*, ed. F. K. Stanzel and Martin Loschnigg (Heidelberg: Carl Winter, 1993): 493–516. Chapter 2 is a revised version of "From Theory to Grammar," which appeared in *New Literary History* 25, no. 4 (Autumn 1994): 899–921. Reprinted by permission of The Johns Hopkins University Press. Part of chapter 5 appeared in *Sulfur* 32. Portions of chapter 6 were published in *Contemporary Literature* 33, no. 2 (Summer 1992). Copyright 1992. Reprinted by permission of The University of Wisconsin.

⊗ The paper used in this publication meets the minimum requirements of the American National Standard for Information Sciences—Permanence of Paper for Printed Library Materials, ANSI Z39.48-1984.

contents

illustrations

BB   *The Blue and Brown Books, Preliminary Studies for the "Philo-sophical Investigations,"* 2d. ed. (New York: Harper and Row, 1965).

CV   *Culture and Value,* ed. G. H. von Wright, in collaboration with Heikki Nyman; trans. Peter Winch (Chicago: University of Chicago Press, 1980).

LCA   *Lectures and Conversations on Aesthetics, Psychology and Religious Belief,* compiled from notes taken by Yorick Smythies, Rush Rhees, and James Taylor; ed. Cyril Barrett (Berkeley and Los Angeles: University of California Press, n.d.).

LEC1   *Wittgenstein's Lectures: Cambridge, 1930–32,* from the notes of John King and Desmond Lee; ed. Desmond Lee (Chicago: University of Chicago Press, 1980).

LEC2   *Wittgenstein's Lectures: Cambridge, 1932–1935,* from the Notes of Alice Ambrose and Margaret Macdonald; ed. Alice Ambrose (Chicago: University of Chicago Press, 1979).

NBK   *Notebooks 1914–1916,* 2d ed., ed. G. H. von Wright and G. E. M. Anscombe (1961; Chicago and London: University of Chicago Press, 1979).

OC   *On Certainty,* ed. G. E. M. Anscombe and G. H. von Wright; trans. Denis Paul and G. E. M. Anscombe (New York and London: Harper and Row, 1969).

PI   *Philosophical Investigations,* 3d ed., trans. G. E. M. Anscombe (New York: Macmillan, 1958).

PO   *Philosophical Occasions 1912–1951,* ed. James Klagge and Alfred Nordmann (Indianapolis and Cambridge: Hackett, 1993).

PR   *Philosophical Remarks* (Chicago: University of Chicago Press, 1975).

SCH   *Schriften: Tractatus logico-philosophicus, Tagebücher 1914–1916; Philosophische Untersuchungen* (Frankfurt: Suhrkamp, 1960).

T   *Tractatus Logico-Philosophicus,* trans. C. K. Ogden, with an introduction by Bertrand Russell (1922; London and New York: Routledge, 1988).

Z   *Zettel,* ed. G. E. M. Anscombe and G. H. von Wright, trans. G. E. M. Anscombe (Berkeley and Los Angeles: University of California Press, 1967).

This book is probably more personal than any of my others. Not that I have written some sort of autobiographical memoir, but *Wittgenstein's Ladder* does mark a return, however circuitously via Gertrude Stein and Samuel Beckett, and via American radical poetries and conceptual art of the late twentieth century, to the Vienna of my childhood, which was still in large measure Wittgenstein's Vienna. My intellectual, upper-middle-class family was hardly in the league of the super-wealthy Wittgensteins, but Ludwig's second cousin Friedrich von Hayek was, like my father, Maximilian Mintz, a member of the so-called Geist Kreis, which met once a month to read work-in-progress to one another and counted among its members Eric Voegelin, Alfred Schütz, Felix Kaufmann, Emmanuel Winternitz, and Fritz Machlup—all of whom were to make major names for themselves in various intellectual disciplines relating to philosophy.

Transported to the U.S. in 1938 as a refugee from Hitler, and growing up in very different circumstances in the Bronx, I wanted for a good part of my life to get away from the Germanic culture of those Austrian visitors who came for *Jause* (open-faced sandwiches, little cakes, coffee rather than cocktails) to our small apartment on Oxford Avenue in Riverdale. Indeed, my brother Walter and I rebelled against having to speak German at home, balked at having Schiller's *Wallenstein* and Goethe's *Götz von Berlichingen* read to us by my great-grandmother, and when my grandmother took me to see my first opera, *Lohengrin,* when I was twelve, I was mortified because she spoke what seemed like very loud German on the subway. By the time we filed for our citizenship papers in 1944, I wanted nothing so much as to be a typical American teenager. I even changed my name from Gabriele (I had been named for the writer Gabriele von Bülow) to Marjorie, which was the name of the most popular girl in my class at the Fieldston School.

When, after graduate school, I began to write about modern poetry, I chose subjects about as far removed from Wittgenstein's Vienna (or even his Cambridge) as possible: the Anglo-Irish W. B. Yeats, the "Mayflower screwball" Robert Lowell, the Irish-American, Catholic, gay poet Frank O'Hara. It was not until the late seventies, when I was working on *The Poetics of Indeterminacy: Rimbaud to Cage,* that I began to take an interest in Wittgenstein's *Tractatus,* and even then, the poet Joan Retallack, who wrote a long and telling review-essay on my book in conjunction with Cage's own writings for *Parnassus,* pointed out that I had misunderstood the famous proposition #7, "Whereof one cannot speak, thereof one must be silent." But having said this, Retallack (who had majored in philosophy) went on to suggest just how apropos Wittgenstein's writings were to the concerns of Cage as of Gertrude Stein and other avant-gardists. And so she planted the seeds for an investigation I was to follow years later.

At the annual meeting of the Western Humanities Institute held at Berkeley in October 1984, Jerome J. McGann organized a session called "The Idea of Poetry, the Poetry of Ideas." The speakers were David Antin, Charles Bernstein, and Catharine R. Stimpson. Stimpson spoke on Gertrude Stein's language in relation to gender, emphasizing the inextricability of theory and practice in Stein's work. Bernstein delivered "Living Tissue/Dead Ideas," an eloquent attack on the then current orthodoxy of using literary texts as so many "examples of literary theory." A great critic like Walter Benjamin, Bernstein argued, is himself primarily to be understood as a writer, the contradictions of whose style are not just to be explained away. When "Living Tissues / Dead Ideas" was published two years later in Bernstein's *Content's Dream* (Los Angeles: Sun & Moon, 1986), it appeared side by side with another essay called "The Objects of Meaning: Reading [Stanley] Cavell Reading Wittgenstein," which can be read as a manifesto for the notion that "the activity of knowing ... has its meaning only in use in the context of a language" (*Content's Dream,* p. 170), that there is no "object" of knowledge "outside of the 'language games' of which it is a part," but that, contra Derrida, "In Wittgenstein's accounting, one is not left sealed off from the world with only 'markings' to 'decipher' but rather *located* in a world with meanings to *respond to*"

(p. 181). Interestingly, this notion was borne out by David Antin's improvisational lecture, unfortunately still not available in print, which made a remarkable case for Wittgenstein's own "poetry of ideas," for the extreme elusiveness, strangeness, and "poeticity" of the numbered aphorisms that constitute the *Tractatus*. "The world is everything that is the case" ("Die Welt ist alles, was der Fall ist"): Antin asked us with mock-serious panache, what can this gnomic opening proposition of the *Tractatus* possibly mean?

The Berkeley session marked the beginning of a decade in which more and more poets, novelists, dramatists, and artists were turning out works that were done, whether explicitly or implicitly, under the sign of Wittgenstein. I discuss the range of these works in the introduction, but I cannot catch up with their ongoing proliferation. At this writing, for example, a traveling exhibition of Bruce Naumann's work is featuring such explicitly Wittgensteinian works as the neon tubing piece *One Hundred Live and Die* (1984). And the Wittgensteiniana of the eighties culminated in the 1990 publication of a book to which I owe a very great debt, Ray Monk's brilliant, engaging, and deeply moving biography *Ludwig Wittgenstein: The Duty of Genius*.

One of the beautiful ironies inherent in the story Monk tells (but which, as someone writing explicitly as a philosopher, he does not develop) is that Wittgensteinian practice (for there is, as we shall see, no systematic philosophy in his work) provides us with access to some of the most enigmatic poetries and artworks of the later twentieth century— works Wittgenstein himself would no doubt have dismissed as so much "Hundedreck." His own taste was for the classics of the previous century—Mozart, Beethoven, Goethe, Grillparzer—and by the late thirties, when he was writing the *Philosophical Investigations,* he had no doubt that a culture propitious to the making of art no longer existed. An art of everyday life? Absurd! Especially since Wittgenstein was producing it himself in notebook after notebook.

In reading these many notebooks and lecture transcriptions by his students, I found myself grateful that I had, after all, "kept up my German," as my parents had insisted. For Wittgenstein's translators have managed to transform his colloquial, idiomatic, and eminently "natural" idiom into the stilted, awkward locutions of the ill-at-ease Cambridge don who hasn't quite mastered the decorum of the Common Room. As an Englishman, Wittgenstein cuts a rather absurd figure (witness the Derek Jarman film!); as an Austrian, however, he is, by the late twenties, equally out of place. He is an exile from both sides of the Anglo-German divide. Even the beautiful house he designed for his sister Gretl on the Kundmanngasse in Vienna testifies to that exile: it is now the Bulgarian Cultural Institute, and when I went to see it in 1993, there were big red graffiti on the outer garden walls. "Graffiti!" Wittgenstein would have exclaimed. "How disgusting!" And yet, graffiti artists of our day have paid homage to Wittgenstein as one of their own.

Why should this be the case? On the final page of the *Tractatus* (#6.54), we read:

> My propositions are elucidatory in this way: he who understands me finally recognizes them as senseless, when he has climbed out through them, on them, over them. (He must so to speak throw away the ladder, after he has climbed up on it.)

This famous metaphor, which has given me my title, contains in embryo three critical aspects of what I take to be a distinctively Wittgensteinian poetics. First, its *dailyness:* for Dante's purgatorial staircase, for Yeats's "ancient winding stair," Wittgenstein substitutes a mere ladder—a ladder, moreover, whose origin (unlike that of the ladder in Yeats's "Circus Animals' Desertion") is as equivocal as its destination. Second, the movement "up" the ladder can never be more than what Gertrude Stein called "Beginning again and again"—a climbing "through," "on," and "over" its rungs that is never finished. Hence Wittgenstein's suspicion of generalization, of metalanguage, indeed of *theory* itself as an imposition on *practice.*

And third—and most important—one cannot (shades of Heraclitus!) climb the same ladder twice. Which is to say that each philosophical "proposition," however much it depends on the propositions that have laid its foundations, always bears some sign of difference, even if the exact same words are repeated in the same order. Repetition, after all, always entails a shift in context as well as in use.

There is, in other words, no vision—only revision—both for Wittgenstein himself and for his reader. And in the course of the climbing that occurs, the rungs of the language ladder manifest their inherent strangeness. It is the strangeness of the language we actually use—Wittgenstein's own language and that of the poets and artists who have climbed through, on, and over the rungs of his ladder—that is my subject.

Some of the following chapters have been tried out at conferences in the U.S. and abroad, specifically, "The First World War in English and German Literature: A Comparative View" (University of Graz, convened by Franz Karl Stanzel), "Futurism and the Avant-Garde" (University of Iowa, convened by Cinthia Blum), "The End of Language? Toward a Visual Poetics" (Yale University, convened by David L. Jackson), "Wittgenstein's Children: Peter Handke's Theatre" (Catholic University, convened by Gita Honegger), and at sessions on Modernism and Postmodernism at the International Association of University Professors of English (convened by Ihab Hassan), the International Association of Philosophy and Literature (Christie MacDonald), and International Comparative Literature Association (Gerald Gillespie and Milan Dimiç). Sections from the book were also delivered as lectures on my tour as a Phi Beta Kappa scholar in 1995: for the Poetics Program at SUNY-Buffalo (convened by Charles Bernstein and Susan Howe), the University of Illinois-Chicago (Donald Marshall), the University of Oregon (Roland Greene), and the University of Hawaii (Susan Schultz).

I want to thank those editors who published earlier versions of individual chapters: Jeffrey Perl of *Common Knowledge;* Wolfgang Iser, who edited a special issue of *New Literary History;* Thomas Gardner, who edited a special issue of *Contemporary Literature;* and Clayton Eshleman, the editor of *Sulfur.* For permission to use the materials indicated, I want to thank the following persons and publishers: for Ingeborg Bachmann's "Im Gewitter der Rosen," R. Piper GmbH & Co.KG Verlag, and the Heirs of Ingeborg Bachmann, and for Mark Anderson's English rendering of this poem as "In the Storm of Roses," Princeton University Press; for Ingeborg Bachmann's "Schatten Rosen Schatten," R. Piper GmbH & Co.KG Verlag, and Marsilio Publishers Corporation for Peter Filkin's

English rendering of this poem as "Shadow Roses Shadow"; for Paul Celan's "Stehen im Schatten," from *Atemwende,* Suhrkamp Verlag, Frankfurt am Main, © 1967, and John Johnson, Ltd. (U.K.) and Persea Books (U.S.) for the English rendering of this poem, "To Stand in the Shadow," from *Poems of Paul Celan,* translated by Michael Hamburger, © 1972, 1980, 1988, by Michael Hamburger; for Thomas Bernhard's "Unten liegt die Stadt," Suhrkamp Verlag, Frankfurt am Main.

For Robert Creeley's "Away," "Water," "Up in the Air," and "Here," New Directions Publishing Corporation; for portions of Ron Silliman's "Sunset Debris," the Segue Foundation; for portions of Rosmarie Waldrop's "The Reproduction of Profiles," Rosmarie Waldrop and Burning Deck Press; for portions of Lyn Hejinian's "The Composition of the Cell" and *The Cell,* © 1992 by Lyn Hejinian, the Sun & Moon Press, Los Angeles, 1992.

I am deeply grateful to the Huntington Library which awarded me a fellowship to work on this manuscript; at the Huntington, I especially profited from conversations and exchanges with a fellow Wittgensteinian, Stanley Stewart. Other friends and colleagues whose conversation helped me to clear up gray areas include Charles Altieri, Charles Bernstein, Ulla E. Dydo, Albert and Barbara Gelpi, Robert Harrison, Van Harvey, Renée and Judd Hubert, Herbert Lindenberger, Ming-Qian Ma, Steve McCaffery, Jerome J. McGann, Tyrus Miller, Jann Pasler, Joan Retallack, and Cole Swensen.

Finally, special thanks go to four colleagues who read part or all of the manscript and made invaluable suggestions: Gerald Bruns, whose own knowledge of philosophy and literature has for years been an inspiration to me; Daniel Herwitz, art theorist and professor of philosophy, who, more than anyone else, could keep me honest so far as Wittgenstein's meanings are concerned; Guy Davenport, a great writer-critic, whose remarks on Wittgenstein and Gertrude Stein in *The Geography of Imagination* first suggested to me a way of approaching the "poetic" Wittgenstein; and finally, Herman Rapaport, who could, at the drop of a hat, provide me with information about anything from Paul Celan's view of Ingeborg Bachmann, to Adorno's passing comments on Wittgenstein in various obscure places, to the new critique of Wittgenstein now coming out of

France, especially in the writings of Jacques Bouveresse. Herman Rapaport's detailed reading of the entire manuscript was an author's dream come true.

My husband, Joseph K. Perloff, much more adept at philosophy than I am, read every word of the manuscript and gave superb advice. Alan Thomas has once again been the exemplary editor—much more than an editor, really, in making the right suggestions at the right time; and Morris Philipson, the director of the University of Chicago Press, offered just the right early encouragement.

Because it marks at least a partial return to origins, to the world of Viennese thought and sensibility in all its ironies and contradictions, this book is dedicated to the memory of my parents, Maximilian Mintz and Ilse Schüller Mintz. I would want them to know that, in Wittgenstein's words, "The world of the happy is a happy world."

Do not forget that a poem, although it is composed in the language of information, is not used in the language-game of giving information.

—Ludwig Wittgenstein, *Zettel*

Philosophy ought really to be written only as a form of poetry. (Philosophie dürfte man eigentlich nur *dichten.*)

—Ludwig Wittgenstein, *Culture and Value*[1]

In the autumn of 1939, Ludwig Wittgenstein and his young Cambridge student and friend Norman Malcolm were walking along the river when they saw a newspaper vendor's sign announcing that the Germans had accused the British government of instigating a recent attempt to assassinate Hitler. When Wittgenstein remarked that it wouldn't surprise him at all if it were true, Malcolm retorted that it was impossible because "the British were too civilized and decent to attempt anything so underhand, and . . . such an act was incompatible with the British 'national character.'" Wittgenstein was furious. Some five years later, he wrote to Malcolm:

Whenever I thought of you I couldn't help thinking of a particular incident which seemed to me very important. . . . you made a remark about 'national character' that shocked me by its primitiveness. I then thought: what is the use of studying philosophy if all that it does for you is to enable you to talk with some plausibility about some abstruse questions of logic, etc., & if it does not improve your thinking about the important questions of everyday life, if it does not make you more conscientious than any . . . journalist in the use of the DANGEROUS phrases such people use for their own ends.[2]

What *is* the use of studying philosophy if it doesn't improve your thinking about the important questions of everyday life? It is the pressing question Wittgenstein asked himself throughout his career as a philosopher. As early as 1913 in the *Notes on Logic,* he wrote, "In philosophy there are no deductions: *it* is purely descriptive. Philosophy gives no pictures of reality."[3] And a few years later, he made the following riddling entry in the manuscript that was to become the *Tractatus Logico-Philosophicus:*

We feel that even if *all possible* scientific questions be answered, the problems of life have still not been touched at all. But of course there is then no question left, and just this is the answer. (T #6.52)

Thus, when Wittgenstein chides Malcolm for accepting as "true" the proposition that assassination attempts are alien to the British "national character," the issue is not whether the British government did or did not participate in a plot to assassinate Hitler, but whether it is meaningful to assert that it was too "civilized" and "decent" to do so. Ethical propositions, propositions about such things as "national character," Wittgenstein held, are always questionable: "nothing we could ever think or say should be *the* thing."[4] Imagine, then, what Wittgenstein would have made of our current propensity for sloganizing, the predilection, not just on the part of television journalists, but in intellectual life, for pious phrasemaking about "the end of history," "the age of Reagan," "the cold war mentality," "the Me decade," "the Vietnam syndrome," and so on.

One such set of "primitive" propositions has to do with poetry. A recent book by Vernon Shetley bears the ominous title *After the Death of Poetry;* another recent book, this one by Dana Gioia, is called *Can Poetry Matter?*—the author noting sadly that "American poetry now belongs to a subculture," that "Daily newspapers no longer review poetry," and that "although there is a great deal of poetry around, none of it matters very much to readers, publishers, or advertisers—to anyone, that is, except other poets."[5]

Are such "DANGEROUS phrases" to be taken at face value? Wittgenstein might have responded by asking Shetley or Gioia what the "it" is that no longer "matters," the "it" that is by the critics' testimony so sadly "diminished," so marginalized, so evidently beside the point in the culture of late twentieth-century America. And he would have been equally suspicious of the critics' prescriptions for change (e.g., Gioia's argument that if we could only get rid of Creative Writing programs, poetry might once again belong to the "public"), asking to *whom* poetry *should* matter and why? It all depends, after all, on what questions one chooses to ask in a given instance. As Wittgenstein put it in a notebook entry of 1942, "A man will be *imprisoned* in a room with a door that's unlocked and opens inwards; as long as it does not occur to him to *pull* rather than to push it" (CV 42). Or again:

> Earlier physicists are said to have found suddenly that they had too little mathematical understanding to cope with physics; and in almost the same way young people today can be said to be in a situation where ordinary common sense no longer suffices to meet the strange demands life makes. Everything has become so intricate that mastering it would require an exceptional intellect. Because skill at playing the game is no longer enough; the question that keeps coming up is: can this game be played at all now and what would be the right game to play? (CV 27)

What, we might ask, extrapolating from Wittgenstein's question, is the "right" poetry game to be played today and, if "skill"—let us say, the ability to use meter, rhyme, and "vivid" imagery—is no longer enough, how should it be reformulated? To put it more concretely: what role does the interrogation of language that *dichten* (composing poetry) entails play in the mass culture of the later twentieth century? Theodor Adorno, after all, had famously declared in 1967 that "Cultural criticism finds itself faced with the final stage of the dialectic of culture and barbarism. To write poetry after Auschwitz is barbaric. And this corrodes even the knowledge of why it has become impossible to write poetry today."[6] What, then, replaces the "poetic" in cultural consciousness?

Wittgenstein would have had no answers to these and related questions. On the contrary, his writing of "philosophy" *as if* it were "poetry" dramatizes the process of working through particular questions so as to test what can and cannot be said about literary forms (e.g., poetry), concepts (e.g., barbarism), and facts of life (e.g., death). "A philosopher," he wrote in 1944, "is a man who has to cure many intellectual diseases in himself before he can arrive at the notions of common sense" (CV 44). And again, "My account will be hard to follow: because it says something new but still has egg-shells from the old view sticking to it" (CV 44). Perhaps it is this curious mix of mysticism and common sense, of radical thought to which the "egg-shells" of one's old views continue to "stick," that has made Wittgenstein, who had no interest at all in the "poetry" of his own time, paradoxically a kind of patron saint for poets and artists.

In the introduction to the screenplay he wrote for Derek Jarman's 1993 film on Wittgenstein, Terry Eagleton remarks:

The library of artistic works on Ludwig Wittgenstein continues to accumulate. What is it about this man, whose philosophy can be taxing and technical enough, which so fascinates the *artistic* imagination? Frege is a philosopher's philosopher, Bertrand Russell every shopkeeper's image of the sage, and Sartre the media's idea of an intellectual; but Wittgenstein is the philosopher of poets and composers, playwrights and novelists, and snatches of his mighty *Tractatus* have even been set to music.[7]

Eagleton himself had fallen under Wittgenstein's spell some years earlier when he wrote a witty novel called *Saints and Scholars* (1987), in which Wittgenstein, fleeing the insularity and hypocrisy of Cambridge, rents a cottage on the Irish coast with his friend, the Russian émigré linguistic philosopher Nikolai Bakhtin (the great critic Mikhail's brother), who, unlike the austere Wittgenstein, happens to be a great gourmet.[8] No sooner have the two dons settled in than they are forced to grant asylum to the Irish patriot James Connolly, on the run from the British government, and to Leopold Bloom, on the run from anti-Semitism in Joyce's Dublin. The conversation between these principals on the value of revolution and related topics is the substance of the novel, Wittgenstein taking the hard line. "Revolution," he tells Connolly, "is the dream of the metaphysician," and again, "the idea of a total break in human life is an illusion. There's nothing *total* to be broken. As though all we know now could stop, and something entirely different start."[9] And yet, the novel suggests, it is Wittgenstein who emerges as perhaps the true radical of the group in his clear-eyed assessment of what the situation really warrants.

A similar, if more stylized, fantasy is found in Guy Davenport's short story "The Aeroplanes at Brescia," published in the collection *Tatlin!* in 1974. Davenport imagines that in 1909, when Kafka and his friends Max and Otto Brod are (as in fact they were) vacationing at Como, they decide to attend the great air show at Brescia, where the aviators Louis Blériot, Glenn Curtiss, and the brothers Wright are scheduled to perform. As they watch Blériot preparing his plane ("a yellow dragonfly of waxed wood, stretched canvas, and wires"), they become aware of a stranger:

Near them a tall man with thick chestnut hair held his left wrist as if it might be in pain. It was the intensity of his eyes that caught Kafka's attention more than his tall leanness which, from the evidence about, marked the aeronaut and the mechanic. This was the age of the bird man and of the magician of the machine. Who knows but that one of these preoccupied faces might belong to Marinetti himself? This was a crane of a man. The very wildness of his curly brown hair and the tension in his long fingers seemed to speak of man's strange necessity to fly. He was talking to a short man in a mechanic's blue smock and with an eye-patch. From his mouth flew the words *Kite Flying Upper Air Station, Höhere Luftstazion zum Drachensteigenlassen.* Then the small man raised his square hands and cocked his head in a question. *Glossop,* was the answer, followed by the green word *Derbyshire.*[10]

From 1908 to 1911, the real Wittgenstein studied aeronautics at the University of Manchester; his main research project on the design and construction of kites was carried on at the Kite Flying Upper Atmosphere Station near Glossop.[11] Davenport, evidently fascinated by the very unusual but apposite practical training the future philosopher received (Wittgenstein did not have a university education), posits what might have happened if Wittgenstein and Kafka, two of the great avant-gardists to come out of the assimilated Jewish world of the Austro-Hungarian empire, two writers who, however, were never to know each other's work, had met (or rather, almost met) at the Brescia air show. "Who," Davenport has Franz Kafka ask the Italian reporter, "[is] that tall man with the deep eyes and chestnut hair?" (GDAB 65). The *giornalista* doesn't know, but later, after Blériot's flight, he hands Franz a piece of paper: "Kafka looked at the name. It read, in light pencil, the kind meticulous men used to jot down fractions and the abbreviated titles of learned journals, volume, number, and page, probably a thin silver pencil with fine lead, *Ludwig Wittgenstein*" (GDAB 67).

That's all that happens. The two men never meet. But after Curtiss's daredevil flight, which wins him the grand prize, "The man named Wittgenstein was again holding his left wrist, massaging it as if it were in pain," even as, on the other side of the field, Max asks Franz, "why are there tears in your eyes?" and Franz responds, "I don't know . . . I don't know" (GDAB 70).

Davenport's story is a parable about the avant-garde art of Mitteleuropa in the pre–World War I years, an art in love with the technology that was soon to destroy it. The air show, for that matter, takes place on what was soon to be Fascist ground and hence off-limits for both Wittgenstein and Kafka. No doubt it is ironies like these that have made the figure of Wittgenstein so appealing to writers such as Davenport and Eagleton, and theirs are only two examples of the growing body of Wittgensteiniana that includes such diverse novels and plays as Peter Handke's *Kaspar* (1968), Ingeborg Bachmann's *Malina* (1971), Thomas Bernhard's *Wittgenstein's Nephew* (1982) and *Ritter, Dene, Voss* (1984), Bruce Duffy's mock biography *The World as I Found It* (1987), and David Markson's *Wittgenstein's Mistress* (1988). Among poets, Wittgenstein's presence is even more startling. In the last decade or so, the following poetry books (all published in the U.S. or Canada) may be said to have been written under the sign of Wittgenstein: Charles Bernstein's *The Sophist* and *Dark City,* Allen Davies's *Signage,* Steve McCaffery's *Evoba: The Investigation Meditations 1976–78,* Tom Mandel's *Realism,* Michael Palmer's *Notes for Echo Lake,* Joan Retallack's *Circumstantial Evidence,* Ron Silliman's *The Age of Huts,* Rosmarie Waldrop's *Reproduction of Profiles* and *A Key into the Language of America,* and Jan Zwicky's *Wittgenstein's Elegies.* The list grows even longer when we include performance pieces; for example, Laurie Anderson's "Language Is a Virus from Outer Space," David Antin's "The Poetry of Ideas and the Idea of Poetry," John Cage's *I–VI* (The Charles Eliot Norton Lectures), and Johanna Drucker's installation piece *The Wittgenstein Variations. Fluxus,* for that matter, now recognized as one of the most important international art movements of the later 1960s and 1970s, is inconceivable without the example of Wittgenstein, as are the recent poetic experiments of Emmanuel Hocquard and Claude Royet-Journoud in France and the *Gruppo 93* in Italy. In 1992 Joseph Kosuth, whose series of "Art Investigations" are directly modeled on Wittgenstein's writings, published a remarkable artist's book called *Letters from Wittgenstein, Abridged in Ghent.* Like Cage or the Tom Phillips of *A Humument,* Kosuth has produced a "writing through," in this case of the well-known bilingual edition of Wittgenstein's letters to Paul Engelmann, a "writing through" composed of enigmatic black-

and-white photographs of Ghent cityscapes. How, Kosuth challenges the viewer to determine, do these dreary images of factories, canals, parking lots, and nondescript office buildings relate to the passionate dialogue about the meaning of life contained in the correspondence between Wittgenstein and Engelmann?

Like Wallace Stevens's blackbird, Wittgenstein's shadow thus marks "the edge / of one of many circles." But why? Is it primarily the life that has fascinated literary artists? Yes and no, for Wittgenstein's life is curiously bound up with his work. "He was," writes Eagleton, "an arresting combination of monk, mystic and mechanic: a high European intellectual who yearned for Tolstoyan *simplicitas,* a philosophical giant with scant respect for philosophy, an irascible autocrat with a thirst for holiness" (WTE 7–8). The Wittgenstein paradoxes are indeed the stuff of legend. A fabulously rich man who gave away all his money so he wouldn't have to bother with it; a man, three of whose brothers committed suicide and who frequently contemplated suicide himself and yet told friends, on his deathbed, that he had had a wonderful life; a Jew baptized in the Catholic church, with strong leanings toward Protestant piety; a Viennese exile who made his home in Cambridge, England, but insisted that he was "German through and through"; a misogynist who counted among his most brilliant and devoted students Elizabeth Anscombe and Alice Ambrose; a closeted homosexual who lived an outwardly austere life but was intimate with a series of much younger men; a gentle man who abhorred violence but became a decorated hero in World War I; an intellectual genius who, in his thirties, worked first as a gardener and then as an elementary school teacher in rural Austria, an apolitical man who went to the Soviet Union in his forties in the hopes of becoming an ordinary worker and declared, "I am a communist, at heart"; a man who had no interest in modernist art movements and lived in Spartan rented rooms furnished with assorted deck chairs, but who designed for his sister Margarete Stonborough a starkly beautiful ultramodernist house and attended to every detail of its construction from radiators to doorknobs[12]— it is, no doubt, a life that lends itself to dramatic and fictional representation, to the making of myths. For Wittgenstein comes to us as the ultimate modernist outsider, the changeling who never stops reinventing himself, who never really "belongs," and whose presence is nevertheless so overwhelming that we can immediately identify it as Wittgenstein's.

Perhaps it is this very contradictoriness, this refusal to stay in one place, that has made Wittgenstein so appealing. His "ladder" of propositions, as we know from the *Tractatus,* has no sooner been climbed than it must be replaced. "If I am thinking about a topic just for myself," Wittgenstein remarks in a notebook of 1937, "and not with a view to writing a book, I jump about all round it; that is the only way of thinking that comes naturally to me. Forcing my thoughts into an ordered sequence is a torment for me. Is it even worth attempting now?" (CV 28).

The example Wittgenstein thus set writers from Samuel Beckett (who insisted that he hadn't read any Wittgenstein until the late fifties, long after he had completed such "Wittgensteinian" works as *Watt* and *Waiting for Godot*)[13] to Ingeborg Bachmann and beyond is that he never gave up the struggle, both with himself and with language, never allowed himself to accept this or that truth statement or totalizing system as *the* answer. "Language," he wrote in his notebook, "sets everyone the same traps. . . . What I have to do then is erect signposts at all the junctions where there are wrong turnings so as to help people past the danger points" (CV 18). And one of the implications of the famous aphorism "*The limits of my language* mean the limits of my world" (T #5.6) is that the cult of personality, of a subject somehow *outside* language, that dominated American poetry from the confessionalism of the fifties to the "scenic mode" (Charles Altieri's apt phrase) of the seventies has now begun to give way to a resurgence of what was known in the heyday of the New Criticism (which regarded it with some asperity) as the "poetry of ideas."[14]

But not the "poetry of ideas" in the traditional sense, in which it meant the expression of significant "content" in appropriate language and verse form. For if we accept Wittgenstein's premise that "The results of philosophy [and hence, by analogy, of poetry] are the uncovering of one or another piece of plain nonsense and of bumps that the understanding has got by running its head up against the limits of language" and that "These bumps make us see the value of the discovery" (PI #119), the "poetry of ideas" becomes the site of discovery, where the "bumps" we receive by running our heads up against the walls and ceilings of the rooms we dwell in are interrogated. And that process of interrogation is of necessity tentative, self-canceling, and self-correcting, even as it deals with the most ordinary aspects of everyday life. Take the following two examples:

Why can't a dog simulate pain? Is he too honest? Could one teach a dog to simulate pain? Perhaps it is possible to teach him to howl on particular occasions as if he were in pain, even when he is not. But the surroundings which are necessary for this behaviour to be real simulation are missing. (PI #250)

"You can't hear God speak to someone else, you can hear him only if you are being addressed."—That is a grammatical remark. (Z #717)

"Wittgenstein," says Guy Davenport in a discussion of these fragments, "did not argue; he merely thought himself into subtler and deeper problems."[15] As such, his Heraclitean epigrams easily shade into poetry. But the paradox—a paradox of a piece with the ones I cited above—is that this poet formulated no poetics, had no "theory" of literature or art, and repeatedly insisted that it was impossible to define the "beautiful" or to say what the "essence" of "art" might be. Such professed skepticism, coupled with what seemed to be simple ignorance about literature, was greeted with suspicion, first by his Viennese, and then by his English, contemporaries. "Cultivated as he was," declared his Cambridge colleague F. R. Leavis, Wittgenstein's "interest in literature had remained rudimentary." Indeed, aside from his knowledge of Dickens's *The Uncommercial Traveller* and *A Christmas Carol,* Leavis reports, "I never discovered that he took any other creative writing seriously. It may of course be that in German the range and quality of his literary culture were more impressive, but I can't give any great weight to that possibility."[16]

In one sense, Leavis was surely right. Cyril Barrett and others have tried to defend Wittgenstein against such charges by noting that he certainly knew his German classics, that, for example, when he was stationed on the eastern front, he asked his friend Paul Engelmann to send him the novellas of Gottfried Keller, the historical dramas of Franz Grillparzer, and the lyric poems of Uhland and Mörike.[17] But it is not a question of listing the literary works Wittgenstein had or had not read—he insisted, for that matter, that he had never read Aristotle or, closer to home, Hegel either—but of outlook and sensibility. Just as Wittgenstein, who had received extensive training in music, would not listen to any composer later than Brahms, so he was indifferent to, if not openly hostile toward, his poetic contemporaries. True, in an impulsive act of legendary generosity, he bequeathed, in 1914, one hundred thousand kronen (roughly the equivalent of one hundred thousand dollars today) to Ludwig von Ficker, the editor of the literary magazine *Der Brenner,* instructing Ficker to distribute the money "among Austrian artists who are without means." But of the three main beneficiaries—Rilke, Trakl, and Carl Dallago—Rilke was the only poet with whose work Wittgenstein was at all familiar. Of Trakl's poems, he wrote Ficker, "I do not understand them, but their *tone* makes me happy. It is the tone of genius." Some months later, however, when Ficker sent him a posthumously published edition of Trakl's works, Wittgenstein's only comment was that they were "probably very good" but that, just now, he had "no desire to assimilate foreign thoughts" (RM 118–20, 126).

During his Cambridge years, Wittgenstein became even less responsive to the artistic production of his contemporaries. In conversations with friends, he was given to pessimistic representations of modernism. "I was walking about in Cambridge," he remarked in 1930, "and passed a bookshop, and in the window were portraits of Russell, Freud, and Einstein. A little further on, in a music shop, I saw portraits of Beethoven, Schubert, and Chopin. Comparing these portraits I felt intensely the terrible degeneration that had come over the human spirit in the course of only a hundred years" (RR 112). If this almost comically exaggerated Spenglerianism (how can one compare Einstein to Chopin?) sounds a bit like the epitaphs for poetry made by critics today, the difference is that Wittgenstein offered no explanations or panaceas. He merely stayed out of the fray: there is no indication that he ever read T. S. Eliot or Ezra Pound, D. H. Lawrence or W. H. Auden, and, with the exception of John Maynard Keynes, he studiously avoided Bloomsbury. As Ray Monk puts it, "There was little common ground between the peculiarly English, self-consciously 'civilized' aestheticism of Bloomsbury and the [Cambridge] Apostles, and Wittgenstein's rigorously ascetic sensibility and occasionally ruthless honesty."[18]

When, in his notebooks and lectures, Wittgenstein does comment directly on the nature of "art," his remarks tend to be modernist commonplaces. "A work of art," he observed in 1930, "forces us—as one might say—to see it in the right perspective but, in the absence of art, the object is just a fragment of nature like any other" (CV 4). Here Wittgenstein echoes, no doubt unwittingly, Viktor Shklovsky's famous doctrine of "making it strange" or "defamiliarization," with its emphasis on the "artistic" removal of the object from its usual surroundings so as to recharge its potency, the object itself being "unimportant." Or again, Wittgenstein will pay lip service to the romantic/modernist doctrine of artistic uniqueness: "Every artist has been influenced by others and shows traces of that influence in his works; but his significance for us is nothing but *his* personality" (CV 23).

One does not, then, go to Wittgenstein for a systematic poetics. His writing (so much of it not *his* writing at all but a re-creation of his talk made by his students and colleagues) has nothing interesting to say about the "big" issues like "the aesthetic," much less the specifics of tropes or genres, fictionality or narrative form, sound structures or verse forms. No wonder, then, that theory (as opposed to formal philosophy, on the one hand, poetry on the other) has largely ignored Wittgenstein's existence. The *Tractatus* (1922), for example, seems to have been wholly unknown to the Russian Formalists, the Prague Linguistic Circle, and the Frankfurt School of the thirties, even though Wittgenstein's questions about language and culture had so much in common with, say, Roman Jakobson's or Walter Benjamin's. No doubt this neglect has much to do with the original presentation and reception of Wittgenstein's book: the *Tractatus Logico-Philosophicus* was, after all, first presented to the world by Bertrand Russell (in C. K. Ogden's translation) as a treatise on the logical structure of propositions and the nature of logical inference. As such, its interest was for philosophers and mathematicians—hardly for literary theorists.

Benjamin, in any case, died long before the *Philosophical Investigations* was published in 1952. But Theodor Adorno, who read it soon after publication, was generally hostile to this book as he was to the *Tractatus*. In *Against Epistemology,* he declares:

As long as philosophy is no more than the cult of what 'is the case,' in Wittgenstein's formula [the reference is to T #1.1, "The world is everything that is the case"] it enters into competition with the sciences to which in delusion it assimilates itself—and loses. If it dissociates itself from the sciences, however, and in refreshed merriment thinks itself free of them, it becomes a powerless reserve, the shadow of shadowy Sunday religion.[19]

And, more pointedly, in *Hegel: Three Studies:*

Wittgenstein's maxim, 'Whereof one cannot speak, thereof one must be silent' [T #7], in which the extreme of positivism spills over into the gesture of reverent authoritarian authenticity, and which for that reason exerts a kind of intellectual mass suggestion, is utterly antiphilosophical. If philosophy can be defined at all, it is an effort to express things one cannot speak about, to help express the nonidentical despite the fact that expressing it identifies it at the same time. Hegel attempts to do this.[20]

Here, as I shall be suggesting in later chapters, a critique like Adorno's mistakes the famous (perhaps too-famous) conclusion of the *Tractatus*. Far from being a "gesture of reverent authoritarian authenticity," Wittgenstein's aphorism "Whereof one cannot speak, thereof one must be silent" is no more than the commonsense recognition that there are metaphysical and ethical aporias that no discussion, explication, rationale, or well-constructed argument can fully rationalize—even for oneself. In this sense, Wittgenstein's "philosophy" is indeed intentionally "antiphilosophical," its purpose being precisely to determine in what circumstances philosophy should be "against" philosophy and why.

The refusal, in any case, of the "effort to express things one cannot speak about" has made Wittgenstein equally suspect (if not merely irrelevant) in French poststructuralist circles. This is not the place to take up the vexed question of Wittgenstein's relationship to Jacques Derrida; suffice it to say that whatever homologies betwen the two have been posited,[21] Wittgenstein plays little role in the work of Derrida or Michel Foucault, Maurice Blanchot or Roland Barthes, Julia Kristeva or Paul de Man. And in such rare exceptions as Jean-François Lyotard's *The Differend* (1983), a book that not only cites Wittgenstein on page after page but even models its discourse on his short, numbered aphoristic units, the

Wittgensteinian proposition is given a curious moral spin. Consider Lyotard's preliminary definition:

As distinguished from a litigation, a differend [*différend*] would be a case of conflict, between (at least) two parties, that cannot be equitably resolved for lack of a rule of judgment applicable to both arguments. One side's legitimacy does not imply the other's lack of legitimacy. However, applying a single rule of judgment to both in order to settle their differend as though it were merely a litigation would wrong (at least) one of them (and both of them if neither side admits this rule). Damages result from an injury which is inflicted upon the rules of a genre of discourse but which is reparable according to those rules. A wrong results from the fact that the rules of the genre of discourse by which one judges are not those of the judged genre or genres of discourse.[22]

This sounds Wittgensteinian enough, Lyotard concluding the paragraph with the assertion that "a universal rule of judgment between heterogeneous genres is lacking in general" (DIF xi). But this seeming rejection of essentialism is more apparent than real, for the Lyotardian "differend" is less a paradox than a sophistry. For example: "To have 'really seen with his own eyes' a gas chamber would be the condition which gives one the authority to say that it exists and to persuade the unbeliever. Yet it is still necessary to prove that the gas chamber was used to kill at the time it was seen. The only acceptable proof that it was used to kill is that one died from it. But if one is dead, one cannot testify that it is on account of the gas chamber" (DIF 3).

Wittgenstein would have dismissed this "argument" as specious. Since when, to begin with, is our "knowledge" of what happened in the past based primarily on what we have "seen with our own eyes"? As for the meaning of the term "gas chamber," "We may say: only someone who already knows how to do something with it can significantly ask a name" (PI 31). To ask whether a gas chamber could cause death, in other words, is to admit the gas chamber's existence. Thus the doubt as to its efficacy says more about the questioner than about the gas chamber's purpose. "The definition ... will depend on the circumstances under which it is given, and on the person I give it to" (PI 29).

The reliance on common sense and context displayed in these propositions, the repeated demonstration that "the meaning of a word [e.g., "gas chamber"] is its use in the language" (PI 43), has evidently proved to be a stumbling block, even for those deconstructionist theories that take language to be a differential system. The criterion of *use,* we read in one of the less genial passages in *The Differend,* is "prey to anthropological empiricism" (DIF 76). Like Adorno, Lyotard cannot, in the end, accept the anticlosural bent of Wittgenstein's investigative mode, his refusal to press toward theoretical definition. A similar discomfort may well motivate such Anglo-American Marxist critics as Raymond Williams, David Harvey, and Fredric Jameson—critics who have largely ignored Wittgenstein's existence. In his important early critique of Russian Formalism, *The Prison-House of Language* (1972), Jameson groups Wittgenstein with the Formalists under the "empiricist" umbrella, arguing that "The vice of Anglo-American empiricism lies indeed in its stubborn will to isolate the object in question from everything else, whether it be a material thing, an 'event' in Wittgenstein's sense, a word, a sentence, or a 'meaning.'" Indeed, given his own Marxist conviction that "philosophy [must] include within itself a theory of its own particular situation," Wittgenstein is found wanting, for "what the philosopher is describing is not language in the absolute, but only the peculiar linguistic habits of philosophers."[23]

Ironically, this distinction is quite accurate, the odd thing being that, as late as 1972 when these words were written, a theory of "language in the absolute" should still have been considered a desirable possibility. Jameson may well have been thinking of Heidegger, whose philosophy does "include within itself a theory of its own particular situation," and who, unlike Wittgenstein, had specifically written on poetic subjects, most notably in his now classic essays on Hölderlin. But with the breakdown of disciplinary boundaries that has characterized the last decade, a shift is beginning to occur, a shift, I shall want to argue, that poets, novelists, dramatists, and artists had anticipated a good deal earlier.

"You often quote Wittgenstein—why is that?" an interviewer asked the sociologist Pierre Bourdieu in 1985. And Bourdieu replied, "Wittgenstein is probably the philosopher who has helped me most at moments of difficulty. He's *a kind of saviour for times of great intellectual distress*—as when you have to question such evident things as 'obeying a rule.' Or when you have to describe such simple (and, by the same token, practically ineffable) things as putting a practice into practice."[24]

Strong words, these, coming as they do from a writer as "scientific" and as generally impersonal as Bourdieu. No doubt the "times of great intellectual distress" are associated in Bourdieu's mind with what he dismissively refers to, in the same interview, as "the totalizing ambition that is usually identified with philosophy" (PBOW 19). For example:

I've always had a pretty ambivalent relationship with the Frankfurt School: the affinities between us are clear, and yet I felt a certain irritation when faced with the aristocratic demeanor of that totalizing critique which retained all the features of grand theory, doubtless so as not to get its hands dirty in the kitchens of empirical research. The same goes for the Althusserians, and for those interventions, both simplistic and peremptory, that philosophical arrogance enables people to make. (PBOW 19)

"Totalizing critique," "grand theory"—in our post-Marxist era, these have increasingly come under suspicion. "I wanted," says Bourdieu, "to reintroduce agents that Lévi-Strauss and the structuralists, among others Althusser, tended to abolish, making them into simple epiphenomena of structure. And I mean agents, not subjects. Action is not the mere carrying out of a rule, or obedience to a rule. Social agents, in archaic societies as well as in ours, are not automata, regulated like clocks, in accordance with laws which they do not understand" (PBOW 9).

The critique of "grand theory," with its concomitant turn to the examination of the "ordinary," has been carried further in the remarkable writings of Jacques Bouveresse. In half a dozen books, written between the early 1970s and the present, Bouveresse has painstakingly distinguished Wittgenstein's writings from those of logical positivism on the one hand and Husserlian phenomenology on the other. His close readings of the *Tractatus* and the *Philosophical Investigations* trace Wittgenstein's dismantling of the metaphysical tradition "in order to preach and practice the spirit of radical poverty in philosophy," and he remarks that Wittgenstein's way of tackling philosophical problems is best called "aesthetic" in its imaginative deployment of exempla, apposite images, parataxes, and sudden leaps of faith.[25]

In this regard, Bouveresse's Wittgenstein recalls Stanley Cavell's. Indeed, among Anglo-American philosophers, Cavell is surely the central disseminator of the notion that, in the case of Wittgenstein, the "philosophical" and the "literary" are inseparable. In *This New Yet Unapproachable America* (1989), for example, Cavell writes movingly of Wittgenstein's antitotalizing stance, his "leaving the world as it is," which he relates to Heidegger's *Gelassenheit.*[26] For Wittgenstein, he argues, the most "simple" thing—like "putting a practice into practice," as Bourdieu puts it—is understood to be the most ineffable. "The *Investigations,*" writes Cavell, "exhibits, as purely as any work of philosophy I know, philosophizing as a spiritual struggle, specifically a struggle with the contrary depths of oneself, which in the modern world will present themselves in touches of madness" (SCUA 37). Cavell is referring to the struggle between competing emphases in the consideration of human discourse—"an emphasis on its distrust of language or an emphasis on its trust of ordinary human speech" (SCUA 32). Both emphases are quite proper, and therein madness lies, for which is it to be? Ordinary language procedures, Cavell notes, "inherently partake of the uncanny" (SCUA 47), for example:

> Of course, if water boils in a pot, steam comes out of the pot and also pictured steam comes out of the pictured pot. But what if one insisted on saying that there must also be something boiling in the picture of the pot? (PI #297)

Here logic is indeed both foolproof and perhaps therefore slightly mad. And Cavell proceeds, as he did in his earlier studies,[27] to relate Wittgenstein's sense of "poverty as a condition of philosophy" to Emerson's "recognition of the power of ordinary words . . . to be redeemed, to redeem themselves" (SCUA 82).

The emphasis on spiritual struggle and redemption should not, however, obscure what we might call the *côté avant garde* of Wittgenstein, the obsession not only with the "power of ordinary words," as in Emerson's case, but with their *strangeness:*

> Imagine that a child was quite specially clever, so clever that he could at once be taught the doubtfulness of the existence of all things. So he learns from the beginning: "That is probably a chair."
>
> And now how does he learn the question: "Is it also really a chair?" (Z #411)

Such riddling is what Guy Davenport seems to have in mind when he links the author of the *Tractatus* to Kafka. This Wittgenstein is an obsessively playful grammarian, whose riddling, disconnected sentence sequences bring to mind those of a fellow avant-gardist Wittgenstein never read, never met (and would probably have thoroughly disliked if he had met!)—namely, Gertrude Stein. "Strangely simultaneous in their stylistic concerns," writes Guy Davenport in *The Geography of the Imagination,* "the two were at work from 1917 onwards on identical linguistic phenomena: the splashed meaning of chattered language, language which is gesture, politeness, and social formula. . . . Gertrude Stein is not interested in the absurdity of language but in the astounding implications that can be flushed from its ordinariness."[28] And Davenport cites the early Stein play *An Exercise in Analysis* (1917), which ends with the lines:[29]

Part LX

Not disappointed.

Act II

Not in there.

Act III

Call me.

Act IV

Call me Ellen.

"Call me," "Call me Ellen"—no sentences could be more "ordinary" and yet "call me" means one thing in Act III and quite another in Act IV, when it is followed by a proper name, Ellen. In the first instance, we could substitute "phone" for "call," but obviously the construction "Phone me Ellen" (without a pause, represented in writing by a comma, after "me") makes no sense. A similar situation obtains in the case of "Not disappointed" and "Not in there": the first "not" functions as a qualifier, the second as a more emphatic negative, as the stress and pitch contour of the sentences suggests. And further: these two acts (or "parts") have no visible relationship to Acts III and IV.

"Distrust of grammar," Wittgenstein had posited in the early *Notes on Logic,* "is the first requisite of philosophizing" (NBK 106). And, by extension, of poeticizing as well. For although the later Wittgenstein was to argue that grammar is precisely the key to understanding a given prop-osition, that there is no essence above and beyond a specific grammatical structure, one nevertheless must "distrust" grammar in the sense of inter-rogating it as stringently as possible.

It is in this sense that grammar may be said to replace theory. In 1931, when his Cambridge colleague C. D. Broad was lecturing on the three "theories of truth"—the Correspondence Theory, the Coherence Theory, and the Pragmatic Theory—Wittgenstein remarked dismissively, "Phi-losophy is not a choice between different 'theories.'" For:

> We can say that the word ["truth"] has at least three different meanings; but it is mistaken to assume that any one of these theories can give the whole grammar of how we use the word, or endeavour to fit into a single theory cases which do not seem to agree with it.[30]

In the same year, Gertrude Stein wrote in her "Arthur a Grammar," "What is a grammar ordinarily. A grammar is question and answer an-swer undoubted however how and about."[31]

"Call me. Call me Ellen." Such conundrums provide a baseline for a whole series of texts that act out, as it were, Wittgenstein's obsession with the "distrust of grammar." From the Stein of *Stanzas in Meditation* to such post–World War II works as Samuel Beckett's *Watt,* to Thomas Bernhard's *Wittgenstein's Nephew* and Ingeborg Bachmann's *Malina,* to the recent experiments in "language poetry" and conceptual art, we find a poetics based on what Wittgenstein called the "enormously difficult" "synopsis of trivialities" (LEC1 26). For example: "A dog believes his mas-ter is at the door. But can he also believe his master will come the day after to-morrow?" (PI 174). "Face to face with this literalness," says the French poet Claude Royet-Journoud, "face to face with this manifestation of a demented logic, you tell yourself that through the literal you can perhaps recover a sense of your body and of the displacement of your body."[32]

"The world which is baldly whatever is the case," writes Terry Eagleton with reference to the famous opening sentence of the *Tractatus,* "whose value and meaning is always elusively elsewhere, is familiar enough to us from the great experimental art of the early twentieth century" (WTE 6–7). In exploring the relationships between Wittgenstein's own avant-garde practices and those of his contemporaries and later versions, I want to begin, as Wittgenstein himself began, with the composition of the *Tractatus,* and specifically with that book's departure from the work of Wittgenstein's mentor Bertrand Russell. The contrast between Russell and Wittgenstein in the World War I years is particularly instructive, the former preaching *on* war from the sidelines, the latter engaging *in* war in the trenches, an engagement that led to the particular form the *Tractatus* took. The status of the *Tractatus* as a war book as well as an avant-garde one has received little attention from philosophers, whose central concern has primarily been to make sense of the "picture-theory" of language that Wittgenstein's "treatise on logic" expounds. My own interest is less in what the *Tractatus* "says" about propositionality, tautology, etc., than in what it *is,* especially in its later sections, which break abruptly with the "clarity" of its opening and turn to matters of ethics and religion in a series of gnomic utterances—"The world of the happy is quite another than that of the unhappy" (T #6.43); "Not *how* the world is, is the mystical, but *that* it is" (#6.44)—whose formulations "solve" nothing.

The genesis of the *Tractatus* from the notebooks Wittgenstein kept during the war is the subject of chapter 1. In chapter 2, I turn to the great work of Wittgenstein's maturity, the *Philosophical Investigations.* Again, I am less interested in the central "argument" of the *Investigations*—a topic on which philosophers have produced a huge library—than in what Cavell calls the "spiritual struggle" dramatized in its pages, as well as in those earlier versions such as the Cambridge lectures of the early 1930s and the jottings collected in *The Blue and Brown Books,* in which Wittgenstein tested and endlessly revised his formulations. What makes Wittgenstein, in Bourdieu's words, such a "saviour in times of intellectual distress" is his gradual recognition that everything happens exactly as it does, but that, at any given moment, we also conjecture that it might have happened otherwise (see CV 37). In the same vein, the question that has dogged literary theory throughout the twentieth century—"Is there a distinction between ordinary and literary language, and, if so, what is it?"—disappears, Wittgenstein demonstrating that (1) there is in fact *no* material difference, but that (2) the *use* to which we put language varies so much that words and sentences become, as it were, unfamiliar when they reappear in a new context. When I say "I have a pain," to take one of Wittgenstein's favorite examples, does the word "have" mean the same thing as when I say "I have an apple"? And since the "pain" in this sentence is obviously "mine" (otherwise, how could I recognize it as pain?), why not just use the single word "Pain!" to express my feelings?

The concept of the "language-game," which is as central to the *Investigations* as it is ultimately undefinable, can be discussed from at least four different, though interrelated, perspectives, all of them applicable to the poems and fictions and artworks produced in the wake of Wittgenstein's writing: (1) the emphasis on the strangeness, the enigmatic nature, of everyday language; (2) the awareness that "the world is *my* world [which] shows itself in the fact that the limits of the language (*the* language which I understand) mean the limits of *my* world" (T #5.62), a proposition the later Wittgenstein never abandoned, although the solipsism of "my" gradually gave way to "our," to the continuous struggle everyone encounters in the "bumping of one's head" against the walls of one's language cage in the drive to understand one's world; (3) the recognition of the self as, in no small measure, a social construct, a cultural construction. Wittgenstein was not a Marxist, but, as we shall see, he shares with Marx and with later cultural materialists the notion that the languages of the self depend on social context, culture, and class. "The subject does not belong to the world but it is a limit of the world" (T #5.632). There is no unique "I" ("The thinking, presenting subject; there is no such thing" [T #5.63]), subjectivity always depending upon a language that belongs to a culture long before it belongs to me. Language is thus a set of rule-governed practices, but one that can be adapted in a myriad of ways. And finally (4), the discovery that there are no propositions of absolute value, no causal or even temporal explanations. "When we think of the world's future, we always mean the destination it will reach if it keeps going in the direction we can see it going in now; it does not occur to us that its path is not a straight line but a curve, constantly changing direction" (CV 3e). Humean as this rejection of causality may sound, it differs from Hume's skepticism in that, for Wittgenstein, such rejection of "straight lines" is a compositional as well as an epistemological principle, his own "conclusions" never being more than tentative, open, and to-be-revised.

Again—and here is where Wittgenstein's "mysticism" comes in—however impossible it may be to formulate ethical principles, it *is* possible to engage in ethical actions. In the "Lecture on Ethics" Wittgenstein gave shortly after his return to Cambridge in 1929, he describes ethics as the running against the boundaries of language and gives the following example. If someone says, after a tennis game, "I play badly but I don't care to play better," this is not analogous to the sentence "I behave badly but I don't care to behave better" (PO 38–39). The difference is clear to anyone who speaks English and suggests that we know instinctively what it means to "behave badly."

The first two of these four perspectives—the strangeness of the ordinary and the "bumping of one's head" against the limits of language—are central to the work of Gertrude Stein, which I discuss in chapter 3. Indeed, the writings of both Stein and Wittgenstein represent a side of modernism markedly different from the Futurist and Imagist collage paradigm, which has set the stage for so much of the discussion of modernism: witness the *parole in libertà* of Marinetti, which Stein takes on in her own oblique, tongue-in-cheek manner. The other two—the social construction of the subject and the articulation of an ethics outside the norms of causality or explanation—come to the fore more fully in what Wittgenstein referred to as the "dark time" in which he published the *Investigations*. In chapters 4 and 5, I take up the ethical dimensions of the language game as they manifest themselves in the works of three great postwar writers whose names begin with *B*—Beckett (who had nothing to say about Wittgenstein but writes the most Wittgensteinian of parables) and the Austrian writers Ingeborg Bachmann and Thomas Bernhard, for whom Wittgenstein's method, transferred to narrative, became something of an obsession.

In Wittgensteinian terms, Beckett's characters—*Watt* is my example—suffer from what we might call a context disorder; Watt, for instance, doesn't know what to do with orders like "You may give the left-overs to the dog," given that there is no dog on the premises. The "resistance to language," I argue in Beckett's case, must be understood in terms of the "language of Resistance," the elaborate game of coding used by Beckett and his co-workers in the underground in the early 1940s, right before he began work on *Watt*. In this setting, the most ordinary sentence—for example, the piano tuner's remark that "The strings are in flitters"—becomes suspect. And in the postwar Austrian writing of the following decades (Bachmann, Bernhard, to some extent Peter Handke), incomplete sentences like "Are you really ... " or "Later on we might ... " have the power to drive their users mad, as do proper names like Ivan and Malina, Hermann Pavilion and Ludwig Pavilion, Ungargasse and Salzkammergut.

Finally, in chapter 6, I turn to recent Wittgensteinian experiments, this time in the United States, in the articulation of a poetics of everyday life. I am less interested in "influence," always a nebulous quality, than in analogue. It is fascinating to see that Wittgenstein's stringent and severe interrogation of language has provided an opening for the replacement of the "autonomous," self-contained, and self-expressive lyric with a more fluid poetic paradigm—a paradigm based on the recognition that the poet's most secret and profound emotions are expressed in a language that has always already belonged to the poet's culture, society, and nation, the irony being that this "belonging" need not make the poetry in question— Robert Creeley's and Rosmarie Waldrop's, Ron Silliman's and Lyn Hejinian's, the *Fluxus* box and the Joseph Kosuth "investigation"—any less moving.

As someone trained in literary criticism rather than philosophy, I make no claim to contributing to the ongoing (and enormous) body of writing that seeks to *explain* the difficult meanings in Wittgenstein's endlessly riddling philosophical writings. Rather, I want to examine the relationship of Wittgenstein's mode of *investigation,* in all its contradictoriness, its stringent and severe self-revision and critique, its cryptic and aphoristic formulations and epiphanies, to the "ordinary language" poetics so central to our own time. For if, as Wittgenstein posits, "Language is not *contiguous* to anything else" (LEC1 112), then its most trivial manifestations become interesting. For example:

Someone who doesn't know English hears me say on certain occasions: "What marvelous light! [*Welch herrliche Beleuchtung!*]" He guesses the sense and now uses the exclamation himself, as I use it, but without understanding the three individual words. Does he understand the exclamation? (Z #150)

Well, does he? Questions like this one have no "answer," at least not a correct (or incorrect) one. They merely open up new spaces, as "poetic" as they are "philosophical," in which to take a deep breath.

When we think of the world's future, we always mean the destination it will reach if it keeps going in the direction we can see it going in now; it does not occur to us that its path is not a straight line but a curve, constantly changing direction.

—Wittgenstein, *Culture and Value*

The fascination of philosophy lies in its paradox and mystery.

—Wittgenstein, *Lectures: Cambridge*

1930–32

one

The Making of the *Tractatus*: Russell, Wittgenstein and the "Logic" of War

The *Tractatus Logico-Philosophicus* is not usually read as a war book. Unlike the countless novels, poems, plays, and memoirs that constitute what is known as the "literature of World War I," Wittgenstein's treatise on logic, begun in the prewar years, would seem to lead a life quite independent of the specific political events of its day. Yet, as I hope to show here, it was primarily Wittgenstein's war experience that transformed the *Tractatus* from logical, scientific treatise to something quite different—a book closer to the avant-garde poetic fictions of the teens and twenties than to the philosophical work that first brought Wittgenstein to the Cambridge of Bertrand Russell and G. E. Moore, the monumental *Principia Mathematica,* produced by Russell, together with Alfred North Whitehead, between 1903 and 1910.

In *Portraits from Memory* (1956), Russell recalls his decision in August 1914 to protest, in any and all forms possible, the participation of England in the First World War:

Love of England is very nearly the strongest emotion I possess, and in appearing to set it aside at such a moment, I was making a very difficult renunciation. Nevertheless, I never had a moment's hesitation as to what I must do. I have been cynical, at

25

times indifferent, but when war came I felt as if I heard the voice of God. I knew it was my business to protest, however futile protest might be. My whole nature was involved.[1]

And in a letter to the *Nation* on 15 August, he declared: "All this madness, all this rage, all this flaming death of our civilization and our hopes, has been brought about because a set of official gentlemen, living luxurious lives, mostly stupid, and all without imagination or heart, have chosen that it should occur rather than that any one of them should suffer some infinitesimal rebuff to his country's pride."[2] Within less than a year Russell was writing to Lady Ottoline Morrell: "My real ambition has quite deserted philosophy and gone into writing about war and peace" (CPBR xxxii).

Or was it the other way around? Did Russell turn to "writing about war and peace" perhaps because philosophy, in its more demanding forms, had deserted *him*? On 4 March 1916, he writes to Lady Ottoline:

... what wanted doing in logic was too difficult for me. So there was no real vital satisfaction of my philosophical impulse in that work, and philosophy lost its hold on me. That was due to Wittgenstein more than to the War. What the war has done is to give me a new and less difficult ambition, which seems to me quite as good as the old one.[3]

Ironically, the very month that Russell confessed that Wittgenstein and the war were drawing him away from philosophy, Wittgenstein himself was serving as an engineer on a workshop train near Lwów on the eastern front. Having enlisted as a volunteer in the Austrian army as soon as war broke out, Wittgenstein never had the slightest doubt that it was his duty to fight. Not that he had any rational argument for war or for German "rights": on the contrary, just a few months into the war, he wrote in his diary: "I feel ... more than ever the tragedy of our—the German race's—situation! For that we cannot defeat England seems to me as good as certain. The English—the best race in the world—*cannot* lose! We, however, can lose and will lose, if not this year then the next! The thought that our race will be defeated depresses me terribly because I am German through and through!"[4]

This racial self-identification may seem ironic, the then twenty-five-year-old Wittgenstein having spent the previous five years avoiding his native Vienna as much as possible, and having formed what was his most serious personal relationship to date with his young Cambridge colleague David Pinsent. Feeling "German through and through," moreover, had nothing to do, in Wittgenstein's case, with any kind of fellow-feeling for his countrymen: repeatedly he complained, both in letters and in his diary, about the "bunch of delinquents" (*Gaunerpack*) with whom he had to serve, the all-but-subhuman crew mates on the *Goplana,* whose "stupidity, rudeness, and malice . . . know no bounds."[5]

Wittgenstein's identification with what he calls "the tragedy of our— the German race's—situation" was, as I shall suggest later, less a question of politics than of a particular view of culture. He had faith neither in the official British position that the war was being fought to "save" civilization, nor in the antithetical conviction, animating Russell's wartime writings, that the war would spell the "flaming death of our civilization"—a conviction that was a central article of faith of British intellectual thought throughout the war and its aftermath. The *saving of civilization,* the *conservation of values,* the *nobility of tradition*—these were concepts alien to Wittgenstein's thinking. Even as Russell was producing pamphlet after pamphlet analyzing the causes of war, the likely results of this particular war, and the steps that might have been taken to prevent it, on the assumption that an enlightened Europe should and would eventually rise above individual and national self-interest, Wittgenstein longed, not for national or cultural "improvement"—an improvement he regarded cynically as, in any case, absurd and impossible—but for his own improvement, both mental and spiritual. His hope was that war might, as he put it, "turn [him] into a different person."[6] The war, he told a nephew many years later, "saved my life; I don't know what I'd have done without it" (BMG 204).

The paradox is that, whereas Russell felt a need to renounce philosophy because of the war, a war he studied from the sidelines, Wittgenstein's actual war experience became one of the mainsprings of his philosophy. In March 1916 he realized his long-expressed wish to be posted to the front as an ordinary soldier and was assigned to an artillery regiment stationed in Galicia near the Romanian border. It was here, in the midst of heavy fighting, that, unbeknownst to Russell, the *Tractatus* was transformed from a treatise on the logic of propositions into something quite different. As Ray Monk puts it:

> If Wittgenstein had spent the entire war behind the lines, the *Tractatus* would have remained what it almost certainly was from its first inception of 1915: a treatise on the nature of logic. The remarks in it about ethics, aesthetics, the soul and the meaning of life have their origin in . . . an impulse that has as its stimulus a knowledge of death, suffering and misery. (RM 137)

It may be useful to review the steps in this evolution. The first step— and here Wittgenstein is still, so to speak, on Russell's wavelength—was the discovery, made in September 1914, at a time when the Austrian army was in retreat on the eastern front, of what came to be known as the picture theory of language.[7] On 22 October, Wittgenstein wrote to Russell that he was completing a book (the hypothetical proto-*Tractatus*) but that he did not want to publish it until Russell had seen it. Since this obviously couldn't happen until after the war, Wittgenstein added:

> But who knows whether I shall survive until then? If I don't survive, get my people to send you all my manuscripts: among them you'll find the final summary written in pencil on loose sheets of paper. It will perhaps cost you some trouble to understand it all, but don't let yourself be put off by that.[8]

Russell responded on 25 November—"I am enormously pleased that you are writing a treatise which you want to publish"—and said he was impatient to see it. He urged Wittgenstein to send it to a mutual friend in the still neutral United States, who would then forward it to Russell in England. "Had Wittgenstein followed Russell's suggestion," Monk observes, "the work would have been published in 1916," and "it would have contained the Picture Theory of meaning, the metaphysics of 'logical atomism,' the analysis of logic in terms of the twin notions of tautology and contradiction, the distinction between saying and showing . . . and the method of Truth-Tables. . . . In other words, it would have contained almost everything the *Tractatus* now contains—*except* the remarks at the end of the book on ethics, aesthetics, the soul, and the meaning of life" (RM 134).

But Wittgenstein didn't send the manuscript to the U.S.; indeed, he had no further contact with Russell until February 1919, after he had been taken prisoner of war on the Italian front.[9] In this three-year interim, Wittgenstein had his initiation into battle. On 4 June 1916, during the heavy fighting of the Brusilov offensive, he won his first decoration for bravery. A week later he wrote in his *Notebook*:

> What do I know about God and the purpose of life?
> I know that this world exists.
> That I am placed in it like my eye in its visual field.
> That something about it is problematic, which we call its meaning.
> That this meaning does not lie in it but outside it.
> That my life is the world.
> That my will penetrates the world.
> That my will is good or evil.
> Therefore that good and evil are somehow connected with the meaning of the world. . . .
> The meaning of life, i.e. the meaning of the world, we can call God. . . .
> To pray is to think about the meaning of life.
> I cannot bend the happenings of the world to my will:
> I am completely powerless.

Or, as he rephrases this last sentence in a proposition that was to be included in the *Tractatus:* "The world is independent of my will" (NBK 73).

Thus, in contrast to Russell's apocalyptic conviction that "When war came I felt as if I heard the voice of God," Wittgenstein, who was *in* the war, was coming to the conclusion that, as he put it in a notebook entry for 8 July, "To believe in God means to see that life has a meaning" (NBK 74). And again: "To believe in a God means to see that the facts of the world are not the end of the matter" (NBK 74). But meaning (God) could only be defined negatively. "Meaning does not lie in [the world] but outside it" (73). This proposition is repeated almost verbatim in the *Tractatus,* followed by the sentences "In the world everything is as it is and happens as it does happen. *In* it there is no value—and if there were, it would be

of no value" (T #6.41). The corollary, which was to become one of the
most famous propositions of the *Tractatus,* is that "there can be no ethical
propositions" (T #6.42):

> The first thought in setting up an ethical law of the form "thou shalt ... " is:
> And what if I do not do it? But it is clear that ethics has nothing to do with punish-
> ment and reward in the ordinary sense. This question as to the *consequences* of an
> action must therefore be irrelevant.... There must be some sort of ethical reward
> and ethical punishment, but this must lie in the action itself. (T #6.422)

Here was a side of the *Tractatus* wholly unanticipated by Russell, G. E.
Moore, and the Cambridge Apostles.[10] After the war, when Russell and
Wittgenstein had their long-planned reunion in The Hague (December
1919), communication between the two had become somewhat strained.
Writing to Lady Ottoline on 20 December, Russell called Wittgenstein's
book "wonderful," although he had doubts that what it said was "right."
He also reports a certain dismay at the "mystic" strain in his friend:

> I was amazed to learn that he has become a complete mystic. He reads people like
> Kierkegaard and Angelus Silesius and is thinking seriously of becoming a monk.
> This all began with William James's *Varieties of Religious Experience.* ... he has pene-
> trated deep into mystical modes of thought and feeling, but I think (although he
> would not agree), that what he likes best in mysticism is its power to stop him from
> thinking.[11]

Despite his mistrust of Wittgenstein's "religious" turn, however, Russell
offered to write an introduction to the *Tractatus* and to arrange for its
publication in 1921.[12] By this time, though, the rift between Russell and
Wittgenstein had become serious, Russell declaring in his introduction
(which Wittgenstein evidently hated)[13] that, despite the author's claim to
the contrary, "he manages to say a good deal about what cannot be said,"
a situation that, Russell admits, "leaves me with a certain sense of intellec-
tual discomfort" (T 22).

Wittgenstein was never, of course, a "complete mystic," but it is true
that his wartime experience (five full years from enlistment to release
from prison camp) had made an irrevocable difference in his thinking on
ethical and religious matters. In the notebook entries for 1916 we read,

"A man who is happy must have no fear. Not even in face of death" (NBK 74), and again, "Fear in face of death is the best sign of a false, i.e., a bad, life" (NBK 75). "Happiness," then, depends upon the willingness to *accept* one's situation. Such acceptance is not a matter of Christian resignation ("To love one's neighbor," Wittgenstein remarks in his notebook, "would mean to will!") but, more accurately, a form of discipline that trains one to extract value from whatever situation one happens to be in. "Only a man who lives not in time but in the present is happy" (NBK 74). And some thirty years later, when his young American friend Norman Malcolm expressed the view that serving in the wartime (World War II) navy was "a boredom," Wittgenstein reproached him with the words "I can't help believing that an enormous lot can be learnt about human beings in this war—*if* you can keep your eyes open. And the better you are at thinking the more you'll get out of what you see."[14]

It is, in any case, the will to *change* that lies behind the well-known letter (January 1918) Wittgenstein wrote to his close friend Paul Engelmann, who had been awarded the Silver Medal for Valor:

It is true there is a difference between myself as I am now and as I was when we met in Olmütz [winter 1916]. And, as far as I know, the difference is that I am now *slightly* more decent. By this I only mean that I am slightly clearer in my own mind about my lack of decency. If you tell me now that I have no faith, you are perfectly right, only I did not have it before either. . . . *I am clear about one thing:* I am far too bad to be able to theorize about myself; in fact I shall either remain a swine or else I shall improve, and that's that! Only let's cut out the transcendental twaddle. . . . (PE 10–11)

Nur kein transzendentales Geschwätz: Wittgenstein had always had a distaste for pretentious chit-chat on philosophical subjects, for pontificating generalizations on questions of metaphysics and ethics, but the war years, during which he read Tolstoy and Dostoyevsky, Schopenhauer and Kierkegaard, intensified this particular aversion to what we would call, in current parlance, bullshit. In a letter of autumn 1919 to Ludwig von Ficker, written after the editor of *Der Brenner* had expressed interest in publishing the *Tractatus,* Wittgenstein explained:

... the point of the book is ethical. I once wanted to give a few words in the foreword which now actually are not in it, which however, I will write to you now because they might be a key for you: I wanted to write that my work consists of two parts: of the one which is here, and of everything which I have *not* written. And precisely this second part is the important one. For the Ethical is delimited from within, as it were, by my book; and I'm convinced that *strictly* speaking it can ONLY be delimited in this way. In brief, I think: All of what *many* are *babbling* today [*was Viele heute schwäfeln*], I have defined in my book by remaining silent about it.[15]

This letter has often been cited as testimony of Wittgenstein's overriding preoccupation with ethics. But for our purposes here, what is particularly interesting is the reference to the "many others [who] are just *babbling* [*schwäfeln*]." For wasn't a penchant for *transzendentales Geschwätz* finally the quality in Russell that Wittgenstein found hard to stomach, the former turning out books, pamphlets, essays, and lectures with whirlwind rapidity and sounding off (*schwäfeln*) as to what England should or shouldn't do (or might have done), what philosophy consists of, and so on, even as the latter published almost nothing during his lifetime and was never satisfied that he had formulated a given question quite correctly?

The difference is not just between two individuals with such-and-such psychological profiles but also between two cultures. I don't want to suggest that Russell and Wittgenstein were representative of their respective nations; far from it. But it is precisely because both were extremely privileged, by family background as well as by wealth, and because both began as students of logic and mathematics, that the opposition of their responses both to war and to work becomes so telling.

Culture Wars

Russell's biographer Ronald W. Clark provides us with an interesting account of Russell's return to England in June 1914, after three months on a lecture tour in the United States:

Russell sailed back across the Atlantic in the comfort of the *Megantic,* idly observing how the sea "was beautiful beyond belief, with the rare gentleness of fierce things"; enjoying the relaxation excited by his first sight of an iceberg, "sticking up in a conical shape, just as they do in pictures," and joyfully adding as a P.S., "I have now seen four icebergs." It was still only June 1914, and England to the east was still the untroubled country he had known since boyhood ... the England which was fashioned in the time of Queen Anne—a land of leisure and beauty, of aristocratic culture, of tolerance and good humour.[16]

This image of prewar England, found as it is in memoir after memoir of the period, has become the stuff of later historical accounts; witness Paul Fussell in *The Great War and Modern Memory:*

The prewar summer was the most idyllic for many years. It was warm and sunny, eminently pastoral. One lolled outside on a folding canvas chaise, or swam, or walked in the countryside. One read outdoors, went on picnics, had tea served from a white wicker table under the trees. . . . Siegfried Sassoon was busy fox hunting and playing serious county cricket. Robert Graves went climbing in the Welsh mountains. Edmund Blunden took country walks near Oxford, read Classics and English, and refined his pastoral diction. Wilfred Owen was teaching English to the boys of a French family living near Bordeaux. David Jones was studying illustration at Camberwell Art School. And for those like Strachey who preferred the pleasures of the West End, there were splendid evening parties, as well as a superb season for concert, theater, and the Russian ballet.[17]

Leonard Woolf, recalling that ballet season in his autobiography, remarks: "One's pleasure was increased because night after night one could go to Covent Garden and find all round one one's friends, the people whom one liked best in the world, moved and excited as one was oneself."[18]

This was the "civilized stability" into which the war intruded. "I think," writes Woolf, "the main difference in the world before 1914 from the world after 1914 was in the sense of security and the growing belief that it was a supremely good thing for people to be communally and individually happy" (BA 44). And throughout the autobiography, the war is regularly mourned as "the destruction of the civilization, the way of life, which existed in . . . vast stretches of England before 1914."[19]

It is this theme that animates Russell's own war writings, with the difference that Russell was an aristocrat, descended from a great Whig family. His mother, Kate Stanley, traced her ancestry to the French invaders who had landed at Hastings in 1066 and whose successors had been granted the reward of an earldom for good work on Bosworth Field. His father, Lord Amberley, was the son of John, 1st Earl Russell, who had fought the Reform Bill through Parliament in 1832 and had served as Victoria's prime minister during the Mexican War and during the revolutions of 1848; an earlier ancestor, William, Earl Russell, had defied Charles II in the Rye House plot of 1683 and had been executed. "I was taught," Russell recalls in *Portraits from Memory,* "a kind of theoretic liberalism which was prepared to tolerate a monarch so long as he recognized that he was an employee of the people and subject to dismissal if he proved unsatisfactory" (PM 7). As for the expectations of his class and time, Russell remarks wryly:

> There was to be ordered progress throughout the world, no revolutions, a gradual cessation of war, and an extension of parliamentary government to all those unfortunate regions which did not yet enjoy it.... There was to be democracy, but it was assumed that the people would always be ready to follow the advice of wise and experienced aristocrats. There was to be a disappearance of imperialism, but the subject races in Asia and Africa, whom the British would voluntarily cease to govern, would have learnt the advantage of a bi-cameral legislature composed of Whigs and Tories in about equal numbers.... The idea of any insecurity to British power never entered anybody's head. Britannia ruled the waves, and that was that. (CPBR 8)

In *Portraits from Memory,* Russell admits that these hopes and expectations "now seem a little absurd," but certainly they colored his own attitudes toward war. In "The Ethics of War" (1915), for example, having begun by spelling out the evils of war, Russell goes on to distinguish between four kinds of war: (1) Wars of Colonization; (2) Wars of Principle; (3) Wars of Self-defence; and (4) Wars of Prestige, arguing that the first two are often justified, the third seldom, and the fourth, which is the category to which World War I belongs, never.

Wars of Colonization, Russell argues, are now largely in the past and they are "totally devoid of *technical* justification." Nevertheless, if we are to judge by results, we cannot regret that such wars have taken place. They have the merit, often quite fallaciously claimed for all wars, of leading in the main to the survival of the fittest, and it is chiefly through such wars that the civilized portion of the world has been extended from the neighborhood of the Mediterranean to the greater part of the earth's surface.... We cannot at this date bring ourselves to condemn the process by which the American continent has been acquired for European civilization. In order that such wars may be justified, it is necessary that there should be a very great and undeniable difference between the civilization of the colonizers and that of the dispossessed natives. It is necessary, also, that the climate should be one in which the invading race can flourish. When these conditions are satisfied the conquest becomes justified. (CPBR 67)

Judging from such arguments—and there are many in Russell's writings of the period—we may surmise that his greatest objection to World War I was that it was so unnecessary, a mere "War of Prestige." What, for example, was the concern for the hegemony of the Balkans if not "entirely a question of prestige" (CPBR 71)? But the reasoning as to what might have been or what should have been is based on a set of rather questionable assumptions. In "The War and Non-Resistance" (1915), for example, Russell argues:

The chief crime of Germany in invading Belgium lies less in the legal fact that a treaty was broken than in the fact that terrible cruelty was inflicted on an unoffending nation. But the question which England had to consider was, not whether Germany had committed a crime, but whether we should do anything to mitigate the bad consequences of that crime by going to war. If we had not come in, the Belgians would in all likelihood not have resisted the German arms. In return for a free passage and for our neutrality, the Germans would have respected Belgian independence, and Belgium would have been spared almost all that it has suffered (CPBR 187).

And in a later discussion he suggests that if England had let Germany have Belgium, then England would have remained "strong and prosperous," the United States would never have been drawn into the war, and the terrible bloodshed and misery would never have occurred.

On the surface, such an argument sounds reasonable enough. But the "ifs" are less than reassuring: suppose (1) that the Germans had not respected Belgian independence, (2) that they had not stopped with Belgium but moved on to France, or (3) that they had challenged England's naval power as well as its right to certain colonies? Is it so sure that, given these scenarios, England would have remained so "strong and prosperous"? Or is Russell banking on a rationalism that is part of his aristocratic Whig heritage, a rationalism that has proved to be increasingly unable to cope with the upheavals of the twentieth century?

Here is another example from the same essay:

> The doctrine of non-resistance . . . is only applicable to wars between civilized states. It rests upon the belief that what is valuable in a European nation is more likely to be destroyed by war—even successful war—than by anything that another nation is likely to do if it is not resisted. A nation sufficiently numerous and strong to resist successfully by force of arms will also be able, if it choose, to resist by the method of the strike, by mere refusal to obey. No one seriously supposes that the Germans would undertake to govern England, even if we had no army or navy. The mere political difficulties would be insuperable. And if ordinary peaceful citizens in Germany could not be incited by fear of England, there would be no such public opinion in Germany as would sanction an invasion of England. (CPBR 188–89)

The alleged "insuperability" of "political difficulties" and the faith in "public opinion" as being reasonable and fair-minded are likely to strike a reader of the 1990s as dangerously naive. Wittgenstein may well have put his finger on the problem when he remarked, in a passage from *Culture and Value* that gives me my epigraph, "When we think of the world's future, we always mean the destination it will reach if it keeps going in the direction we can see it going in now; it does not occur to us that its path is not a straight line but a curve, constantly changing direction."

Not a straight line but a curve. Wittgenstein's own experience had prepared him for such deviation. "We do not advance towards our goal by the direct road," he wrote Paul Engelmann shortly after he had been released from his prison camp in 1919, "for this we (or at any rate I) have not got the strength. Instead we walk up all sorts of tracks and byways, and so long as we are making some headway we are in reasonably good shape. But whenever such a track comes to an end we are up against it;

only then do we realise that we are not at all where we ought to be"
(PE 21).

The sense of *difficulty* expressed here, a difficulty that demands constant struggle and self-discipline, was not just Wittgenstein's own; it was
characteristic of his particular cultural and political moment. Like Russell, he came from a leading family, though in his case the prominence
was one of industrial wealth rather than aristocracy. Whereas Russell had
been brought up to believe that it was his natural duty to engage in the
larger political life of his country, Wittgenstein, far from being able to
trace his ancestry back to the princes or political leaders of the Habsburg
dynasty, was three-quarters Jewish, a fact that, despite his baptism and
upbringing in the Catholic faith, mitigated against any large-scale identification with Austrian history or traditions. Accordingly, the devotion to
public life of the Russells was replaced, in the case of the Wittgensteins,
by a devotion to Culture.

There is, of course, nothing "typically Viennese" about Wittgenstein,
and yet, as in the case of Russell, it is difficult to dissociate his attitude
toward the Great War from the opulent, highly cultured, secretive, technologically efficient yet strangely unstable society in which he moved in
his youth. In their classic study *Wittgenstein's Vienna,* Allan Janik and
Stephen Toulmin provide the intellectual/social background for Wittgenstein's philosophy: the decadence and hypocrisy of the Habsburgs, the
writings of Karl Krauss and Arthur Schnitzler, the sexual theories of Otto
Weininger and the psychosexual theories of Freud, the music of Schönberg, the philosophy of Fritz Mauthner and Ernst Mach. "The *Tractatus,*"
write Janik and Toulmin, "epitomized the philosophical and intellectual
problems of Viennese art and culture, as they existed *before* 1918."[20] Accurate as this claim may be in its generalities, it must also be qualified. Born
in 1889, Wittgenstein belonged, after all, less to the Viennese *fin de siècle*
(Freud, born in 1873, and Schönberg, born in 1874, are Russell's age, not
Wittgenstein's) than to what Apollinaire was to call, in his poem
"Guerre," "les jeunes de la classe 1915." Indeed, the enigmatic *Tractatus*
may be closer to the language games of Duchamp or Gertrude Stein than
to the erotic exhibitionism characteristic of Klimt and Schiele, much less

the witty, amoral ironies of Schnitzler. The avant-garde connection is, in any case, the one I now want to consider.

TRACTATUS AND AVANT-GARDE

In a recent provocative study called *Rites of Spring* (1989), Modris Ecksteins reminds us how different the German prewar period was from the French and especially the English *avant guerre,* which was its antithesis. Whereas England, on the eve of World War I, was the major conservative power in the world, Germany regarded itself as the country of the future. Having been unified only since 1871 and having in the thirty years between unification and the war industrialized and modernized itself with almost unbelievable rapidity, the new urbanized Germany was committed to change, to a *Flucht nach vorne.*[21] From the German point of view, Ecksteins observes, "British pronouncements about the rule of law, about democracy and justice, were, given her foreign policy, obviously a sham. In the international context Germans were inclined to regard their country as a progressive, liberating force that would introduce a new honesty into power arrangements in the world" (ME 87). Indeed, when war broke out, the Germans responded to it in what they considered "spiritual terms":

Although matériel was important, war was regarded, especially in Germany, as the supreme test of spirit, and, as such, a test of vitality, culture, and life. War, wrote Friedrich von Bernhardi in 1911 in a volume that was to go through six German editions in two years, was a "life-giving principle." It was an expression of a superior culture. "War," wrote a contemporary of Bernhardi's, was in fact *"the price one must pay for culture."* (ME 90, my emphasis)

Another epithet frequently applied to war was *eine innere Notwendigkeit,* an inner, so to speak, spiritual necessity. "It was a quest," writes Ecksteins, "for authenticity, for truth, for self-fulfillment, for those values, that is, which the avant-garde had evoked prior to the war and against those features—materialism, banality, hypocrisy, tyranny—which it had attacked.... For many the war was also a deliverance—from vulgarity, constraint, and convention. Artists and intellectuals were among those most gripped by war fever" (ME 92).

Such war fever was, as I suggested in *The Futurist Moment,* character-istic of the Italian and Russian avant-garde as well, and even in France such marginalized poets as Blaise Cendrars and Apollinaire, neither of whom could claim to be "genuine" Frenchmen, were eager to prove them-selves war heroes, at least in the early stages of the conflict.[22] The German *Flucht nach vorne* seems to have been more deep-seated, a by-product of the violent industrialization and too-rapid urbanization of the prewar years, but whatever the precise relationship of the German paradigm to that of its Continental neighbors, we should bear in mind that the story, told by such leading cultural historians as Paul Fussell, of a benign, or-dered, and "innocent" society destroyed by a meaningless and terrible war, accurate as it may be with regard to the British *avant-guerre* (and even here some qualification is surely in order), has little to do with the realities of the German (or Austro-Hungarian) situation. For prewar Germany, war evidently meant revolution or, at the very least, necessary change. Internalized, war became the quest for authenticity and self-fulfillment, that is, putting to the test one's manhood in the face of death. It is in his intuitive acceptance of this paradigm that Wittgenstein may be said to be, as he put it, "German through and through."

I say "intuitive" because, at the conscious level, Wittgenstein had nothing but contempt for the avant-garde cult of violence, revolution, and the *Flucht nach vorne.* Had he attended Marinetti's London music-hall performances, this lover of Beethoven and Goethe would no doubt have been thoroughly disgusted. Indeed, it is less in the aesthetic than in the ethical realm that Wittgenstein's "Germanness" manifests itself. Ac-cording to Ray Monk, he and Russell frequently quarreled about personal morality. In June 1912, for example, Russell tells Lady Ottoline, "Witt-genstein went on to say how few there are who don't lose their soul. I said it depended on having a large purpose that one is true to. He said he thought it depended more on suffering and the power to endure it. I was surprised—I hadn't expected that kind of thing from him" (RM 51). When Russell explained that his own inclination was to look outside him-self for something to sustain him, Wittgenstein insisted, in Ray Monk's words, "that the possibility of remaining uncorrupted rested entirely on one's self—on the qualities one found within. If one's soul was pure . . . then no matter what happened to one 'externally' . . . nothing could happen to one's *self*" (RM 52–53).

This central difference is hardly surprising when one remembers that Wittgenstein was brought up in a household that placed individual initiative far above social action. Karl Wittgenstein had, after all, run away to America when he was seventeen, establishing his business credentials and then coming back to Vienna to make his fortune. In this context, to dwell on history seems entirely beside the point. "What has history to do with me?" Wittgenstein writes in a notebook entry of 2 September 1916. "Mine is the first and only world!" Indeed, "What others in the world have told me about the world is a very small and incidental part of my experience of the world" (NBK 82).

Thus, when Wittgenstein writes to Paul Engelmann (January 1918) that he now feels "slightly more decent" than he had two years earlier, he is expressing the conviction that the challenge of war has helped him to fulfill himself, to become more authentic. As Engelmann recalls, "When [Wittgenstein] heard that his friend Bertrand Russell was in prison as an opponent of the war, he did not withhold his respect for Russell's personal courage in living up to his convictions, but felt that this was heroism in the wrong place."[23]

In fact, one way to read the *Tractatus* is as a critique of "heroism in the wrong place." As early as 1912, Wittgenstein had expressed violent objection to an essay of Russell's called "The Essence of Religion," which argued that there is such a thing as an "infinite part of our life, [whose] . . . impartiality leads to truth in thought, justice in action, and universal love of feeling" (RM 62). The war essays carried on this mode—a mode Wittgenstein would dismiss, in his letter to Ficker, as so much *schwäfeln,* idle talk. And increasingly the urgency of *not* saying what *cannot be said* came to dominate Wittgenstein's thinking.

The *Tractatus* was evidently completed in the summer of 1918, when Wittgenstein was on leave at his Uncle Paul's house near Salzburg. The news of David Pinsent's death in a plane accident reached him in early

July. The dedication to Pinsent, "my first and my only friend," as he wrote to Pinsent's mother (RM 154), becomes significant in light of the fact that in its final version the "logical" core of the *Tractatus* was subordinated to a larger scheme that is both poetic and at least subliminally elegiac.

Consider the preface, evidently added after the rest of the manuscript had been completed (BMG 265). Imagine a treatise on truth tables, on tautology and contradiction, that begins with the paragraph:

> This book will perhaps only be understood by those who have already thought the thoughts which are expressed in it—or similar thoughts. It is therefore not a text-book. Its object would be attained if it afforded pleasure to one who read it with understanding. (T 27)

Pleasure is the word I find most remarkable here—the *pleasure* of finding thoughts one has already thought. Such a pleasure is bound to be at least in part aesthetic, depending as it does on the reader's participation in an intriguing process of elimination whereby, so we are told in the preface, we will come to see that, although "the problems" taken up in the treatise "have in essentials been finally solved . . . the value of this work secondly consists in the fact that it shows how little has been done when these problems have been solved" (T 29).

From this curious invitation, we turn to the text itself, with its elaborately numbered aphorisms. Brian McGuinness explains:

> The work was to consist . . . of propositions, aphorisms or remarks of at most paragraph length, numbered so as to show their logical relations. n.1 was to be a comment on n, n.11 on n.1, and so on. The most obvious exemplar of this system of numbering is *Principia Mathematica*. . . . The implication that these philosophical propositions have the lack of ambiguity and the quite definite logical relations of the lemmata, definitions, axioms, and theorems of a logical system is, though paradoxical, quite certainly intended. For composition this method of numbering . . . has the merit that a number, an afterthought, can always be inserted between any two existing numbers—thus between n.11 and n.12 we can insert first n.111 then n.112 (or n.1101) . . . and so on. (BMG 265)

This makes perfect sense but it doesn't quite describe what happens in the *Tractatus*. Consider the numbering of the opening:

1	The world is everything that is the case.
1.1	The world is the totality of facts, not of things.
1.11	The world is determined by the facts, and by these being *all* the facts.
1.12	For the totality of facts determines both what is the case, and also all that is not the case.
1.13	The facts in logical space are the world.
1.2	The world divides into facts.
1.21	Any one can either be the case or not be the case, and everything else remains the same.
2	What is the case, the fact, is the existence of atomic facts.
2.01	An atomic fact is a combination of objects (entities, things).

The neatly numbered propositions provide the reader with a sense of calm and order: #1, 1.1, 1.11, 1.12, and so on. But why does, say, #1.2 ("The world divides into facts") not follow #1.1 ("The world is the totality of facts, not of things") or #1.11 ("The world is determined by the facts, and by these being *all* the facts")? Or again, why is the proposition "An atomic fact is a combination of objects," which is a comment on #2 ("What is the case, the fact, is the existence of atomic facts"), numbered #2.01 rather than #2.1?

Critical commentary on the *Tractatus* has shed little light on this subject.[24] Perhaps the best way to regard the number anomaly is as a kind of *clinamen,* a bend or swerve where logic gives way to mystery. And that mystery comes to a head in Section 5 where, after the very technical discussion of truth functions, with elaborate tables such as the one in #5.101, which provides the schema for the truth functions of any number of elementary propositions, we come, in #5.134ff, to the negative critique of inference and causality:

5.134	From an elementary proposition no other can be inferred. . . .
5.135	In no way can an inference be made from the existence of one state of affairs to the existence of another entirely different from it.

> 5.136   There is no causal nexus which justifies such an inference.
>
> 5.1361   The events of the future *cannot* be inferred from those of the
>   present. Superstition is the belief in the causal nexus.

The third of these propositions (#5.136) was adumbrated in a notebook entry made at Olmütz on 15 October 1916: "It is clear that the causal nexus is not a nexus at all" (NBK 84); the same entry contains the aphorism "What cannot be imagined cannot even be talked about," which becomes *Tractatus* #5.61.

The causal nexus is not a nexus at all. Indeed, belief in the causal nexus is called "superstition," there being no way the events of the future can be *inferred* from those of the past. Was Wittgenstein thinking of Russell here, the Russell who, in his war tracts (e.g., *The Principles of Social Reconstruction*) was increasingly given to finding solutions based on his reasoned deductions as to the successes and failures of past actions? There is no way of knowing, but what is clear is that for Wittgenstein the war had become, not a subject to be analyzed but the condition for what might best be called textual breakthrough. The mysterious aphorisms of the #5.6s ("*The limits of my language* mean the limits of my world"; "Everything we see could also be otherwise," and so on)—which make little sense individually—achieve a special aura in the context, arrived at as they are with so much difficulty and pain.

Take the proposition (#6.43) "The world of the happy is quite another than that of the unhappy." It first appears in a notebook entry of 29 July 1916, made during the heavy fighting of the Brusilov Offensive:

It seems one can't say anything more than: "Live happily!"
The world of the happy is a different world from that of the unhappy.
The world of the happy is *a happy world.*
Then can there be a world that is neither happy nor unhappy? (NBK 78)

The permutations of the word "happy" remind me of Gertrude Stein's portrait of Picasso, with its charged repetitions of the words "charming," "working," and "following," each instance of the word in question introducing a slight shift in meaning. "The world of the happy is *a happy world*": what looks like tautology turns out to raise some central questions about the *Tractatus*'s opening premises. If, as the treatise's first proposition tells us, "The world is everything that is the case," then there is no question of its being "happy" or "unhappy," both attributes being "of the world." Or again, if what "is the case" is "happiness," then happiness is obviously a quality of the world and it is tautological to assert its existence. But third, if "happiness" is not a property of the world but lies outside it, then it makes no sense to talk of "*a happy world.*"[25] The permutations of the word "happy," far from making Wittgenstein's meaning clearer, thus produce a sense of enigma, an enigma even more marked in the German original, "*Die Welt des Glücklichen ist eine glückliche Welt,*" where the subject nominative implies ownership, the world *belonging* or *pertaining* or *attributed* to the happy one, even as the predicate emphasizes what is simply a state of affairs—*a happy world.* Such foregrounding of syntactic difference is closer to avant-garde writing than to the style of the *Principia Mathematica* or even to the philosophical writings of Mauthner and Mach, to which Janik and Toulmin link Wittgenstein. Schopenhauer is a more plausible precursor,[26] but Schopenhauer's meditations on desire and will are not embedded, as are Wittgenstein's, in dry passages of logical analysis. Indeed, what is uniquely Wittgensteinian is the sudden break, the lack of connection, between two kinds of operation, as when, having established in *Tractatus* #6.3751 that "a particle cannot at the same time have two velocities, *i.e.,* that at the same time it cannot be in two places, *i.e.,* that particles in different places at the same time cannot be identical," Wittgenstein suddenly breaks off, leaves a space, and then gives us:

6.4   All propositions are of equal value.

6.41   The sense of the world must lie outside the world. In the world everything is as it is and happens as it does happen. *In* it there is no value—and if there were, it would be of no value.

How did the mind make the jump from the world of fact ("a particle cannot at the same time have two velocities") to the world of value, more accurately the world of resignation that "everything is as it is and happens as it does happen"? If "the sense of the world must lie outside the world," what are we doing measuring and assessing what lies inside? It is this note of irresolution, this recognition of a mystery that cannot be solved, that places the *Tractatus* with, say, the gnomic and aphoristic manifestos of Malevich or the meditative poems of Wallace Stevens rather than with the writing of *fin de siècle* Vienna, much less the Bloomsbury of G. E. Moore or Maynard Keynes.

But what, specifically, is the relation of this way of putting things to the reality of war? The *Tractatus* is not, of course, overtly a book "about" World War I; it contains no brief against war as such, no images of horror or bloodshed, no transcendental truths about violence and slaughter. But it is a war book nevertheless, illustrating, as it does, its own theory that certain things cannot be *said,* they can only be *shown:* "There is indeed the inexpressible. This *shows* itself; it is the mystical" (#6.522). To put it another way, when we come to the proposition "Death is not an event of life. Death is not lived through" (#6.4311), we feel that we have witnessed the process whereby this "mystical" insight has been earned. The diarist has witnessed countless deaths, but they are not, he feels obliged to insist, "events" of his own life. The point cannot be argued; it can merely be felt. And in this sense the *Tractatus* must be understood as a poetic construct.

In a practical sense, however, Wittgenstein's "war book" portrays a state of mind that could not be maintained. Even if "The sense of the world must lie outside the world" (#6.41), the world that is "everything that is the case" reasserts its claim on one's attention. In 1929 Wittgenstein returned to Cambridge to teach philosophy and remained in England the rest of his life. He was never again close to Russell: M. O'C. Drury recalls that in the early thirties, when he was an undergraduate, Wittgenstein told his weekly discussion group, "Russell's books should be bound in two colours: those dealing with mathematical logic in red, and all students of philosophy should read them; those dealing with ethics and politics in blue, and no one should be allowed to read them."[27] As for Russell's pronouncements on sexuality and marriage, Wittgenstein remarked, "If a person tells me he has been to the worst places I have no right to judge him; but if he tells me it was his superior wisdom that enabled him to go there, then I know he is a fraud" (RR 127).

But didn't such "fraud" open up new possibilities? *Schwäfeln*—the high-minded babble on this or that subject, the insistence on speaking about that of which *one cannot speak*—could itself become a fascinating subject for philosophical/poetical investigation. The next step, therefore, was to take the language actually used in such discourse and put it to the test:

When philosophers use a word—"knowledge," "being," "object," "I," "proposition," "name"—and try to grasp the *essence* of the thing, one must always ask oneself: is the word ever actually used in this way in the language-game which is its original home?

What *we* do is to bring words back from their metaphysical to their everyday use.

This is #116 of the *Philosophical Investigations,* whose long first part Wittgenstein completed (but did not publish) in 1945 at the conclusion of yet another war. Compiled from notes that go back many years, perhaps it too can be read as something of a war book, although now seen from the other side of darkness, through the eyes of a survivor. By this time, of course, the notion of war as *Flucht nach vorne* had been utterly discredited, and yet Wittgenstein was still trying to "become a different person," still insisting that philosophy could be only a method, not a science, because it has nothing to discover.[28] In the preface to the *Philosophical Investigations* (PI vi), he writes:

It is not impossible that it should fall to the lot of this work, in its poverty and in the darkness of this time, to bring light into one brain or another—but, of course, it is not likely.

The skepticism of that last disclaimer is deeply moving, for Wittgenstein understood, as many of his exegetes have not, that the study of philosophy could not make one a better person. But if not better, at least wiser? The *Philosophical Investigations* is almost always read by academic philosophers as an advance over the youthful *Tractatus:* a view confirmed by Wittgenstein himself, who, by the late twenties, had rejected its theory of logical inference and its claim that atomic propositions are independent. "What was wrong about my conception," he told Moritz Schlick and Friedrich Waismann during a meeting with the Vienna Circle in 1929, "was that I believed that the syntax of logical constants could be laid down without paying attention to the inner connection of propositions." The task ahead, therefore, was to describe that "more comprehensive syntax about which I did not yet know anything at the time" (RM 284–85).

The gradual development of that "more comprehensive syntax" is the subject of the next chapter. But we should bear in mind that the seeming failure of the *Tractatus* to articulate the "inner connection of propositions" is, from another angle, the source of its peculiar strength, its poetic power. On its penultimate page, we read:

> The temporal immortality of the human soul, that is to say, its eternal survival after death, is not only in no way guaranteed, but this assumption in the first place will not do for us what we always tried to make it do. Is a riddle solved by the fact that I survive for ever? Is this eternal life not as enigmatic as our present one? The solution of the riddle of life in space and time lies *outside* space and time. (T #6.4312)

"Is [the] eternal life not as enigmatic as our present one?" Wittgenstein came to this epiphany only very gradually. Two entries in the secret notebook, made on the retreat from the Russians in the "icy cold, rain and fog" of the Carpathian mountains (GT 69) are revealing. The first dates from 26 July 1916 and refers to a "deeply moving letter from David [Pinsent]." "He writes that his brother has been killed in France. How terrible! This kind, friendly letter opens my eyes to the fact that I am living in *exile* here. It may be a healing exile, but I now feel it as an exile all the same." To speak of exile is, of course, to admit that one has a home, that, in Wittgenstein's case, perhaps one is, after all, at home in the world. And the next entry (29.7.16) reads: "Yesterday, I was shot at. I was in despair. I was afraid of death. What desire I now have to live! And it is hard to deny oneself life when one finally comes to value it."[29]

Here, after two years of notebook entries expressing thoughts of suicide, is a turn toward life. The immortality of the soul, it now seemed to the author of the *Tractatus,* is "not only in no way guaranteed, but this assumption in the first place will not do for us what we always tried to make it do." Philosophy, in other words, cannot discover the Truth; its propositions cannot provide a picture of "reality," as the *Tractatus* had originally argued. But if the "eternal life" is as "enigmatic as our present one," that present one deserves to be studied closely. As Wittgenstein puts it in #6.52: "We feel that even if *all possible* scientific questions be an-

swered, the problems of life have still not been touched at all." All the
more reason to pay attention to the ways we formulate these problems.

In this context, the famous ladder metaphor that concludes the
Tractatus has been enacted by the very narrative we have just finished
reading:

> My propositions are elucidatory in this way: he who understands me finally rec-
> ognizes them as senseless, when he has climbed out through them, on them, over
> them. (He must so to speak throw away the ladder, after he has climbed up on it.)

So much for the riddling aphorisms that have led up to this page of the
Tractatus. But that page also looks ahead to the writings of the thirties,
when Wittgenstein would exchange one ladder, one form of exile, that of
the war and postwar years in Austria, for another—the exile of teaching
the mysteries of ordinary language in a country and language not his own.
Trying to write a colloquial English, he was given to epistolary locutions
such as "Dear Gil (old beast)" and the signature "So long!" (see RM 294;
PO 11). No wonder grammar was to become an obsession. "The choice
of our words," wrote Wittgenstein in 1933, "is so important, because the
point is to hit upon the physiognomy of the thing exactly, because only
the exactly aimed thought can lead to the correct track. The car must be
placed on the tracks precisely so, so that it can keep rolling correctly"
(PO 165).

But since the car track can be thought of as a horizontal ladder, and
ladders, once used, are to be discarded, how do we identify that "correct
track"? The question would have to be posed otherwise.

If I say A has beautiful eyes someone may ask me: what do you find beautiful about his eyes, and perhaps I shall reply: the almond shape, long eye-lashes, delicate lids. What do these eyes have in common with a gothic church that I find beautiful too?

—Wittgenstein, *Culture and Value* 24

You might think Aesthetics is a science telling us what's beautiful—almost too ridiculous for words. I suppose it ought to include also what sort of coffee tastes good.

—Wittgenstein, *Lectures and Conversations*

on Aesthetics, Psychology, and Religious Belief

… to imagine a language means to imagine a form of life.

—Wittgenstein, *Philosophical Investigations*

two

The "Synopsis of Trivialities": *The Art of the Philosophical Investigations*

Wittgenstein's lectures on aesthetics, given at Cambridge in the summer of 1938, were designed to show that words like "good" and "beautiful" have no intrinsic meaning, that, on the contrary, what matters is the "occasion" on which these words are said, the uses to which they are put. "In order to get clear about aesthetic words," he remarks, "you have to describe ways of living" (LCA 11). Yet, as we have already noted, the Wittgenstein who scoffed at the very notion of a "science" of aesthetics is also the one who said, "Philosophie dürfte man eigentlich nur *dichten*" ("Philosophy ought really to be written only as a *form of poetry*"; CV 24). What sense can this statement make if we don't know what "poetry" is, more broadly, what art is? It is this paradox which lies at the heart of the radically "poetic" *Philosophical Investigations* and which I want to examine in the present chapter. I begin with the vexed question of the relationship of "poetic" to "ordinary" language.

(Un)Defining the "Ordinary"

In 1916, the year Wittgenstein, stationed at the Russian front, was writing the later "mystical" sections of the *Tractatus,* in Moscow Lev Jakubinsky, one of the members of the newly formed Russian Formalist circle, wrote a treatise called "On Sounds in Verse Language":

> The phenomena of language ought to be classified according to the purpose for which the speaker uses his language resources in any given instance. If the speaker uses them for the purely practical purpose of communication, then we are dealing with a system of *practical language* (discursive thought), in which language resources . . . have no autonomous value and are merely a *means* of communication. But it is possible to conceive in fact to find language systems in which the practical aim retreats to the background (it does not necessarily disappear altogether), and language resources acquire autonomous value.[1]

This distinction between the "practical" language of "ordinary" communication and the "autonomous" language of poetry was, we know, to become an article of faith of modernist poetics. As Roman Jakobson, the most important Russian Formalist theorist, put it:

> . . . the content of the concept *poetry* is unstable and temporally conditioned. But the poetic function, *poeticity,* is . . . an element sui generis. . . . For the most part poet-icity is only a part of a complex structure, but it is a part that necessarily transforms the other elements and determines with them the nature of the whole. . . .
>
> But how does poeticity manifest itself? Poeticity is present when the word is felt as a word and not a mere representation of the object being named or an outburst of emotion, when words and their composition, their meaning, their external and inner form, acquire a weight and value of their own instead of referring indifferently to reality.[2]

There have been a good many variants of this basic formulation. In the Cambridge of the early thirties, Wittgenstein's contemporary I. A. Richards interpreted the ordinary language/literary language dichotomy more broadly as the distinction between the scientific and the artistic, the cognitive and the emotive, the denotative and the connotative, the literal and the figurative—a distinction largely taken over by the American New Criticism.³ Other Formalists, notably Viktor Shklovsky, formulated the dichotomy less on textual than on affective grounds, as an opposition between the reader's (or viewer's) habituation and the possibility of "fresh" perception, the enabling concept here being that of *defamiliarization* or *making strange* (*ostranenie*), the ability of the artistic construct to slow down perception and make the audience see the object in question as if for the first time.⁴

The concept of defamiliarization was not, of course, invented by the Russian Formalists; Romantic writers from Goethe and Wordsworth to Proust and Walter Benjamin had discussed the power of particular linguistic forms to create the *ostranenie* that gives a literary text its particular *aura* in opposition to the *instrumental* (with its cognates "literal," "propositional," "logical," "neutral," "representational"), information-bearing language of "ordinary" prose. But what is less well understood is that the various deconstructionisms of the post–World War II era never quite dispelled the notion that there is a basic opposition between "ordinary" and "literary" discourse. True, the literary, or *fictive,* now became the property of *all* writing, there being no *hors-texte,* no presence to which the play of signifiers might point with any assurance. But although *différance* (Derrida's term derived from the doubleness of the pair "differ"/"defer") now marks the sign not only in texts marked as "literary" but in all forms of writing, there is, as Pierre Bourdieu has shrewdly noted, one form of discourse that seems to be exempt from the aporias of undecidability, a discourse in which the fabled slippage of the signifier does not seem to preclude the formulation of authoritative statements—namely, the philosophical (theoretical) discourse itself.⁵ Open a text like Derrida's *Of Grammatology* at random, and you will find passages like the following:

The hinge [*brisure*] marks the impossibility that a sign, the unity of a signifier and a signified, be produced within the plenitude of a present and an absolute presence. That is why there is no full speech, however much one might wish to restore it by means or without benefit of psychoanalysis.

Or this one:

The end of linear writing is indeed the end of the book, even if, even today, it is within the form of a book that new writings—literary or theoretical—allow themselves to be, for better or for worse, encased.[6]

Language may never have access to a reality that exists outside the text, may never be able to avoid the slippage of the signifier, and yet the argument that this is the case is made in a series of defining statements that, however oblique and stylized, are meant to be accepted as belonging to a coherent theoretical discourse. "That is why," says Derrida in the first example above, "there is no full speech" explaining or accounting for the status of the sign to the reader. "Derrida," Fredric Jameson noted as long ago as 1974, "is condemned to the impossible situation (which resembles Barthes's description of the impossibility of literature) of denouncing the metaphysic of presence with words and terminology which, no sooner used, themselves solidify and become instruments in the perpetuation of that illusion of presence which they were initially designed to dispel."[7]

But how should theory deal with what was increasingly felt to be an unsatisfactory binary opposition between instrumentality and poeticity? In his famous essay called "How Ordinary Is Ordinary Language?" (1973), Stanley Fish tried to solve the problem by moving the locus of *literariness* from text to reader. In the headnote to the essay, added when it was reprinted in *Is There a Text in This Class?,* Fish declares:

In this essay I challenge the ordinary-language/literary-language distinction, first by pointing out that it impoverishes both the norm and its (supposed) deviation, and second by denying that literature, as a class of utterances, is identified by formal properties. Literature, I argue, is the product of a way of reading, of a community agreement about what will count as literature, which leads the members of the community to pay a certain kind of attention and thereby to *create* literature. Since that way of reading or paying attention is not eternally fixed but will vary with cultures and times, the nature of the literary institution and its relation to other institutions whose configurations are similarly made will be continually changing. Aesthetics, then, is not the once and for all specification of essentialist literary and nonliterary properties but an account of the *historical* process by which such properties emerge, in a reciprocally defining relationship. The writing of this aesthetics, of a truly new literary history, has hardly begun.[8]

This argument seems nothing if not reasonable. In the essay itself, Fish is able to show, without too much difficulty, that *"deviation theories always trivialize the norm"* (ITT 101). Such theories fall into two classes: "message-plus" theories, "committed to downgrading works in which the elements of style do not either reflect or support a propositional core," and "message-minus" theories, which are "forced to deny literary status to works whose function is in part to convey information or offer propositions about the real world" (ITT 103–4). What, then, *is* "literature"? "Literature is language but it is language around which we have drawn a frame, a frame that indicates a decision to regard with a particular self-consciousness the resources language has always possessed." And Fish adds parenthetically, "(I am aware that this may sound very much like Jakobson's definition of the poetic function as the *set toward the message;* but his set is exclusive and aesthetic—toward the message *for its own sake*—while my set is toward the message for the sake of the human and moral content all messages necessarily display.) What characterizes literature then is not formal properties but an attitude. . . . The difference resides not in the language but in ourselves" (ITT 108–9). And Fish goes on to make his now-familiar argument about "interpretive communities" as the locus of meaning and value.[9]

The name Wittgenstein does not appear in the index to *Is There a Text in This Class?* Asked in a recent interview whether he thought Wittgenstein had significantly influenced his work, Fish replied, "No I don't, because I don't know him well enough."[10] This seems to be a fair self-appraisal. At Johns Hopkins in the late seventies, Fish recalls, talk of Wittgenstein was very much in the air, but his own ideas were developed independently of the *Philosophical Investigations.* A comparison of the two bears this out: indeed, Wittgenstein's own analysis of the ordinary paradoxically moves the "literary" into quite a different arena.

From a Wittgensteinian perspective, perhaps the first thing to note about Fish's argument is that, however much Fish wants to redefine what literature is and whence its authority comes, he never seems to doubt that definition (more accurately, redefinition) is possible. Take the declaration in the headnote, "Literature, I argue, is the product of a way of reading, of a community agreement about what will count as literature, which leads the members of the community to pay a certain kind of attention and thereby to *create* literature." "*Literature, I argue, is . . .*": the sentence assumes that there is such a thing as *literature* and that this thing is in urgent need of redefinition. "The nature of the literary institution," Fish goes on to say, "will be continually changing"—again a proposition based on a particular assumption, namely, that a "literary institution" has a basic nature, subject to change. And furthermore, "Aesthetics . . . is not the once and for all specification of essentialist literary and nonliterary properties but an account of the *historical* process by which such properties emerge." "*Aesthetics is not . . .*": Fish's sentence never questions for a moment that there is such a thing as aesthetics; it merely attacks a particular notion of aesthetics ("the once and for all specification of essentialist literary and nonliterary properties") and corrects it: "[Aesthetics is] an account of the *historical* process by which such properties [literary properties] emerge." But if "literature" cannot be specified, how can it have "properties"? More important: if we cannot, according to Fish, define the *literary,* how is it that we know what the term *historical* means?

Now let us reread the passage cited above in which Fish distinguishes his own procedure from Jakobson's:

> . . . literature is language . . . but it is language around which we have drawn a frame, a frame that indicates a decision to regard with a particular self-consciousness the resources language has always possessed. (I am aware that this may sound very much like Jakobson's definition of the poetic function as the *set toward the message;* but his set is exclusive and aesthetic—toward the message *for its own sake*—while my set is toward the message for the sake of the human and moral content all messages necessarily display.)

Here Fish boxes himself into the untenable position of maintaining that the *aesthetic* is not fully "human," whereas the "moral" (ethical) is so. And further: Fish implies that the "human and moral" (now equated) are somehow specifiable in ways that the aesthetic is not. But what *is* the "human and moral content" that "all messages necessarily display"? If I say, to use one of Wittgenstein's most common examples, "This chess piece is called a king," is this a "human and moral" message? If "all messages necessarily display" a "human and moral content," the answer must be that it is. But if "all messages" have this property, then "aesthetic" messages must have it too. How then are they "exclusive"?

By now it should be clear that Fish merely replaces one set of binary oppositions with another, the "interpretive community" now becoming the locus of literary interpretation and value judgment as against the "ordinary" or random readership that presumably does not confer meaning and value on a given text. Milton, in either case, remains the great English poet (which means that, for an Anglo-centered critic like Fish, he is *the* great poet), and the issue becomes how and why one interpretive community (say, our own in the late twentieth century) interprets Milton differently from the way an earlier one (say, that of his contemporaries or of the New Critics of the 1950s) read him.

But suppose one scraps the notion that the ordinary must be defined in relation to its opposite, the extraordinary, or indeed in relation to anything outside it. Wittgenstein's *ordinary* is best understood as quite simply *that which is,* the language we do *actually* use when we communicate with one another. In this sense, the ordinary need not be literal, denotative, propositional, neutral, referential, or any of the other adjectives with which it has been equated in the ordinary/literary debate. On the contrary, our actual language may well be connotative, metaphoric, fantastic, the issue being quite simply whether and in what context people use it. "I have a pain," "I want to talk to you," "I'm afraid of lions": these sentences seem ordinary enough. But what about "If a lion could talk, we could not understand him" (PI, p. 223)? An ordinary enough sentence but one not used in everyday conversation and therefore less familiar than "I have a pain." But then "I have a pain" is, so Wittgenstein shows us (see especially PI #244–56), itself an enigma, it being impossible for X to convey to Y or Z precisely what the pain he/she feels is like. And what about the gnomic sentence "Imagine someone saying: 'But I know how tall I am!' and laying his hand on top of his head to prove it" (PI #279)? All the words here are perfectly "ordinary" as is the grammatical construction, and yet the notion of an actual person behaving in this way is absurd, Wittgenstein using this particular example to show how oddly we use the verb *to know*.

The Wittgenstein who returned to Cambridge in 1929, after a fifteen-year absence during which he had experienced life at the front and in an Italian prison camp and had worked as a gardener, a village schoolmaster, and an architect, seems to have lost his faith in the power of a given proposition to "picture" that which it describes. "Philosophy," we read on the first page of the first lecture he gave during Lent term 1930, "is the attempt to be rid of a particular kind of puzzlement. The 'philosophic' puzzlement is one of intellect and not of instinct. Philosophic puzzles are irrelevant to our every-day life. They are puzzles of *language*. Instinctively we use language rightly; but to the intellect this use is a puzzle" (LEC1 1). It is the formation of this "instinctive" use of language, a set of habits that might, as his Cambridge friend, the Italian Marxist economist Piero Sraffa, argued, be studied anthropologically, that became Wittgenstein's new focus.[11] And here he turned to *grammar,* the actual construction of words and phrases in a given context. For "there are no gaps in grammar; grammar is always complete." Complete in that "we can only have incompleteness *in* a space," whereas the grammar of a sentence—say, "The door is open"—*is* the space (LEC1 16). "You cannot justify grammar" (LEC1 48); it merely *is*.

Description thus replaces explanation. We begin to look at sentences very closely. "When I say 'The door is not open' and 'The chair is not yellow', is it the same *not* in both sentences?" (LEC1 54). The first states a condition, the second an attribute of the noun modified, but we have no trouble understanding what "not" means in either case. Again, "We say 'Twice two is four' and 'This is red'. But when we point to a rose and say this, do we mean that it is identical with red? Of course not. All we can do is to show that the two signs are used differently; and the person to whom we are explaining can only be satisfied" (LEC1 86–87). No form of language, in other words, is inherently meaningful; "it has no sense to say that language is 'important' or 'necessary' to communicate our meaning. But it may be important for building bridges and doing similar things" (LEC1 61).

Here is Wittgenstein the engineer, the former student of aeronautics, arguing that *praxis* must be central to any philosophical investigation. "What is striking about the diversity of responses which philosophers have given to the question of the specificity of the work of art," says Bourdieu, "is not so much the fact that these divergent answers often concur in emphasizing the absence of function, the disinterestedness, the gratuitousness, etc. of the work of art, but that they all (with the possible exception of Wittgenstein) share the ambition of capturing a transhistoric or an ahistoric essence" (FCP 255). Even Derrida, Bourdieu argues, is not exempt from this charge. For the very insistence that there is, say, no transcendental signified, no "origin," no speech that has priority over writing, no "inside" superior to an "outside," and so on, makes the assumption that it is meaningful to *theorize* about such relationships in the abstract, to explain how and why speech is or is not necessarily prior.[12]

The later Wittgenstein, on the other hand, takes the tack that "Philosophy is not a choice between different 'theories.' It is wrong to say that there is any one theory of truth, for truth is not a concept" (LEC1 75). Assessing truth claims (or ethical or aesthetic claims), after all, depends on what it is one wants to do. " 'Arbitrary,' " Wittgenstein remarked in a lecture given during Easter term 1931, "as we normally use it always has a reference to some practical end: e.g. if I want to make an efficient boiler I *must* fulfill certain specifications, but it is quite arbitrary what colour I paint it" (LEC1 60). As for such oppositions as signifier/signified, "Language is not *contiguous* to anything else. We cannot speak of the use of language as opposed to anything else. So in philosophy all that is not gas is grammar" (LEC1 112).

From Theory to Language Game

But if "language is not *contiguous* to anything else," how can we talk about such abstractions as art or ethics, truth or beauty? In the *Tractatus,* we recall, Wittgenstein concluded that "The sense of the world must lie outside the world. . . . *In* it there is no value," and that hence "there can be no ethical [or aesthetic] propositions" (T #6.4, #6.42, #6.421). But by the early thirties, when Wittgenstein was rethinking these questions, he adopted a more pragmatic perspective. True, the sense of the world must lie outside the world; true, "Ethics is transcendental" and hence "cannot be expressed" (T #6.421), but the fact is that in actual communication, whether spoken or written, we do make ethical and aesthetic judgments that, even if they don't "capture" the "truth," do communicate something to someone. Here the "form of life" Wittgenstein calls the *language game* comes into play. The term, now widely disseminated, is difficult to understand because Wittgenstein characteristically never fully defines it, but he uses it so frequently that his use becomes ours.[13] The term first turns up in a Cambridge lecture of 1932:

> In teaching a child language by pointing to things and pronouncing the words for them, where does the use of a proposition start? If you teach him to touch certain colors when you say the word 'red', you have evidently not taught him sentences. . . . What is called understanding a sentence is not very different from what a child does when he points to colors on hearing color words. Now there are all sorts of *language-games* suggested by the one in which color words are taught: games of orders and commands, of question and answer, of questions and "Yes" and "No." We might think that in teaching a child such *language games* we are not teaching him a language but are only preparing him for it. But these games are complete; nothing is lacking. (LEC2 11; my emphasis)

Note that the language game, as Wittgenstein uses the term here, is neither a genre nor even a particular form of discourse; rather, it is a paradigm, a set of sentences, let us say, selected from the language we actually use so as to describe how communication of meaning works in specific circumstances. Thus, in the slightly later set of lectures known as *The Blue Book,* we read:

> I shall in the future again and again draw your attention to what I shall call *language games.* These are ways of using signs simpler than those in which we use the signs of our highly complicated everyday language. *Language games* are the forms of language with which a child begins to make use of words. The study of *language games* is the study of primitive forms of language or primitive languages. . . . When we look at such simple forms of language the mental mist which seems to enshroud our ordinary use of language disappears. We see activities, reactions, which are clear-cut and

transparent. On the other hand we recognize in these simple processes forms of language not separated by a break from our more complicated ones.[14]

And lest we think we now have a fixed definition, Wittgenstein adds:

We are inclined to think that there must be something in common to all games, say, and that this common property is the justification for applying the general term "game" to the various games; whereas games form a *family* the members of which have family likenesses. Some of them have the same nose, others the same eyebrows and others again the same way of walking; and these likenesses overlap. The idea of a general concept being a common property of its particular instances connects up with other primitive, too simple, ideas of the structure of language. It is comparable to the idea that *properties* are *ingredients* of the things which have the properties; e.g. that beauty is an ingredient of all beautiful things as alcohol is of beer and wine, and that we therefore could have pure beauty, unadulterated by anything that is beautiful. (BB 17)

Here Wittgenstein takes on one of the central pieties of aesthetic theory—the notion that one cannot say X is beautiful unless one has a notion of what "beauty" is in the abstract. The fact is that we normally feel quite confident in callings things "beautiful," even though we cannot name a "common property," a general term that will cover all instances. In this sense, "Aesthetics is descriptive. What it does is to *draw one's attention* to certain features, to place things side by side so as to exhibit these features" (LEC2 38). Such description—and this is perhaps the most striking aspect of the language game—is culturally constructed: *"What belongs to a language game is a whole culture.* In describing musical taste you have to describe whether children give concerts, whether women do or whether men only give them, etc. etc. In aristocratic circles in Vienna people had [such and such] a taste, then it came into bourgeois circles and women joined choirs, etc. This is an example of tradition in music" (LCA 8). Take the case of the so-called "ideal Greek profile":

What made the ideal Greek profile into an ideal, what quality? Actually what made us say it is the ideal is a certain very complicated role it played in the life of people. For example, the greatest sculptors used this form, people were taught it. Aristotle wrote on it. Suppose one said the ideal profile is the one occurring at the height of

Greek art. What would this mean? The word "height" is ambiguous. To ask what "ideal" means is the same as asking what "height" and "decadence" mean. You would need to describe the instances of the ideal in a sort of serial grouping. And the word is always used in connection with one particular thing, for there is nothing in common between roast beef, Greek art, and German music. (LEC2 36).

In such examples, Wittgenstein oddly anticipates some of the arguments of recent cultural theory: compare the statement above to the following in Bourdieu's "The Historical Genesis of a Pure Aesthetic":

> . . . the "subject" of the production of the art-work—of its value but also of its meaning—is not the producer who actually creates the object in its materiality, but rather the entire set of agents engaged in the field. Among these are the producers of works classified as artistic (great or minor, famous or unknown), critics of all persuasions. . . . collectors, middlemen, curators, etc., in short all who have ties with art, who live for art and, to varying degrees, from it. (FCP 261)

Like Wittgenstein, whom he cites in this discussion, Bourdieu suggests that the reason the concepts used to discuss artworks are so slippery, so indeterminate and contradictory, is that "they are inscribed in ordinary language and are generally used beyond the aesthetic sphere," so that inevitably they are "completely resistant to essentialist definition" (FCP 261). As such, *description* takes on a new role, for to describe the structure and function of a particular language game is to clear the air of misconception. "Language," says Wittgenstein, "sets everyone the same traps; it is an immense network of easily accessible wrong turnings. . . . What I have to do then is erect signposts at all the junctions where there are wrong turnings so as to help people past the danger points" (CV 18).

One of Wittgenstein's most interesting compositions, in this regard, is his relatively little-known commentary on Sir James Frazer's *The Golden Bough*.[15] Wittgenstein objected strongly to what he took to be Frazer's basic premise:

> Frazer's account of the magical and religious views of mankind is unsatisfactory: it makes these views look like *errors*.
>
> Was Augustine in error, then, when he called upon God on every page of the *Confessions*?

But—one might say—if he was not in error, surely the Buddhist holy man was—or anyone else—whose religion gives expression to completely different views. But *none* of them was in error, except when he set forth a theory.

The very idea of wanting to explain a practice [*Gebrauch*]—for example, the killing of the priest-king—seems wrong to me. All that Frazer does is to make them plausible to people who think as he does. It is very remarkable that in the final analysis all these practices are presented as, so to speak, pieces of stupidity [*Dummheiten*].

But it will never be plausible to say that mankind does all that out of sheer stupidity. (PO 119)

Here Wittgenstein takes on one of the articles of faith of modernity: the metanarrative of progress, of a gradual evolution from "primitive" barbarism to modern enlightenment. *The Golden Bough* tries to "explain" primitive magic and religious ritual—and, by implication, Christian ritual—as a form of ignorance, to be dispelled by "us," who know so much more than "primitive" peoples did. Wittgenstein's response is not to justify this or that practice or to argue that Augustine's belief system was either true or false, but to submit Frazer's arguments to a series of simple language games: he puts himself in the place of the external observer, an observer outside the specific cultural frame, who would have to assume that, if Augustine was not in "error," then the Buddhist holy man *is* in error, and so on, with the result that all religious practices emerge as no more than *Dummheiten*.

In such instances, Wittgenstein suggests, "one can only *describe* and say: this is what human life is like" (PO 121). Take, for example, Frazer's account of the elaborate prayers to rain gods found in early African cultures. For Frazer, these are rituals exemplifying "primitive" and "savage" superstitions that attributed natural phenomena like rainfall or fire to some sort of divine intervention. But, Wittgenstein suggests, suppose we interpret the accounts of these rituals quite literally. If so, we notice a curious detail in Frazer's account: the prayers to the "Kings of the Rain" take place not during the long dry season, when the land is a "parched and arid desert; and the cattle, which form the people's chief wealth, perish for lack of grass," but, on the contrary, *"when the rainy period comes."*[16] "Surely," writes Wittgenstein, "that means that they do not really believe that he [the god] can make it rain, otherwise they would do it in the dry periods of the year." Rather, he argues, the prayer rituals are timed for the season when the rains usually begin; in other words, these are rituals appropriate for the season, and it does not necessarily follow that the natives believe prayer *causes* rain. Indeed, these "primitive" rituals are not all that different from our own. "When I am furious about something," notes Wittgenstein, "I sometimes beat the ground or a tree with a walking stick. But I certainly do not believe that the ground is to blame or that my beating can help anything. 'I am venting my anger'. And all rites are of this kind" (PO 137).

In these instances, Wittgenstein's aim is not to "disprove" Frazer's facts by adducing other, more up-to-date ones, but to pay closer attention to what a given description can and cannot actually tell us. If "certain races of mankind venerate[d] the oak tree, it is not necessarily the case that they thought there was anything special about the oak, but only the fact that they and the oak were united in a community of life" (PO 139). And Wittgenstein remarks: "The nonsense here is that Frazer represents these people as if they had a completely false (even insane) idea of the course of nature, whereas they only possess a peculiar interpretation of the phenomena. That is, if they were to write it down, their knowledge of nature would not differ *fundamentally* from ours. Only their *magic* is different" (PO 141). Magic, in this context, means *practice.* And a particular practice, appearing in a different context, may have "*nothing whatever* sinister about it" (PO 145). Take the ancient game in which little pieces of cake are drawn out of a bowl, one of the pieces having been dipped in charcoal, the decree being that "Whoever draws the black bit, is the *devoted* person who is to be sacrificed to *Baal*" (PO 150). The same *practice* might be used by children to pick the leader of a team or to choose who will be the one to hide in a game of hide-and-go-seek. The practice, in other words, is not inherently "deep and sinister"; it is what Wittgenstein calls "Die *Umgebung* einer Handlungsweise," the environment in which an interchange takes place,[17] that makes it seem so.

We are now in a better position to understand why Wittgenstein's own writing was so fragmentary and provisional, why he used the same or similar examples over and over again and felt himself unable to produce a "finished" book. The preface to the *Philosophical Investigations* opens with the following disclaimer:

> The thoughts which I publish in what follows are the precipitate of philosophical investigations which have occupied me for the last sixteen years. They concern many subjects: the concepts of meaning, of understanding, of a proposition, of logic, the foundations of mathematics, states of consciousness, and other things. I have written down all these thoughts as *remarks,* short paragraphs, of which there is sometimes a fairly long chain about the same subject, while I sometimes make a sudden change, jumping from one topic to another. —It was my intention at first to bring all this together in a book whose form I pictured differently at different times. But the essential thing was that the thoughts should proceed from one subject to another in a natural order and without breaks.
>
> After several unsuccessful attempts to weld my results together into such a whole, I realized that I should never succeed. The best that I could write would never be more than philosophical remarks; my thoughts were soon crippled if I tried to force them on in any single direction against their natural inclination.—And this was, of course, connected with the very nature of the investigation. (PI v)

How radical these prefatory remarks are has not always been recognized, especially by those of Wittgenstein's followers who have wanted to find a coherent, organizing scheme in the *Investigations.* Wittgenstein himself understands that his mode of "investigation" cannot have a beginning, middle, and end, that it cannot have organic unity, a causal, logical, or sequential structure, an underlying theme or master plot. "Sudden change, jumping from one topic to another," is the lifeblood of the work, as is what Gertrude Stein has called "beginning again and again." Indeed, the notebook entries and lectures produced in the sixteen-year period that begins in 1929 and ends in 1945 with the "completion" of Part I of the *Investigations* should actually be looked at as a single, ongoing, revisionary composition. Revisionary in both senses: Wittgenstein repeatedly draws on the same corpus, revising and adjusting his examples so as to make meaning as precise as possible, and revisionary in the sense of inventing a new way of "doing" philosophy that is no longer quite philosophy. Such "re-vision," I take it, is what Wittgenstein had in mind when he said that "Philosophy ought really to be written only as a *form of poetry*" (CV 24).

"This book," Wittgenstein says apologetically in the preface, "is really only an album," in which "the same or almost the same points were always being approached afresh from different directions" (PI v). One thinks of such postmodern poetic fictions as Georges Perec's *La Vie mode d'emploi* or Lyn Hejinian's *Oxota,* works in which the "same points"—the inventory of a particular room, a childhood memory, a meeting between lovers—are also "always being approached afresh from different directions." Even when Wittgenstein tried, as he did in Part I of the *Investigations,* to have his "thoughts . . . proceed from one subject to another in a natural order and without breaks," he couldn't do it because a "natural order" in this context would mean some kind of linearity, a logical progression, rational synthesis, and so on. Indeed, it is a delicious irony that this iconoclast, who refused to listen to Mahler and Schönberg and paid little attention to the great art movements of his day, was himself the most radical of modernist writers, a writer for whom any totalizing scheme must always give way to "travel over a wide field of thought criss-cross in every direction." Only such "criss-cross" advances our thinking; hence, a Wittgenstein text is alternately anecdotal and aphoristic, repetitive and disjunctive, didactic and jokey, self-assertive and self-canceling. "I should not like," he says toward the end of the preface, "to spare other people the trouble of thinking. But, if possible, to stimulate someone to thoughts of his own" (PI vi).

Not an overarching theory, then, but a *method* for "going on"—this is what makes the *Investigations,* along with *Culture and Value, The Blue and Brown Books,* and the various lectures and notebooks published posthumously, so interactive a text. For here, *in* language always to be rephrased, recomposed, or charged with a new metaphor or example, is the deconstruction *of* our own language usage at its most insidious, baffling—and yet its most ordinary. "The *Tractatus,*" says Terry Eagleton, "may have the shimmering purity of an Imagist poem or Suprematist canvas; but the *Investigations* read more like an assemblage of ironic fables or fragments of a novel, deceptively lucid in their language but teasingly enigmatic in their thought. . . . Like all good artists, Wittgenstein is selling us less a set of doctrines than a style of seeing; and that style cannot be abstracted from the feints and ruses of his language, the rhetorical questioning and homely exemplifying, the sense of a mind in ceaseless ironic dialogue with itself" (WTE 9).

What makes this "style of seeing" so challenging for the reader is that Wittgenstein's paratactic structures are not metonymically organized, as are, say, Ezra Pound's lyric sequences in the *Cantos,* or Apollinaire's verse paragraphs in "Zone." In the *Investigations,* to the contrary, parataxis is a matter of what Herman Rapaport calls negative serialization. "Two and two is four" is a simple sentence, as is "The rose is red," but there is nothing in the first sentence to make the second follow. "In each sentence," as Rapaport puts it, "there is compulsory connectivity. But in thinking of the sentences serially, the question of reciprocity becomes vexed. In short, despite appearances, they are Other to one another."[18] Given this otherness, the *Investigations* cannot possibly constitute any sort of whole; its negative seriality is an index to the inherent provisionality of the text. Indeed, had Wittgenstein lived to do so, he would surely have reworked the book.[19]

An Assemblage of Ironic Fables

The *Investigations* begins with a famous passage from Augustine's *Confessions* (I, 8):

When they (my elders) named some object, and accordingly moved toward something, I saw this and I grasped that the thing was called by the sound they uttered when they meant to point it out. Their intention was shewn by their bodily movements, as it were the natural language of all peoples. . . . Thus, as I heard words repeatedly used in their proper places in various sentences, I gradually learnt to understand what objects they signified; and after I had trained my mouth to form these signs, I used them to express my own desires. (PI #1)

The rest of the book will be devoted to a refutation of this "way of seeing," but since the theory that words name things, that every word must refer to or "stand" for something in the "real" world, is, after all, the normative semantic theory in Western culture, the question immediately arises why

Wittgenstein chose Augustine as its exponent. Norman Malcolm explains: "[Wittgenstein] revered the writings of St. Augustine. He told me he decided to begin his *Investigations* with a quotation from the latter's *Confessions,* not because he could not find the conception expressed in that quotation stated as well by other philosophers but because the conception *must* be important if so great a mind held it."[20] Nor did Wittgenstein set out to refute Augustine's theory: "Augustine, we might say, does describe a system of communication; only not everything that we call language is this system" (PI #3).

The Augustine example thus sets the stage for the "criss-cross" (cross-country) trip through the network of fragments that is the *Investigations,* a trip that will gradually make it impossible for us to trust, ever again, the full authority of a given word or group of words to *name* a particular thing. It is not a trip that can be rushed; indeed, the first few language games in the *Investigations* are not especially impressive. When, for example, Wittgenstein describes the language game involving "five red apples" (PI #1), in order to show that the grocer's response to the customer's request illustrates how the word "five" is used in this particular instance but not what "five" itself *means,* the reader may well conclude that the account is too ordinary and commonsensical to be interesting. Don't we all know that a number cannot be defined except relationally? And doesn't the word "apple" nevertheless point to that thing we see in the fruit bin and hence name it just as Augustine supposed?

If Wittgenstein's language games are deceptively simple, so are his "homely" metaphors. In #11, language is compared to a "tool-box" ("there is a hammer, pliers, a saw, a screw-driver, a rule, a glue-pot, glue, nails and screws"), and the author comments, "The functions of words are as diverse as the functions of these objects"; in #18, language is described as "an ancient city: a maze of little streets and squares, of old and new houses, and of houses with additions from various periods; and this surrounded by a multitude of new boroughs with straight regular streets and uniform houses." No one could quarrel with either metaphor: yes, language may be said to resemble a "tool-box," and yes, language is a complicated structure like a city with buildings of different sizes and periods, but so what?

As we make our way through the *Investigations,* we begin to see that the text itself is a complex language game, to "play" which we must practice the easier moves before we learn the more difficult ones. This is why Wittgenstein is so notoriously difficult to excerpt, even though all his posthumous writings are composed of fragments that would seem, on the face of it, easily excerptible. But the *Investigations* is neither a book of proverbs nor a systematic argument. Confronted with a selection—as, say, in Hazard Adams's *Critical Theory* textbook[21]—students are often baffled by what seems to them an almost simpleminded discussion of the everyday use of language. "Is that all there is to it?" they ask in disappointment. "We thought Wittgenstein was supposed to be a major philosopher and here all he has to tell us is that the word 'handle' may be 'the handle of a crank which can be moved continuously,' or it may be 'the handle of a switch, which has only two effective positions, it is either off or on' (PI #12), and so on. But we all knew that 'handle' had both these meanings, so what is all the fuss about?"

The rhetoric that creates this "is that all?" mood is probably quite intentional. "The work of the philosopher," we read in #27, "consists in assembling reminders for a particular purpose." At first that purpose may be hidden, but gradually we are initiated into the process whereby we begin to question the generalizations and abstractions we have hitherto accepted as normative. Take #31:

> When one shews someone the king in chess and says: "This is the king," this does not tell him the use of this piece—unless he already knows the rules of the game up to this last point: the shape of the king. You could imagine his having learnt the rules of the game without ever having been shewn an actual piece. The shape of the chessman corresponds here to the sound or shape of a word.
>
> One can also imagine someone's having learnt the game without ever learning or formulating rules. He might have learnt quite simple board-games first, by watching, and have progressed to more and more complicated ones. He too might be given the explanation, "this is the king,"—if, for instance, he were being shewn chessmen of a shape he was not used to. This explanation again only tells him the use of the piece because, as we might say, the place for it was already prepared. Or even: we shall only say that it tells him the use, if the place is already prepared. . . .

We may say: only someone who already knows how to do something with it can significantly ask a name.[22]

Even this example doesn't seem to "refute" Augustine's claim as to naming. "Yes," we may respond, it's true that in chess the names "king" and "queen" have no meaning except in the game in which they function, but that is a special case, isn't it? It doesn't prove that the meaning of any word is necessarily defined by its use. Anticipating this response (and Wittgenstein has used all these examples in earlier sketches), the author now gives us an example from everyday life that is the antithesis of the special case. In #33, he takes sample sentences in which the word "blue" appears:

"Is this blue the same as the blue over there? Do you see any difference?"
You are mixing paint and you say "It's hard to get the blue of this sky."
"It's turning fine, you can already see blue sky again."
"Look, what different effects these two blues have."
"Do you see the blue book over there? Bring it here."
"This blue signal-light means...."
"What's this blue called?—is it 'indigo'?"

What makes such a list so fascinating—and we can provide any number of additional examples of our own—is that in ordinary conversation, we have no trouble whatsoever in understanding any of these sentences. They are sentences, moreover, a very young child can and does use. If, for example, a child is trying to find the puzzle piece that fits into a certain hole, she may say, "Is this blue the same as the blue over there?" (sentence 1). If she is out in the garden, making a picture of what she sees, she complains that "It's hard to get the blue of this sky" (2). If she wants to go swimming but it's been raining, she may say hopefully, "you can already see blue sky again" (3). In (4) the child's supposition is that there are different blues; in (5), where blue is a designator, it is that blue means blue; and in (6), she knows that blue arbitrarily stands for something else like "stop" or "go." Finally, (7) "What's this blue called?—is it 'indigo'?" is a question asked when, say, the child has been given a fancy new paint kit and is familiarizing herself with the varieties of color possibilities.

How is it that a child knows that "blue" is sometimes a fixed descriptor (as in the sentence "you can already see blue sky again"), sometimes a class comprising various subsets (e.g., shades of blue), sometimes a reference to the ability of manufactured colors to "match" those in nature, and so on? Because, so Wittgenstein gradually shows us, language has no essence; it is a complex cultural construction, whose variables are articulated according to one's particular intersection with it. "When I talk about language (words, sentences, etc.)," we read in #120, "I must speak the language of every day. Is this language somehow too coarse and material for what we want to say? *Then how is another one to be constructed?*—And how strange that we should be able to do anything at all with the one we have!" And Wittgenstein adds:

> In giving explanations I already have to use language full-blown (not some sort of preparatory, provisional one); this by itself shews that I can adduce only exterior facts about language.
>
> Yes, but then how can these explanations satisfy us?—Well, your very questions were framed in this language; they had to be expressed in this language, if there was anything to ask!...
>
> 124. Philosophy may in no way interfere with the actual use of language; it can in the end only describe it.
>
> For it cannot give it any foundation either.
>
> It leaves everything as it is.

Here Wittgenstein gets around the problem that has beset deconstruction, the problem of denouncing a metaphysic of presence in a metalanguage in which presence is inevitably reinscribed: think of the way terms such as *trace, gramme, differance, transcendental signified, the slippage of the signifier, parergon, logocentrism, supplementarity, episteme*—or, for that matter, *essentialism* itself—have become part of "advanced" theoretical discourse. For Wittgenstein, on the other hand, there need be no metalanguage, for each of us has access to the "language full-blown (not some sort of preparatory, provisional one")," the language that is given to us. Wittgenstein is aware, of course, that the modern disciplines rely on a good deal of technical vocabulary not understood by the layperson, and that this vocabulary, whether in the case of law or medicine, music or symbolic logic, engineering or agronomy, must be mastered by anyone who hopes to succeed in that field. But for him, such language acquisition always takes place in the context of a particular language game, as in the chess example. Thus, if one cardiologist asks another: "Does Mr. Smith have a rhythm disturbance?" and the other replies, "At the moment there is no ectopic rhythm," the meaning of the word *rhythm* is perfectly clear to both parties, although a layperson like myself would not be able to play this particular language game.

But isn't philosophy itself a specialized discourse with its own technical vocabulary? And, by analogy, isn't literary theory such a discourse? Here Wittgenstein parts company with normative theoretical discourse, at least that of the twentieth century. "When we analyse in science," he remarked in an early Cambridge lecture, "we describe some further event. In chemistry we analyse water and find that its chemical composition is H_2O; we find out something new about it. Analysing here means finding something new. But this is not what we mean by analysis in philosophy. . . . philosophical analysis does not give us any new facts" (LEC1 35). Accordingly, its language games cannot have a specific technical vocabulary and so the bifurcation between philosophy (or poetry) as "high" discourse, in which a certain vocabulary is *de rigueur,* and ordinary language—language that even the most arcane philosopher engages in when he or she asks what time it is or when the next train is due to leave—breaks down:

> When philosophers use a word—"knowledge," "being," "object," "I," "proposition," "name"—and try to grasp the *essence* of the thing, one must always ask oneself: is the word ever actually used in this way in the language-game which is its original home?
>
> What *we* do is to bring words back from their metaphysical to their everyday use. (#116)

The most surprising entry in this catalogue of large, abstract nouns whose meanings are not fixed is the pronoun "I." "Solipsism," says Wittgenstein in an analogous passage, "could be refuted by the fact that the word 'I' does not have a central place in grammar, but is a word like any other."[23]

Surely this is a remarkable statement, challenging as it does the entire romantic and postromantic faith in inwardness, in the hidden depths of the unique, individual consciousness, whose desire for expression is thwarted by an impersonal, uncomprehending society, by what Lacan calls "the Law of the Father." Rimbaud's famous "*Je* est un autre" ("*I* is someone else"), with its emphasis on psychological depth, vision, and metamorphosis, gives way to the formula that "I" is a word like any other. But of course for Wittgenstein, the ordinariness of "I" is by no means a sign of its unimportance, pointing as it does to the contexts and constructs that create "ordinary" selves.

"Long before contemporary cultural theory," Terry Eagleton remarks in the preface to his screenplay, "Wittgenstein was teaching us that the self is a social construct—that when I look into my most secret feelings, I identify what I do only because I have at my disposal a language which belonged to my society before it ever belonged to me."[24] But if this is the case—and I think it is—what role can literature, especially the formalized first-person mode we call lyric poetry, play today? The usual answer is that it plays very little role; that once "genius theory" goes by the wayside, poetry assumes a marginal position, largely irrelevant to the central discourses of the time unless of course it performs specific "cultural work," as do the poetries of various subaltern groups.[25] And a corollary, now part of the common wisdom, is that there is no difference between "high" and "low" art, that if the self is socially and culturally constructed, the focus of study should be on culture itself, rather than on the "individuals" who are functions of it.

Indeed—and here is the paradox—a Wittgensteinian "poetics" would seem to be one that denies that "poetry" exists. At the same time, Wittgenstein speaks enthusiastically about specific poems, just as he discusses individual passages of music by Mozart or Mendelssohn and, in general, treats artists with a quasi-religious veneration. "The works of great masters," we read in *Culture and Value*, "are suns which rise and set around us. The time will come for every great work that is now in the descendent to rise again" (CV 15).

Not *poetry* or *art*, those hopelessly indeterminate categories, but *artistic practice*—this is what concerns Wittgenstein. The "greatness" of a work (and Wittgenstein—unlike, say, Fish—is convinced that there *are* "great" works of art) can only be intuited, but the conditions of that work's production, dissemination, and reception can be examined with great profit. Here Wittgenstein anticipates what Bourdieu calls the *habitus,* the "feel for the game" or "set of dispositions" that is *"acquired through experience* [and] thus variable from place to place and time to time," by means of which the individual agent (never a mere "puppet controlled by the strings of structure") responds to a certain practice.[26]

Or, as Wittgenstein puts it more simply and enigmatically, a literary form is a "form of life." For Wittgenstein, even the Latin term *habitus* would be unnecessary (and somewhat pretentious), for what Bourdieu is really expressing, Wittgenstein would say, is the commonsense notion that "cultural construction" is central to any formation of a self, but that such construction is never merely a class definition, that there are always a number of (often conflicting) cultural factors—ethnicity, nationality, social and professional class, gender, and so on—that "construct" a particular subject, who in turn responds according to a particular set of expectations.

A useful case in point is Wittgenstein's own self-representation in the writings that form the core of the *Investigations.* Consider the following passage from Part II:

> If I see someone writhing in pain with evident cause I do not think: all the same, his feelings are hidden from me.
>
> We also say of some people that they are transparent to us. It is, however, important as regards this observation that one human being can be a complete enigma to another. We learn this when we come into a strange country with entirely strange traditions; and what is more, even given a mastery of the country's language. We do not *understand* the people. (And not because of not knowing what they are saying to themselves.) We cannot find our feet with them.
>
> "I cannot know what is going on in him" is above all a *picture.* It is the convincing expression of a conviction. It does not give the reasons for the conviction. *They* are not readily accessible.
>
> If a lion could talk, we could not understand him. (PI, p. 223)

This passage should be read against the German original:

> Wen ich, mit offenbarer Ursache, sich in Schmerzen winden sehe, von dem denke ich nicht: seine Gefühle seien mir doch verborgen.

Wir sagen auch von einem Menschen, er sei uns durchsichtig. Aber es ist für diese Betrachtung wichtig, das ein Mensch für einen andern ein völliges Rätsel sein kann. Das erfährt man, wenn man in ein fremdes Land mit gänzlich fremden Traditionen kommt; und zwar auch dann, wenn man die Sprache des Landes beherrscht. Man *versteht* die Menschen nicht. (Und nicht darum, weil man nicht weiss, was sie zu sich selber sprechen.) Wir können uns nicht in sie finden.

"Ich kann nicht wissen, was in ihm vorgeht" ist vor allem ein *Bild*. Es ist der überzeugende Ausdruck einer Uberzeugung. Es gibt nicht die Gründe der Uberzeugung an. *Sie* liegen nicht auf her Hand.

Wenn ein Löwe sprechen könnte, wir könnten ihn nicht verstehen. (SCH 536)

Ironically—and this happens frequently in the case of the *Investigations*—Wittgenstein's commonsense discussion of the way "ordinary" language works has been translated with some inaccuracy (by G. E. M. Anscombe) into a curiously stilted English. The second paragraph, for example, begins with a misleading reference to "some people," whereas Wittgenstein says, "We say of *someone* that we can see through *him*" (my emphasis). The use of the singular rather than Anscombe's plural is important because, in Wittgenstein's view, it is not *people* but only an individual who can be judged to be "transparent" (or not transparent). Thus in the next sentence—and here the translation is unaccountably literal—Wittgenstein talks of the case in which "one human being can be a complete enigma to another." "Ein fremdes Land" (in sentence 3) refers quite literally not only to a "strange" but to a "foreign" country, and, in this setting, the understated "Man *versteht* die Menschen nicht" points directly to the author himself. It is he who can't understand these foreigners, who mourns that "Wir können uns nicht in sie finden" ("We can't find ourselves in them"), which is oddly metaphorized in the translation as "We cannot find our feet with them."

The "limits of my language" thus ironically include the limits imposed on "my world" by the construction of Wittgenstein as an author-in-translation, an author partially created by the community of Cambridge philosophers who have disseminated his writing. Indeed, the *Investigations* exists in a curious in-between or exile space, not wholly "German" or "English" in its articulation. The exile experience is central to Wittgenstein's own language, which is never quite sure of itself and is therefore all the more concerned with the impossibility of "full" disclosure, much less full understanding. At the same time, Wittgenstein the upperclass, singularly wealthy, culturally superior Viennese male is present even in passages like this one that say nothing explicit about his own culture. It is the imperious tone of the *Investigations* that is a giveaway in this regard. "Man *versteht* die Menschen nicht": there is something authoritative about this articulation, the "Man" ("one") balanced against "die Menschen" ("the people").

National identity, then, is, however obliquely, a defining feature of the Wittgensteinian text. And so is ethnicity. Wittgenstein has little specific to say about the Jews (and when he does, as in *Culture and Value,* his derogatory tone suggests a certain self-hatred, typical of his class and milieu),[27] but Jewishness is, for him, a kind of subtext of difference. Only someone who is not fully at home in the world will talk as much as Wittgenstein does about "the language-game which is [one's] original home." The reference to "foreign traditions" and the "foreign country" refers not only to Wittgenstein's foreignness on English soil but also to his "foreignness," as a Jew, in the Vienna of his birth. The writing of the *Investigations,* we must remember, took place in precisely the years when Wittgenstein was forced to recognize that, despite the baptism and Catholic upbringing that generations of Wittgensteins had undergone, from the perspective of the Nazi regime, they were simply Jews. In this context, even the "mastery" of his chosen "country's language" cannot eradicate the sense of difference Wittgenstein speaks of above. Indeed, it may be the very *distance* from others ("Man versteht die Menschen nicht") that makes this philosopher-poet so determined to live *inside* the *ordinary* language field of his adopted nation, and yet to be so aware of its vagaries.

For the *ordinary* remains strange no matter how thoroughly one shows it up for what it is. "Why can't a dog simulate pain? Is he too honest?" (PI #250). "Why can't my left hand give my right hand money?" (PI #268). To "answer" such questions is to run into new roadblocks the philosopher has set for us. Roadblocks, incidentally, that deflect attention from the one attribute of "I" that evidently cannot be talked about— namely, the author's sexual (which is to say, homosexual) life. "Philosophy," we read in #126, "simply puts everything before us, and neither explains nor deduces anything.—Since everything lies open to view there is nothing to explain. For what is hidden, for example, is of no interest to us." But instinctively, as Wittgenstein regularly reminds us, we always do draw inferences: "If I see someone writhing in pain with evident cause I do not think: all the same, his feelings are hidden from me," but the fact is that those feelings "are not readily accessible." Indeed, "my prediction (in my expression of intention) has not the same foundation as [someone else's] prediction of what I shall do" (PI, p. 224). Doesn't this insistence that no one else can know my feelings with anything approaching certainty have something to do with Wittgenstein's need to protect and disguise his own feelings? And what role does gender play in these "everyday" language games?

Let us come back, for a moment, to the famous Wittgenstein aphorism, "If a lion could talk, we could not understand him," which concludes the passage I cite above. At one level, there is something stubbornly and charmingly childlike about this proposition. For of course it is true: whatever "lion-speak" might be, it couldn't be our speech and so we couldn't understand it. Second, its plainspoken common sense reflects Wittgenstein's early training, not in philosophy or classical literature or art history, but in mechanics and engineering. In this respect, Wittgenstein's *habitus* differs sharply from the Viennese *fin de siècle* poets, painters, composers, and philosophers, whose training was so different from his. *Practice,* as I remarked earlier, is always foremost. And third, the sentence, comical as it is to think of trying to understand a lion's talk, is also somehow sad. The whole passage, after all, has stressed the impossibility of understanding others. Even if one person may strike us as transparent, the very epithet "transparent" wouldn't make sense if that person weren't compared to someone else who is an enigma. And so Wittgenstein, who for the most part stresses those language games in which we do understand perfectly well what the other person is saying, is now emphasizing the solipsism central to human life. But there is not the slightest note of self-pity in the statement; Wittgenstein makes clear that one does feel *as if* one understands what someone else is going through ("If I see someone writhing in pain with evident cause I do not think: all the same, his feelings are hidden from me"). In everyday life, he suggests, one functions well enough and our language is quite adequate. Yet at another level, language remains the greatest mystery, the contact with others that is not really a contact at all.

To say that "I" is "a word like any other" may thus mean, paradoxically, that, like any other "ordinary" word, this one loses its invisibility when we begin really to look at it. For example, "I" is denied by the text the power to act as a vehicle for confession (Wittgenstein never talks about his personal life), the watchword being that language can never relate "what is hidden." In keeping with such "hiding," "I" is deemed to be superfluous: if I say, "I have a pain," subject and verb are really unnecessary because clearly the "pain" I am talking about (perhaps accompanying my statement with frowning or weeping) is *mine*. But the paradox is that, looked at from the reader's angle, every proposition, every formulation in the *Investigations* is the embodiment of this author's "I." Someone of a different class, gender, nationality, profession, and historical/cultural moment would use different examples, different locutions. The predominance of interrogatives, for example, is the prerogative of someone in an authoritative position, someone who is allowed to raise issues and ask questions. Not everyone who writes philosophy or poetry is, we know well enough, so licensed. Is leisure time, perhaps, a requisite for this particular language game? Is the solitary life a requisite? And what about money?

Let me now come back to the question of the *ordinary* versus the *literary* with which I began. Where does the *Investigations* stand in this dialectic? Certainly, it is not "literary" in the generic sense: no one would claim that it is a novel, much less a lyric poem or a drama. A case could be made for the *Investigations* as an autobiography or diary, but the confessional element is so insistently missing that it is hard to see it as related to Augustine or Rousseau. And even stylistically, despite the high incidence of metaphor, aphorism, and proverb, the *Investigations* is hardly an instance of the *poeticity* Jakobson talks of, its orientation not being primarily toward the message.

"Literature," says Stanley Fish, "is the product of a way of reading, of a community agreement about what will count as literature." This formulation seems to come closer than, say, Jakobson's to Wittgenstein's own conception of the literary, but the differences outweigh the similarities. For one thing, Wittgenstein would have scoffed at the notion of an "interpretive community," especially an academic one. For him, such a community was precisely what one sets oneself against, artistic pleasure being of necessity a private experience prompted by an individual practice. Wittgenstein knew what he liked but he neither tried to theorize his own practice nor sought to persuade others as to what makes a particular poem "great." Accordingly, his writing doesn't lend itself to the kind of systematization that theorists like Fish engage in. A systematization, incidentally, that preserves the distinction between a philosophical text like the *Investigations* and a "literary" one like *Paradise Lost.* A contemporary theorist, in Fish's view, might *draw* on Wittgenstein, "applying" his insights to a given literary text, but the possibility of reading the *Investigations* and related lecture notes as themselves poetic is hardly likely to arise.

And yet, as I remarked in the introduction, the library of poems, fictions, plays, artworks, films, and even musical compositions relating to this and other Wittgenstein texts continues to grow. Artists, it seems, have taken to heart the following observation, made in a 1930 notebook:

> . . . it seems to me . . . that there is a way of capturing the world sub specie aeterni other than through the work of the artist. *Thought has such a way*—so I believe—it is as though it flies above the world and leaves it as it is—observing it from above, in flight. (CV 5, my emphasis)

Wittgensteinian "thought" is charged with drama: we witness its continuous unfolding:

> A dog believes his master is at the door. But can he also believe his master will come the day after to-morrow?—And *what* can he not do here?—How do I do it?—How am I supposed to answer this?
>
> Can only those hope who can talk? Only those who have mastered the use of a language. That is to say, the phenomena of hope are modes of this complicated form of life. . . .
>
> "For a second he felt violent pain."—Why does it sound queer to say: "For a second he felt deep grief"? Only because it so seldom happens? (PI, p. 174e)

These last questions have more in common with a Pinter or Beckett dialogue than with a critical essay. "For a second," Didi might exclaim to Pozzo, or Meg to Petey, "I felt deep grief." And the audience would laugh and brace itself for the return shot. Not that such sentences are inherently "poetic," but their *use* renders them so. In this sense, the pursuit of the ordinary may well be the most interesting game in town. Why is it acceptable to say "For a second he felt violent pain," but not "For a second he felt violent grief?" Wittgenstein responds to such questions, not by giving us the dictionary definitions of "pain" and "grief," but by probing the *grammar* of the sentences in which these words appear. "You interpret," he says, "a grammatical movement made by yourself as a quasi-physical phenomenon which you are observing. . . . What you have primarily discovered is a new way of looking at things. As if you had invented a new way of painting; or, again, a new metre, or a new kind of song" (PI #401).

The "ordinary" ("For a second he felt violent pain") thus turns out, after all, to be capable of being *seen as* the "aesthetic." But that aesthetic remains resistant to definition. Hence the futility of asking those habitually posed questions: what makes an ordinary object (e.g., a urinal, a wine rack, a bicycle wheel, *pace* Duchamp) a work of art? What is the difference between "abstract art" and "mere" decorative pattern? Which is better: "abstract" or "figurative" art? And so on. "One must," says Bourdieu, "replace the ontological question with the historical question of the genesis of the universe, that is the artistic field, within which, through a veritable continuous creation, the value of the work of art is endlessly produced and reproduced" (FCP 259). "Continuous" because "language is a labyrinth of paths" (PI #203) and there is no way of getting *outside* it. All the more reason to pay attention to the movements inside the labyrinth. For "the place I really have to get to is a place I must already be at now" (CV 7).

—A grammar relates to not liking to see again those you used to know.

—What is the difference between resemblance and grammar. There is none. Grammar is at best an oval ostrich egg and grammar is far better.

Gertrude Stein, "Arthur a Grammar"[1]

three

"Grammar in Use": Wittgenstein/Gertrude Stein/ Marinetti

"Grammar," Wittgenstein typically remarks in the *Philosophical Investigations,* "only describes and in no way explains the use of signs" (PI #496). And he gives the following account of the way grammar actually works:

498. When I say that the orders "Bring me sugar" and "Bring me milk" make sense, but not the combination "Milk me sugar," that does not mean that the utterance of this combination of words has no effect. And if its effect is that the other person stares at me and gapes, I don't on that account call it the order to stare and gape, even if that was precisely the effect that I wanted to produce.

499. To say "This combination of words makes no sense" excludes it from the sphere of language and thereby bounds the domain of language. But when one draws a boundary it may be for various kinds of reason. If I surround an area with a fence or a line or otherwise, the purpose may be to prevent someone from getting in or out; but it may also be part of a game and the players be supposed, say, to jump over the boundary; or it may shew where the property of one man ends and that of another begins; and so on. So if I draw a boundary line that is not yet to say what I am drawing it for.

500. When a sentence is called senseless, it is not as it were its sense that is senseless. But a combination of words is being excluded from the language, withdrawn from circulation.

More than twenty years before Wittgenstein put forward these propositions, Gertrude Stein was producing poems, fictions, and plays that had sentences like the following:

> Roast potatoes for.
> Loud and no cataract.
> I wish matches.
> Explain whites for eggs.[2]

Confronted by such sentences, early readers of Stein almost invariably went into what Wittgenstein calls, with reference to the sentence "Milk me sugar," the staring-and-gaping mode. "The words in the volume entitled *Tender Buttons,*" wrote the reviewer for the *Louisville Courier-Journal,* "are English words, but the sentences are not English sentences according to the grammatical definition. The sentences indicated by punctuation do not make complete sense, partial sense, nor any other sense, but nonsense."[3] Grammar, in this context, means a set of prescriptions that all "acceptable" sentences must follow, in contrast to Wittgenstein's conception of grammar as the description of how sentences are actually formed. "When one draws a boundary," he cautions, "it may be for various kinds of reason." The so-called "senselessness" of a sentence like "Milk me sugar" is merely the result of such boundary drawing: "a combination of words is being excluded from the language, withdrawn from circulation" (*aus dem Verkehr gezogen*).

Roast potatoes for. The words withdrawn from circulation here are those that would determine whether "roast" is an adjective or a verb and whether Stein's sentence is indicative or imperative: "We're having roast potatoes for dinner" as opposed to "Please roast those potatoes for dinner" or "for me." The sentence's incompletion provides many intriguing semantic possibilities.[4] "Roast potatoes" are "for" what or whom exactly? Why do we cook and eat them? Or are the potatoes an example, "Roast potatoes, for instance"? Furthermore, "for" puns on "four" (i.e., four potatoes, with the further echo of the well-known children's counting game, "One potato, two potato, three potato, four...."). A second pun brings in the language of Stein's adopted nation: *four* is French for "oven." *Pommes de terre au four.* Where else would one expect to find roast potatoes? And further: there is a buried pun on "fore": roast potatoes before the salad, perhaps. Or before they get cold.

In addition, the "withdrawal" of intermediary words "from circulation" creates significant sound patterning. The final "t" of "roast" is moved forward to come between "o" and "a": "*p-o-t-a.*" And then it happens again, chiastically: "*t-o.*" The word "for," moreover, contains the "*r-o*" of "roast," only now in inverted order. The sixteen-letter unit has two *a*'s and four *o*'s, alpha and omega, as it were, as if to say that the potato is the staple of life and hence of articulation. Roast potatoes, after all, are everybody's food. Indeed, the sixteen-letter phrase has only seven phonemes, "simplicity" of sound thus perfectly conveying the reference to this, the "apple of the earth."

Stein thus seems to "draw a boundary," not out of a refusal to "make sense" or a predilection for pure nonsense, but because she wants to draw out specific semantic implications not normally present in culinary discourse. Obviously, if Miss Stein were telling her cook Hélène what to make for dinner, the sentence would be highly inappropriate and the cook would stare and gape, or she would ask, "For how many people?" or "For lunch or for dinner?" But "Roast potatoes for" is being used not in the cooking game but in the game of testing the limits of language, which is, for Stein, *the* game that matters. And in this "poetry game," the locution makes rather good sense.

For one thing, "Roast potatoes for" has been anticipated in an earlier "Food" poem in *Tender Buttons* called "Breakfast":

A change, a final change includes potatoes. This is no authority for the abuse of cheese. What language can instruct any fellow.

A shining breakfast, a breakfast shining, no dispute, no practice, nothing, nothing at all.

A sudden slice changes the whole plate, it does so suddenly. (TB 41)

One pictures a small mound of mashed potatoes on the breakfast tray next to the cheese omelette. But why does this addition constitute a "final change"? What language "instructs," perhaps, is that words are endlessly slippery: the "use" of cheese easily modulates into "abuse," and the "final change" is never really final: "A sudden slice changes the whole plate." However we want to construe the "nothing at all" that happens, the relation of potatoes to cheese is taken up again in the sequence of potato poems that includes "Roast potatoes for":

POTATOES

Real potatoes cut in between.

POTATOES

In the preparation of cheese, in the preparation of crackers, in the preparation of butter, in it.

ROAST POTATOES

Roast potatoes for. (TB 51)

The "cut in between" in #1 refers to potatoes being cut open or cut down the middle and perhaps stuffed with cheese or butter and served with crackers. Then too, the second "POTATOES" is "cut in between" the other two potato poems, and, as Bettina Knapp has noted, it may well be a sexual allusion to the penetration of the female body ("in it"), followed as it is by the sexual punning on "crackers" ("crack hers").[5] And "Roast Potatoes," in this context, recalls Stein's famous line in the love poem "Preciosilla": "Roasted susie is my ice-cream."

In recent years, the sexual coding pervasive in Stein's language has been submitted to intense and rewarding scrutiny by feminist criticism,[6] but what has not been sufficiently recognized is that, in Stein's particular case, issues of gender are closely linked to those of exile. Like Wittgenstein, whom she had never met and whose work she did not know,[7] Stein chose exile in large measure because the familial and cultural pressures of her native country would have made it all but impossible to live a homosexual life, even though, again like Wittgenstein, she remained largely closeted, even in her adopted country.[8] The double bind of sexual and national difference, in any case, produced, in Stein's case as in Wittgenstein's, a very special relationship to language. As Françoise Collin puts it in "L'Ecriture sans rature":

> She has accomplished her *dépaysement* once and for all by the age of twenty, taking up residence in a country where her language isn't spoken. This is her only exoticism but it is a radical one. . . . Living in a foreign environment, Gertrude Stein distances herself from the language that she hears all around her—French—which is not her own, and which is for her an object of fascination to the point where she appropriates any number of its elements and formulae. But she is also distancing herself from her own language, American, which is not spoken around her, which has become the language of the other, even if it is the language of intimacy. The writing of Gertrude Stein is ex-centric with respect to two languages, according to different formulae: it is a third language.
>
> Other than this rupture with her native land, everything enters into the sphere of the familiar. Whatever she confronts, she addresses as "tu." Whatever she touches, whatever she names, whatever she sees, becomes hers.[9]

Here the parallel to Wittgenstein is especially interesting. Both continue to write in their native language, but since much of Wittgenstein's "writing" is in fact the student transcription of his Cambridge lectures (in English), we have a double language base, a base in which, as I noted in chapter 2, a somewhat stilted and convoluted English "translates" (not quite) a much more straightforward German. But even the German, it could be argued on the analogy of Stein's American, is no longer the Austrian German of someone actually living in Vienna but a distanced language, spoken and written self-consciously. In Stein's case, however, the situation is even more schizophrenic, since American is the language of intimacy with Alice, French the language of friendship (for example, with Picasso) and of daily social and domestic contact.

In both cases, accordingly, grammar, taken for granted by most writers who are "at home" in their own language and hence are likely to pay more attention to image and metaphor, to figures of heightening, embellishment, and transformation, becomes a contested site. "Grammar," after all, "does not tell us how language must be constructed in order to fulfill its purpose. . . . It only describes and in no way explains the use of signs" (PI #496). It does not, for example, explain how the "have" in "I have a pain" differs from the "have" in "I have a book" or why one's right hand can't "give" one's left hand money. Or, to turn to Stein's lexicon, grammar cannot explain why it is incorrect to say "I wish matches" (*Pink Melon Joy*). Doesn't "désire" as in "Je désire des allu-mettes" translate as both "want" and "wish"?

"I wish to have matches" or "I wish for matches" would do the trick, although if one went into the drugstore to ask for matches, these con-structions would sound excessively stilted. Can an infinitive or a mere preposition—"for"—make such a difference? "Roast potatoes for" sug-gests that they can. " 'I'," remarks Wittgenstein in the *Investigations,* "is not the name of a person, nor 'here' of a place, and 'this' is not a name. But they are connected with names. Names are explained by means of them. It is also true that it is characteristic of physics not to use these words" (PI #410). One might add that for the nonnative speaker these are the words that cause the most confusion. "Consider," writes Wittgenstein in #411, "how the following questions can be applied, and how settled":

(1) "Are these books *my* books?"
(2) "Is this foot *my* foot?"
(3) "Is this body *my* body?"
(4) "Is this sensation *my* sensation?"

Here the grammatical structure is identical but the words "this" and "my" function quite differently. In (1), "these" is a pointer: I notice some books lying on a desk and wonder whether they are "*my* books." In (2), as Witt-genstein points out, the question can only make sense if, say, my foot has been anesthetized or paralyzed, and the question is then a way of saying "This foot doesn't even feel like my own foot." In (3) the reference may be to a mirror-image, as if to say "Does my body look like *that?*" And (4) is the oddest of all because of course there is no way for me to point to "this sensation" unless it is in fact "*my* sensation."

Gertrude Stein had a predilection for language games that exploited precisely these subtle differences. Like Wittgenstein, she took the naming function of language to be its least challenging aspect. "A noun," she wrote in "Poetry and Grammar," "is a name of anything, why after a thing is named write about it. A name is adequate or it is not . . . things once they are named the name does not go on doing anything to them and so why write in nouns. Nouns are the name of anything and just naming names is alright when you want to call a roll but is it good for anything else."[10]

Here Stein may well be thinking of a particular example of roll calling: namely, the *parole in libertà* of F. T. Marinetti and his Futurist *cénacle*. In "The Technical Manifesto of Futurist Literature" of 1912, Marinetti had declared that "Poetry should be an uninterrupted sequence" of image-bearing nouns, nouns "related by analogy." "Example: man-torpedo-boat, woman-gulf, crowd-surf, piazza-funnel, door-faucet" ("Esempio: uomo-torpediniera, donna-golfo, folla-risacca, piazza-imbuto, porta-rubinetto").[11] The "destruction of syntax" thus effected was to be enhanced by means of a "typographical revolution"—*"three or four colours of ink,* or even twenty different typefaces if necessary. For example: italics for a series of similar or swift sensations, boldface for the violent onomatopoeia, and so on."[12]

The "destruction of syntax" was, of course, also Stein's project, but, as we shall see, for her the phrase meant something quite different. True, she shared Marinetti's dislike of adjectives, but whereas Marinetti declares that "One must abolish the adjective to allow the naked noun to preserve its essential color,"[13] Stein, to the contrary, held adjectives to be too close to nouns. "After all," she writes, "adjectives effect nouns and as nouns are not really interesting the thing that effects a not too interesting thing is of necessity not interesting" (LIA 211). Verbs and adverbs are a little better because "they have one very nice quality and that is that they can be so mistaken. . . . Nouns and adjectives never can make mistakes can never be mistaken but verbs can be so endlessly both as to what they do and how they agree or disagree with whatever they do" (LIA 211–12). Take a sentence like "Return a pigeon seated" in "Arthur a Grammar" (HTW 58). Is "return" a verb or a noun? And what about "Cared for horses are either up or down"? (HTW 58).

But the most "varied and alive" parts of speech, for Stein as for Wittgenstein, are the small words, the connectives that make the sentence fluid and open: prepositions, articles, conjunctions, and especially pronouns:

> Pronouns are not as bad as nouns because in the first place practically they cannot have adjectives go with them. That already makes them better than nouns.
>
> Then beside not being able to have adjectives go with them, they of course are not really the name of anything. They represent some one but they are not its or his name. In not being his or its or her name they already have a greater possibility of being something than if they were as a noun is the name of anything. (LIA 213–14)

A pronoun, it seems, is a way of getting away from the confinement of the label, of a fixed name: "they may be born Walter and become Hub, in such a way they are not like a noun. A noun has been the name of something for such a very long time" (LIA 214), whereas the pronoun opens up all sorts of possibilities for poetry. Traditionally, poetry was conceived as the naming game; its mission was "to know how to name earth sea and sky and all that" (LIA 233). But by the end of the nineteenth century, these names had taken on a fixity that had made it impossible "to feel anything and everything that for me was existing so intensely" (LIA 242). Hence the struggle in *Tender Buttons* "with the ridding myself of nouns, I knew nouns must go in poetry as they had gone in prose if anything that is everything was to go on meaning something" (LIA 242).

This case against the noun (and later in the essay, against all punctuation marks except the period) has generally been construed as no more than Stein's attempt, however charming and witty, to justify her own arbitrary word play.[14] True, the sweeping historical argument—the notion that poetry from Homer through the nineteenth century had been one thing (e.g., "caressing nouns"), a thing that the twentieth century now had to undo—must be taken with a grain of salt. What Stein really means when she makes the case for the superiority of pronouns (and prepositions, conjunctions, etc.) to nouns may be glossed by Wittgenstein's remark, cited above, that "Physics does not use these words" (PI #410). Physics, that is to say, can rely largely on the naming or noun function: $e = mc^2$; its use of pronouns is relatively minimal. But this is not the case in ordinary discourse. "You can't hear God speak to someone else, you can hear him only if you are being addressed," Wittgenstein noted commonsensically, and added, "That is a grammatical remark" (Z #717). Consider, in this regard, the pronouns and prepositions in the following sentences, sentences Stein cites as examples of "successful" emotional balance:

> He looks like a young man grown old.
> It looks like a garden but he had hurt himself by accident.
> A dog which you have never had before has sighed.
> Once when they were nearly ready they had ordered it to close.
>
> (LIA 226)

These short declarative sentences have a Wittgensteinian cast: nonsensical as they look at first glance, they begin to make sense when we see how they are used. Sentence 1, for example, seems ridiculous because every old man was once a young man, but we can conceive of a situation in which X tells Y she is surprised that Z seems suddenly to have aged so much, whereupon Y might reply, "He looks like a young man grown old." Yeats's "Girl's Song," for that matter, ends with the stanza "And that was all my song— / When everything is told, / Saw I an old man young / Or young man old?"[15] In #2 the odd feature is the conjunction "but"; again we could make up contexts that would make this sentence quite plausible, for instance: "Did he fall down on the pavement and break his leg?" "No, it looks like a garden but he has hurt himself by accident." In #3, the seemingly irrelevant subordinate clause ("which you have never had before") makes sense if the speaker is, say, a dog trainer who is explaining the particular habits of a dog to its new owner. And #4 allows for all sorts of narrative possibilities. The "they" might, for instance, own a restaurant, and once, when they were nearly ready to go to a wedding, they ordered "it" (the restaurant) to close for the evening. And so on.

The indeterminacy of pronouns here and in some of Wittgenstein's examples is no doubt motivated, at least in part, by the felt need to encode all overt references to sexual identity;[16] it is a common practice in the love poetry of W. H. Auden and, later, in the writing of John Ashbery. But since many homosexual writers of Stein's time—Marcel Proust and Virginia Woolf, to take just two prominent examples—had no use for this particular pronominal mode, it remains to be specified just how the "theories" put forward in "Poetry and Grammar," and even more complexly in the pieces collected in *How to Write,* operate in the Stein text.

"Thank You for the Difference in Me"

Wittgenstein's discussion of *identity* in the *Philosophical Investigations* provides a useful context for Stein's own "experiments" with language:

> But isn't *the same* at least the same?
>
> We seem to have an infallible paradigm of identity in the identity of a thing with itself. I feel like saying: "Here at any rate there can't be a variety of interpretations. If you are seeing a thing you are seeing identity too."
>
> Then are two things the same when they are what *one* thing is? And how am I to apply what the *one* thing shews me to the case of two things? (PI #215)

Repeat the same and it is no longer the same. This commonsense discrimination forms the basis of Stein's mode of repetition, a mode that is, after all, an extreme form of *literalism.*[17] Stein herself, for that matter, thought of *Tender Buttons* and related compositions as essentially "realistic" in the tradition of Flaubert. In the "Transatlantic Interview" with Robert Bartlett Haas (1946), she explains: "I used to take objects on a table, like a tumbler or any kind of object and try to get the picture of it clear and separate in my mind and create a word relationship between the word and the things seen."[18] And her mentor William James praised *Three Lives* as "a fine new kind of realism."[19]

But how does this relationship work, given the obvious fact that Stein's portraits, whether of persons or objects, do not describe what is seen in any recognizable way? Here again Wittgenstein provides us with a point of entry. "A main source of our failure to understand," he observes, "is that we do not *command a clear view* of the use of our words. . . . A perspicuous representation produces just that understanding which consists in 'seeing connexions' " (PI #122). Such "seeing as" or "seeing something *as something*" (PI p. 213) depends, I think, on our willingness to read Stein both *literally* as well as *contextually,* examining why she puts up a particular "fence" or "boundary line" around certain words and why others are excluded. "Dislocations" of specific words and phrases are, after all, ways of *locating* others.

"But isn't *the same* at least the same?" Consider, for example, the following passage from "Arthur a Grammar":

> Right.
> Right right right right left.
> Right left right left I had a good job and I left.
> Right left right left right I had a good job and I left.
> Told grammar.
> Grammar.
> What is it.
> Who was it.
> Artichokes.
> Articles.
> A version.
> He merely feels.
> Does he.
> Does it.
> He merely feels does it.
> He merely feels does he.
> Makes.
> In prints it.
> Prints prints it.
> Forgotten.
> He has forgotten to count.
> He has forgotten how to count.
> Aid and alike.
> Of account.
> Howard Howard.
> Arthur Arthur.
> Rene Crevel.
> Grammar.

> Our account.
>
> On our account.
>
> (HTW 50–51)

Stein's mock catalogue begins with an allusion to the World War I infantry marching chant "Right, left, right, left, I had a good job and I left. . . . " Verbs, remember, "can be mistaken," as the pun on "left" indicates: such ambiguities are part of a "Told grammar." And, in case you think you know what grammar is, try referring to it as a "who," not a "what."

Nouns, Stein says repeatedly, are not "interesting"—not, at least, if you think of them as names. But suppose you break them down into their components:

> Artichokes
>
> Articles
>
> A version

Phonetically, these three three-syllable units sound alike; the first two are almost identical, "artichokes" sharing the same stress pattern and all but three of its letters—*h, o, k*—with "articles," a plural noun that otherwise has no direct relationship to it, although of course artichokes are articles to be found in the garden or (cooked) on the dinner table. And then line 3 gives us an example of an article in "A," but, coming as it does after the two nouns, one naturally tries to make the next word conform by eliding the space between "A" and "version." And that gives us *aversion*—not exactly a version of things to be expected in this particular catalogue.

Pronouns, Stein believes, "have a greater possibility of being something" than nouns. "He merely feels. / Does he. / Does it. / He merely feels does it. / He merely feels does he." Here the range of possibilities is generated by the period. He merely feels rather than thinks? Or should we complete the sentence? He merely feels rotten? Does he? Does it hurt? Any number of scenarios are written into these childlike constructions. "In prints it" differs from "Prints prints it," in that the first "prints" may be a noun and the sentence therefore lopped off: "In prints it. . . . " And further: when spoken, "In prints it" is all but indistinguishable from "im-

prints it." A related "possibility" arises in the semantic contrast between
"He has forgotten to count" and "He has forgotten how to count," as
well as in the variations between "Of account," "Our account," "On our
account," the meaning shifting each time.

Now consider the proper names:

> Howard Howard
> Arthur Arthur
> Rene Crevel

"Howard" and "Arthur," as their repetition suggests, have no individual
identity; they are used for structural purposes in specific sentences, as in
"How is Howard and how are Arthur and Harold" (HTW, p. 57). "How-
ard" is no more important than "how"; "Arthur" becomes part of the verb
"are" or "Arthur is an author" (HTW, p. 58), and so on. But "Rene
Crevel" designates a real person, the young Surrealist writer who fre-
quented Stein's salon. "Of all the young men who came to the house,"
recalls Alice in the *Autobiography of Alice B. Toklas,* "I think I liked René
the best. He had french charm. . . . He was young and violent and ill and
revolutionary and sweet and tender. Gertrude Stein and René are very
fond of each other."[20] So "Rene"[21] gets extra space: he has a family name
"Crevel" as well as a first name, in contrast to Arthur and Howard and
Harold. His name, moreover, is not as readily absorbable into the sound
structure and grammar of the composition.

"The results of philosophy," we read in the *Philosophical Investiga-
tions,* "are the uncovering of one or another piece of plain nonsense and
of bumps that the understanding has got by running its head up against
the limits of language" (PI #119). It is these "bumps" that Stein takes on
in "Arthur a Grammar," and the related "essays" in *How to Write.* Such
Wittgenstein puzzles as "Why can't my right hand give my left hand
money?" (PI #268) are matched by the implicit question, How is it that
we know that the "account" of "our account" (e.g., bank account or narra-
tive) is not the same as the "account" in "On our account," where "ac-
count" means "behalf"? Or again, why does it sound strange to say "Told
Grammar" or "Grammar will"?

In asking such questions, Stein takes us to the heart of her inquiry into the nature of grammar. Indeed, in the passage above, language is not at all "anarchic" or "nonreferential"; it merely exposes, in what we might call a hyperreal fashion, the implications contained in phrases, word groups, words, and morphemes. Ironically, then, Stein's essay-poem is what it proclaims itself to be: a treatise on grammar—grammar, that is to say, in its relation to human life ("Arthur"). Like Wittgenstein, Stein displays an almost allergic reaction to what she takes to be the misuse of words and phrases: "Forgotten. / He has forgotten to count. / He has forgotten how to count." "Being alone with English and among people who can't read a word of her work" (ABT 66), Stein is sensitive to every preposition, even as Wittgenstein, writing in German but lecturing in the English of his adopted Cambridge, wonders whether the verb "is" in "The rose is red" is the same "is" as that in "twice two is four" (PI #558). Attention to such questions of grammar, both writers insist, is a serious business—perhaps *the* serious business.

"He has forgotten to count. He has forgotten how to count": it is interesting to see how Stein's "destruction of syntax" differs from that of her Futurist contemporaries. Marinetti, as a page from *Les Mots en liberté futuristes* (1919) will show (see fig. 1), was committed to what we might call linguistic mimesis, that is, to the principle that linguistic and visual signs can directly represent and express material sights and sounds. *Après la Marne, Joffre visita le front en auto* (originally titled "Montagnes + val- lées + routes + Joffre"), for example, uses dramatic typographic effects (especially the "LEGER/LOURD" opposition of giant phallic **M**'s and "female" **V**'s and **W**'s), mathematical symbols, and elaborate onomatopoeia to rep- resent what the page itself designates as the "Verbalisation dynamique de la route," the frenzy and excitement of General Joffre's passage through the mountains and valleys. Thus the overscale **S** curves on the left, curves that evoke the shape of the trenches, move from "la BELLE FRANCE" (with "BEL-LE divided by +, −, and × signs) to the confrontation with "GUERRE" and "PRUSSIENS" at bottom left, as if to show the explosion at the Franco-German border. "**Mon AMiiiii**," "**MaAA × AAapetite**," "**ta ta ta ta ta**" : the complex visual arrangement of these words is designed to convey the actual "feel" of battle. The destruction of the linguistic or-

1. F. T. Marinetti, *After the Marne, Joffre Visited the Front in an Automobile* (1915), in *Les Mots en liberté futuristes*, 1919. Beinecke Rare Book and Manuscript Library, Yale University.

der, as Johanna Drucker remarks, stands for the destruction of human life at the front.[22]

From a Wittgensteinian perspective, such correspondence between word and thing, visual layout and verbal referent, reduces meaning to the process of naming. Words, Wittgenstein argues throughout the *Investigations,* are not to be viewed as pointers designating particular objects; their meaning depends on their function in the specific context of action we call the language game. And Stein, as we have seen, was in this respect a thorough if unconscious Wittgensteinian: the substitution of the equal sign (=) for the word "is," she would have posited, cannot change the fact that "is" sometimes means "equals" but sometimes not. To understand Stein's own fix on Marinetti's expressive model, we might look at a short composition she wrote in 1916, a year after Marinetti produced *Après la Marne.* This composition belongs to no fixed genre (being part portrait, part prose poem, part private diary) and has no fixed form, its five pages ranging from short rhyming couplets (e.g., "To make her shine. / We entwine") to paragraphs bearing titles like "SHE WAS. NOT ASTONISHING" or "ANOTHER CHANCE." It is called *Marry Nettie,* and subtitled *Alright Make it a Series and call it Marry Nettie.*[23]

FORMS OF (EVERYDAY) LIFE

In the *Autobiography of Alice B. Toklas,* Alice describes the summer of 1915, when, "to forget the war a little," she and Gertrude Stein went to Mallorca, where they remained until the following spring:

> And we went to Palma thinking to spend only a few weeks but we stayed the winter. First we went to Barcelona. It was extraordinary to see so many men on the streets. I did not imagine there could be so many men left in the world. One's eyes had become so habituated to menless streets, the few men one saw being in uniform and therefore not being men but soldiers, that to see quantities of men walking up and down the Ramblas was bewildering. We sat in the hotel window and looked. I went to bed early and got up early and Gertrude Stein went to bed late and got up late and so in a way we overlapped but there was not a moment when there were not quantities of men going up and down the Ramblas. (ABT 152–53)

This strangely "men-full" Spanish world (the word "men" occurs seven times in the paragraph) is the backdrop for the little-known *Marry Nettie,* written during Stein and Toklas's Mallorcan stay. The title alludes, of course, to Marinetti, of whom Stein writes in the *Autobiography:*

It was about this time [1912] that the futurists, the italian futurists, had their big show in Paris and it made a great deal of noise. Everybody was excited and this show being given in a very well known gallery everybody went. Jacques-Emile Blanche was terribly upset by it. We found him wandering tremblingly in the garden of the Tuileries and he said, it looks alright but is it. No it isn't, said Gertrude Stein. You do me good, said Jacques-Emile Blanche.

The futurists all of them led by Severini thronged around Picasso. He brought them all to the house. Marinetti came by himself later as I remember. In any case everybody found the futurists very dull. (ABT 153)

Futurism, this passage makes clear, was something of a bone of con-tention between Stein and Picasso, she evidently having been annoyed that Marinetti and his friends were brought to her salon and were so much fussed over. Her good friends Apollinaire and Picabia, let us re-member, were strongly influenced by Futurism as was the early Du-champ—this despite the claim, in Marinetti's first (1909) manifesto, that "We will glorify war—the world's only hygiene—militarism, patriotism, the destructive gesture of freedom-bringers, beautiful ideas worth dying for, and scorn for woman" (LMM 50). No doubt Stein would have loved to see the loud, bombastic, charismatic Marinetti put down, but she bided her time.

Marry Nettie, Alright Make it a Series and call it Marry Nettie begins as follows:

Principle calling.
They don't marry.
Land or storm.
This is a chance.
A Negress.
Nurse.
Three years.
For three years.

By the time.
He had heard.
He didn't eat.
Well.
What does it cost to sew much.

A cane dropped out of the window. It was sometime before it was searched for. In the meantime the Negress had gotten it. It had no value. It was one that did bend. We asked every one. No one would be intended or contented. We gave no peace. At last the day before we left I passed the door. I saw a bamboo cane but I thought the joints were closer together. I said this. Miss Thaddeus looked in. It was my cane. We told the woman who was serving. She said she would get it. She waited and was reasonable. She asked if they found it below as it was the cane of my Thaddeus. It was and plain. So there. We leave.

There is no such thing as being good to your wife. (UD 309)

What language game is being played in this oblique and seemingly opaque sentence series? The name *Marinetti* is not just a word to be punned upon here,[24] for the opening section immediately evokes a comic but also mercilessly satiric portrait of the impresario of Futurism, the proponent of *parole in libertà,* the advocate of technology, violence, war, and free love. Indeed, the text cleverly replaces one word ("Marinetti") by two ("Marry Nettie"), as if to say that the domineering *chef d'école* of Futurism must be replaced by two women in dialogue: "Marry who. Marry Nettie. Which Nettie. My Nettie. Marry whom. Marry Nettie. Marry my Nettie."

Consider, to begin with, the grammar of Stein's composition. In anticipation of the argument she would later make in "Poetry and Grammar," the text of *Marry Nettie* depends precisely on those parts of speech abjured by Marinetti in his "Technical Manifesto of Futurist Literature" (1912)—conjunctions, prepositions, auxiliary verbs, adverbs, and especially the dreaded pronoun "I," which Marinetti railed against as a vestige of the "old" psychology (LMM 92–95). Conversely, Stein avoids the prescribed infinitive, with its supposed "elasticity of intuition" (LMM 92), and her nouns tend to be abstract rather than concrete. For Marinetti, as I noted above, lyric was synonymous with a sequence of powerful, con-

crete noun pairs or triads, as in "man-torpedo-boat" or "piazza-funnel."
Stein refuses such pairing: aside from "Land or storm" (line 3), of which
more in a moment, her thirteen-line opener has only six nouns: "Prin-
ciple," "chance," "Negress," "Nurse," "years," and "time," none of them
graphic or particularized.

"One must," declared Marinetti, "destroy syntax and scatter one's
nouns at random just as they are born" (LMM 92). One of the great iro-
nies of Stein's *Marry Nettie* is that she is the one who actually destroys
syntax; Marinetti's roll calls of analogous nouns seem quite tame by com-
parison. Whereas Marinetti's aim, in works like *Zang Tumb Tuuum,* is to
render the sound of things by the look of things, the aural by the visual
as in "**uuuuuuuurlaaare**" (see fig. 2), in Stein's text such mirror effects give
way to unfinished sentences ("For three years," "By the time"), ambiguous
referents ("They don't marry," "This is a chance," "He had heard," "It
was my cane"), and unanswered questions ("What does it cost to sew
much"). Even more remarkably, Stein begins her composition with a play
on Marinetti's demand for a poetry that is "an uninterrupted sequence of
new images, or it is mere anemia and greensickness" (LMM 93). "You
want an uninterrupted sequence?" her narrator seems to be asking. Well,
"Alright make it a series and call it Marry Nettie." But hers is a "series" not
of nouns in parallel constructions but of short, linear units, each with a
slightly different grammatical form and each seemingly unrelated to the
unit that comes before or after.[25]

"Principle calling," the "series" begins, immediately making a
tongue-in-cheek allusion to Marinetti's grandiose pronouncements, an al-
lusion that is also a pun on Marinetti's insistence on being the "principal"
player in all Futurist events. "They don't marry" (line 2) most immedi-
ately refers to the soldiers fighting in the war; "they don't marry" because
they die instead. But it also refers to Marinetti's call for honest lust in
place of romantic love, his attack, for example, on the dancing couple of
"Down with Tango and Parsifal" as having the air of "two hallucinated
dentists" (LMM 77). Similarly, "Land or storm" (line 3) alludes both to
the war (Marinetti's desired "hygiene") and to the frenetic travel of the
impresario known as the "caffeine of Europe," as well as to the celebration
of aggressive military campaigns in the manifestos. And "This is a

nel treno *fogliame vibrante dell'olfatto* odore
fecale della dissenteria **+** puzzo melato dei
sudori della peste **+** tanfo ammoniacale
dei colerosi **+** fetidità zuccherina delle gan-
grene polmonari **+** odore acidulo dei feb-
bricitanti **+** odori di cantina **+** piscio di
gatto **+** olio-rancido pane-caldo **+** aglio **+**
incenso **+** paglia-fradicia **+** stagni **+** frittura **+**
vinacce **+** odori di topo **+** tuberosa **+** ca-
volo-marcio **zang–tumb–tumb tata-**
tatatata stop

        uuuuuuuurlaaare degli
ammalati nel **crrrrrrepitare** delle **palle**
fischi **schianto** di vetri rotttti sportelli-ber-
sagli Adrianopoli interamente accerchiata treno
abbandonato dai meccanici e dai soldati
rabbbbbia degli shrapnels bulgari
fame rapacità mordere mordere i minareti-

2. F. T. Marinetti, from *Zang Tumb Tuuum* (1914), in
Opere di F. T. Marinetti, vol. 2: *Teoria e invenzione futurista,*
p. 689. Rome: Mondadori, 1968. Edizione Futuriste de
"Poesia," 1914. Beinecke Rare Book and Manuscript
Library, Yale University.

chance" (line 4) pokes fun at Marinetti's blatant opportunism, even as the "chance" is also the poet's own.

Now we come to the lines "A Negress. / Nurse." Anyone familiar with Marinetti will recall the passage in the First Manifesto in which the poet describes the accident in which his new motorcar capsizes in a muddy ditch:

> Oh! Maternal ditch, almost full of muddy water! Fair factory drain! I gulped down your nourishing sludge; and I remembered the blessed black breast of my Sudanese nurse. (LMM 48)

The nurse, for that matter, is mentioned frequently in Marinetti's writings, always as an emblem of the exotic, "violent" East (specifically, Egypt), where Marinetti grew up. Stein turns this Sudanese nurse into an American "Nettie" ("Nettie" was, in Stein's day, a common Southern name, especially for "colored girls"), for whom marriage is being proposed. But by whom and how? We only know that "A Negress. Nurse" has somehow been around "For three years. By the time," but we don't, at this point, know by what time and what her role is. Perhaps she has managed to get away, has made "an egress." The "series" of terse, staccato sentence units ("He had heard. / He didn't eat"), in any case, now culminates in a pun on "sew" (the nurse's job?)/"so." "What does it cost," the line implies, "to talk so much?" Or shout so much or whatever other appropriate verb we want to insert into the sentence. And at this point, *Marry Nettie* shifts from "verse" to "prose" with a "description" of a cane that has been "dropped out of the window," where "In the meantime the Negress had gotten it. It had no value."

In the photographs (and some paintings as well) of Marinetti and his *cénacle* (see fig. 3), the black derby hat, the heavy black overcoat, the cigarette dangling from the lips, and the cane held by a black-gloved hand become Futurist insignia. *Marry Nettie* plays on this image, presenting us with a situation in which the cane, which "had no value" (because, Stein seems to suggest, Futurist art had no value), "dropped out of the window." The magic wand passes on to someone else. To whom? To the Negress, of course, the Nettie of the title. "It was one that did bend": someone else (Nettie) could appropriate it. But soon the real owner, a

3. Luigi Russolo, Carlo Carrà, F. T. Marinetti, Umberto Boccioni, and Gino Severini in Paris, 1912. In Caroline Tisdall and Angelo Bozzolla, *Futurism.* New York and Toronto: Oxford University Press, 1978, p. 36. Beinecke Rare Book and Manuscript Library, Yale University.

Miss Thaddeus, turns up and claims it, Miss Thaddeus quite possibly representing one of the American spinster ladies, like the Misses Cone from Baltimore, who tries to come between the "marrying" of Gertrude and Alice. "There is no such thing as being good to your wife."

Thus far, then, Stein's poetic composition is a comic and sometimes devastating send-up of Marinetti's values; it elegantly and wittily deflates its "subject" without making a single overt statement about him. But, someone is sure to object, if Stein wants to produce a satire, why does she need to be so obscure? Or, to make the opposite objection, if she wants to be so obscure, why am I, as her reader, "translating" the passage back into straightforward, "normal" English? Isn't this a violation of her poetic intentions?

My response to the first objection is that Stein's fabled obscurity is, ironically enough, a function of what we might call her hyperrealism. She does not, as the more familiar satirist would, belittle her subject by exposing his foibles or mocking his pretensions. Rather, she stages the subject's self-exposure. Here, as in her portraits of Picasso and Matisse, Stein uses Marinetti's own words and gestures to deprive the artist of his identity. Consider, for example, the shift from short line-units to "normal" prose that accompanies the appropriation of the "dropped" cane by the "negress." From Marinetti to Nettie. Or, more properly—in view of the fact that "They don't marry" (line 2)—a reference to the various single guests at the Mallorca hotel whom the narrator maliciously observes, from Marinetti to Gertrude and Alice, who can't legally "marry" but are "marry-nettied" all the same.

But what of the second objection? Why is it not enough to say of the passage in question that it represents Stein's refusal to "mean," her dislocation or disruption of patriarchal language by means of what Marianne DeKoven and others have described as an "irreducibly multiple, fragmented, open-ended articulation of lexical meaning," whose "primary modes are dissonance, surprise, and play" (MDK 76)? Why violate the *jouissance* of Stein's "pre-Oedipal" language? Because, I would suggest, not all "dislocations" are of equal value. To assume that Stein chooses her words more or less randomly, that she is merely being "playful," is to ignore the careful contextualization that makes such play possible. No two words, after all, are used precisely the same way. Suppose, for example, that in line 1 of *Marry Nettie* we substituted "Conviction calling" for "Principle calling." The pun of "principle"/"principal" would be lost. As for "calling," no synonym (e.g., "shouting," "announcing," "heralding") has precisely the resonance of this ordinary word, which may be present participle or noun. A "principal calling"—it is the artistic vocation Marinetti claimed for his "revolutionary" movement.

Having submitted this vocation to comic critique, Stein now develops the "Marry Nettie" relationship between the "we" who are Gertrude and Alice. First, the ladies go shopping:

She asked for tissue paper. She wanted to use it as a respirator. I don't understand how so many people can stand the mosquitoes.

It seems unnecessary to have it last two years. We would be so pleased.
We are good.
We are energetic.
We will get the little bowls we saw to-day.
The little bowls we saw to-day are quite pretty.
They will do nicely.
We will also get a fan. We will have an electric one. Everything is so reasonable.

It was very interesting to find a sugar bowl with the United States seal on one side and the emblem of liberty on the other.

If you care to talk to the servant do not talk to her while she is serving at table. This does not make me angry nor annoy me. I like salad. I am losing my individuality.

What could be "simpler" than the childlike, regressive grammar of this paragraph? "We would be so pleased," "The little bowls we saw to-day are quite pretty," "We will also get a fan. We will have an electric one"—it seems like the mere recording of the banalities and niceties of everyday "polite" chitchat. The "sugar bowl with the United States seal on one side and the emblem of liberty on the other" is purchased, evidently by Stein herself, and then reappears in the section, some two pages later, entitled, "A New Sugar Bowl with a Cross on Top":

We said we had it. We will take it to Paris. Please let us take everything.

The sugar bowl with a cross on top now has sugar in it. Not soft sugar but the sugar used in coffee. It is put on the table for that.

It is very pretty. We have not seen many things. We want to be careful. We don't really have to bother about it. (UD 311)

But why should the reader care about a silly sugar bowl with the Statue of Liberty on it? And why does it matter that the bowl "now [back in Paris] has sugar in it. Not soft sugar but the sugar used in coffee"? And what is the significance of the social decorum that dictates such things as "If you care to talk to the servant do not talk to her while she is serving at table"?

"The aspects of things that are most important for us are hidden because of their simplicity and familiarity," notes Wittgenstein (PI #129). "(One is unable to notice something—because it is always before one's eyes.). . . . we fail to be struck by what, once seen, is most striking and most powerful." The Stein paragraph I have just cited will strike many readers as merely boring. Who cares whether or not a nameless female customer ("she") "asked for tissue paper" that she wanted to use as "a respirator"? Who cares that there are so many mosquitoes about?

A clue as to what Stein is up to here may be found in the concluding sentences, "I like salad. I am losing my individuality." Like "I have a pain," "I have three dresses," Stein's parallel grammatical units mask an important semantic difference. "I like salad"—these are the polite words of a lady in a dining room, when served by the waitress. So oppressive is the need to say these things, to observe the niceties we have just witnessed, that the speaker shifts gears to "I am losing my individuality." And indeed we have just witnessed this loss: in the sugar bowl/electric fan encounter, it's not clear whether the "I" is Gertrude or Alice or whether it is a third speaker who is overheard. Nor does it matter, the point being that for all the foreigners sitting out the war on the Mallorca hotel scene, individuality is what is lost. Although "All languages" are spoken here (UD 310), a nagging estrangement has set in: "They see English spoken." Note that this sentence subtly deviates from its model, "They hear English spoken." To "see" English spoken is to see a sign on a shop window or in a restaurant or hotel: "English spoken." That's how one sees it. And such seeing is not without its attendant anxieties:

> We will go out in the morning. We will go and bring home fish. We will also bring note-books and also three cups. We will see Palma. Shoes are necessary. Shoes with cord at the bottom are white. How can I plan everything?

So meaningless do the rituals become that we "overhear" vapid statements like:

> Sometimes I don't mind putting on iodine and sometimes I do—

which makes disinfecting one's wounds sound like an "informed" choice to commit an act of real consequence.

The world of *Marry Nettie* is thus one of social ritual and boredom, of niceties and conventions, of proper behavior and meaningless chores. The hotel food is tasty ("It is very edible," on the model of "It is very reasonable"), but "She" (who?) "came upstairs having been sick. It was the effect of the crab." The "issue" of the day is whether "tissue paper" can serve as a "respirator" (note the rhyme), a protection against mosquitoes, or whether towels do or do not "dry down here" as well as they dry up at the Count's place. As a result, confusion sets in: "Was I lost in the market or was she lost in the market" (UD 311)—a curiously Wittgensteinian question, for obviously, if two people go to a market and lose each other, both are equally "lost" or "found," as the case may be.

The loss of "individuality" gradually leads from boredom to anxiety and a degree of claustrophobia. The section called "We Blamed Each Other" begins: "She said I was nervous. I said I knew she wasn't nervous. The dear of course I wasn't nervous. I said I wasn't nervous" (UD 311). The war is always in the background: "Do we believe the germans. We do not" (UD 312). And again, "May the gods of Moses and of Mars help the allies. They do they will." As the days go on, the heat evidently becomes more oppressive and "we" no longer go out or have tea. "We will not have tea. We will rest all day with the electric fan. We will have supper. We can perspire. After supper. This is so humorous."

But what has happened to Marinetti? The section I have just cited ("We Will Walk after Supper") is followed by one called "We Had an Exciting Day," which begins: "We took a fan out of a man's hand." This droll gesture acts as a gentle slap on Marinetti's wrist, a comic dismantling of the pretentiousness Stein discerns in Futurist poetics. Thus, "we" women (specifically, Gertrude and Alice) remove the fan, a traditional emblem of femininity, from the "man's hand" that tries to control it. But more important, given the declaration, on the first page of *Marry Nettie,* that "We will also get a fan. We will have an electric one," the fan taken out of a man's hand represents Stein's assertion that Marinetti and his friends no longer have a corner on technology. On the contrary, electricity, celebrated in countless paeans by the Futurists, now belongs to "us." But its use has to be redefined: Stein wholly subverts the paratactic mode of Futurism (or, for that matter, Imagism and Vorticism), using syntactic context and impersonal pronouns ("They," "this," "he," "it," "What") in a series of short, staccato sentences that, far from creating a constellation of revelatory images, undercut one another. The technique is to take ordinary language ("We said we had it. We will take it to Paris. Please let us take everything") and create a "narrative" in which nothing really changes except our own "Capacity to see something *as* something" (PI p. 213).

As *Marry Nettie* moves to its conclusion, Gertrude and Alice become increasingly detached from the other guests: "You see plenty of french people. You see some foolish people. You hear one boasting. What is he saying." It no longer matters too much, for what counts is their own "marriage":

> YOU LIKE THIS BEST.
>
> Lock me in neatly.
>
> Unlock me sweetly.
>
> I love my baby with a rush rushingly.

After this love scene, *Marry Nettie* concludes with a kind of chant in which *parole in libertà* are nicely replaced by the punning play on Marinetti's name, its dissolution making way for the "I" who speaks:

> Marry who. Marry Nettie. Which Nettie. My Nettie. Marry whom. Marry Nettie. Marry my Nettie.
>
> I was distinguished by knowing about the flower pot. It was one that had tuberoses. I put the others down below. That one will be fixed.
>
> I was also credited with having partiality for the sun. I am not particular. I do not like to have it said that it is so necessary to hear the next letter. We all wish to go now. Do be certain that we are cool.
>
> Oh shut up. (UD 313)

"Marry who. Marry Nettie. Which Nettie. My Nettie." Stein's droll chant has finally turned the grand impresario into a *marionette*. And over against Marinetti's own insistence on the particularity of the image, Stein presents her *own* particularity: "I was distinguished by knowing about the flower pot," "I put the others down below," "I was also credited with . . .," and finally, the double entendre of "I am not particular." Also, the flower pot the narrator is "distinguished by knowing about" is the "one that had tuberoses." Is it a mere coincidence that in the page from *Zang Tumb Tuuum* illustrated above (see fig. 2)—a page Stein might certainly have seen at a Paris exhibition or heard declaimed by Marinetti—we find *tuberosa* in the following context?

> vinacce + odori di topo + tuberosa + ca-
> volo-marcio **zang-tumb-tumb tata-tatatata stop** (TIF 689)

Like the fan Gertrude and Alice have taken "out of a man's hand," the tuberoses, removed from the smells of the battlefield, are now, so to speak, in her own "flower pot."

But the permutations of the "Marry who" sentence have an interesting way of qualifying the identity of Stein's "I." As Wittgenstein put it in the passage from the *Investigations* cited above, "Then are two things the same when they are what *one* thing is?" (#215). Each permutation of "the same" word group—here *Marry Nettie*—creates difference: the relationship of two people is always shifting. Is it correct to say "Marry who" or "Marry whom"? It all depends. "I do not like to have it said that it is so necessary to hear the next letter." There are no prescriptions that fit every situation. The *same* is not the same. And so the text ends on a note of impatience with the line "Oh shut up."

Is Stein addressing Toklas here? One of the other guests who has annoyed her? The chambermaid? Or Marinetti himself, the performance artist who never shuts up? The implied "you" may be any or all of these— in this sense the Stein text is indeterminate. But her indeterminacy, as I have argued elsewhere,[26] is by no means equivalent to nonsense or automatic writing. Indeed, her "ordinary" language constructions, like Wittgenstein's, are always in dialogical relation to the language of the world in which they exist, providing a powerful satire of its pretensions. "A great many philosophical difficulties," remarks Wittgenstein, "are connected with that sense of the expressions 'to wish', 'to think', etc. . . . These can all be summed up in the question: 'How can one think what is not the case?' " (BB 30).

Take the layeredness of *Marry Nettie.* From a modernist literary perspective, it functions as Stein's own counter-Futurist manifesto, her very covert and witty proclamation of difference and subversion. Words, her text suggests, can be torn open and realigned so as to uncover relationships that Marinettian parataxis had tended to ignore. From a historical perspective, the piece provides us with an image of the boredom and malaise experienced by those "private" citizens who tried to escape the realities of wartime France—indeed, in a broader sense, the malaise of any group of people marking time in a comparable situation. And from a personal perspective, *Marry Nettie* is "about" the day-to-day relationship, under the strained circumstances of the Mallorcan idyll, of a never-named Gertrude and Alice—a relationship that is loving but also tense, a "marriage" made in the face of the "they" who "don't marry."

Ironically, then, Stein's text can, as feminist critics have suggested about related texts, be construed as an antipatriarchal, antiauthoritarian, nonlinear, and oblique lesbian fiction. But in Stein's case, such specific gender construction is never the whole story. It would be misleading, for example, to assume from *Marry Nettie* that Stein was the enemy of Futurism; on the contrary, many of the paintings and writings she most admired—say, Duchamp's *Nude Descending a Staircase* or Apollinaire's *Calligrammes*—had close links to Futurist aesthetic. Nor can we assume that Stein's oblique upstaging of Marinetti represents the larger resentment she felt toward male artists in general. Her most important role model—perhaps her only real model—was, after all, the aggressively male Picasso. Indeed, within the poetic construct which is *Marry Nettie,* Stein is much less interested in ideology than in what she calls (in "Composition as Explanation") "using everything."

"Using everything" suggests a further irony. There is, after all, one thing Stein does seem to have learned from Futurist practice. Look at the opening page—for that matter, at any page—of *Marry Nettie.* If the page design is not quite that of, say, *Zang Tuuum Tumb* (fig. 2), it isn't entirely unlike it either. Lineated passages alternate with conventional paragraphs, sentences are often set off and surrounded by white space as in "There is no such thing as being good to your wife." (UD 309), and repeated units are arranged in a column as in

Oil.
Oil.

so as to form visual configurations. Most important, short blocks of text, whether lineated or in paragraph form, are preceded by titles in capital letters: "HOT WEATHER," "PLEASE BE QUICK," "WHY DO YOU LIKE IT," "WHOM DO YOU SAY YOU SEE," and so on.

Such attention to visual poetics was not part of Stein's early practice: neither *Three Lives* nor *The Making of Americans* nor even the early portraits exhibited any sort of break with conventional layout by means of typography, spacing, irregular margins, and so forth. Not until 1914, when she produced *Tender Buttons* and *Pink Melon Joy*, was the standard print block of the conventional book called into question. And by this time Futurist typography, collage, and manifesto format were well known in Stein's Paris. *Marry Nettie* is thus more Marinettian than Stein cared to admit.

Still, it is fair to say that Steinian grammar was never primarily visual; for her, as for Wittgenstein, what mattered was how people actually put words and sentences together and how they understood one another. "We were sure," we read halfway through *Marry Nettie*, "that steam was coming out of the water. It makes that noise" (UD 311). A wonderfully droll pseudoexplanation that may be glossed by the following proposition from the *Philosophical Investigations*:

> Of course, if water boils in a pot, steam comes out of the pot and also pictured steam comes out of the pictured pot. But what if one insisted on saying that there must also be something boiling in the picture of the pot? (#297)

Like Wittgenstein, Gertrude Stein took ordinary language so seriously that she would have appreciated the absurdity (and yet necessity) of the question about water boiling in the pictured pot. As would Samuel Beckett, to whom I now turn.

—Why do I not satisfy myself that I have two feet when I want to get up from a chair? There is no why. I simply don't. This is how I act.

—Wittgenstein, *On Certainty*

—If I am inclined to suppose that a mouse has come into being by spontaneous generation out of grey rags and dust, I shall do well to examine those rags very closely to see how a mouse may have hidden in them, how they may have got there and so on. But if I am convinced that a mouse cannot come into being from these things, then this investigation will perhaps be superfluous.

—Wittgenstein, *Philosophical Investigations*

One of the first things that Watt learned by these means was that Mr. Knott sometimes rose late and retired early, and sometimes rose very late and retired very early, and sometimes did not rise at all, nor at all retire, for who can retire who does not rise?

—Samuel Beckett, *Watt*[1]

four

Witt—Watt: The Language of Resistance/
The Resistance of Language

In 1945, the year Wittgenstein finished Part I of the *Philosophical Investigations,* Samuel Beckett, back in Paris after the war years, when he was living in hiding in the south of France, put the finishing touches on his novel *Watt.* Both books, oddly enough, were not to be published until 1953, the *Investigations* posthumously because Wittgenstein kept adding to the manuscript and delaying the promised delivery to the publisher,[2] *Watt* because no London, Dublin, or New York publisher at the time would touch it.[3] It was only thanks to Richard Seaver, who had become a devoted Beckettian as a result of reading *Molloy, Malone Meurt,* and *En Attendant Godot* (all three published in Paris between 1951 and 1952), that Maurice Girodias's small Olympia Press brought out, in the "Collection Merlin," a limited edition (1,100 copies) of *Watt.* The irony, of course, is that Olympia was known as a publisher of allegedly pornographic books—for example, the novels of Henry Miller—with which *Watt* had little in common. The Grove Press (Olympia's affiliate in the U.S. and still Beckett's publisher today) brought out a larger edition of *Watt* in 1959, but the first British edition (John Calder) was not published until 1963, and the first French translation (Editions de Minuit) not until

1968—seventeen years after *Molloy,* which *Watt* antedated, and almost a quarter century after it was completed.[4]

It is important to keep these dates in mind because the "Beckett" constructed in the Paris of the fifties—the Beckett of Maurice Blanchot and Georges Bataille, of Maurice Nadeau and Ludovic Janvier—was viewed as the chronicler of a postwar, postatomic world of alienation, emptiness, and inevitable despair. Writing in 1951 of the "fathomless misery" that characterizes *Molloy,* Bataille remarked:

> Language is what determines this regulated world, whose significations provide the foundation for our cultures, our activities and our relations, but it does so in so far as it is reduced to a means of these cultures, activities and relations; freed from these servitudes, it is nothing more than a deserted castle whose gaping cracks let in the wind and rain: it is no longer the signifying word, but the defenseless expression death wears as a disguise.[5]

Blanchot, writing of *The Unnamable* the same year, construes Beckett's world as one that does not "spare us the worst degradation, that of losing the power to say *I.*"[6] And, coming from a very different place, Theodor Adorno observes that "Beckett's characters behave in precisely the primitive, behavioristic manner appropriate to the state of affairs after the catastrophe, after it has mutilated them so that they cannot react any differently; flies twitching after the fly swatter has half-squashed them." "*Endgame,*" he declares, "takes up a position at the nadir of what the construction of the subject-object laid claim to at the zenith of philosophy: pure identity becomes the identity of what has been annihilated, the identity of subject and object in a state of complete alienation."[7]

Degradation, loss of subjectivity, the emptying out of being, death: these topoi, drawn from the *Trilogy* and the early plays and still largely accepted by Beckett commentators, have, not surprisingly, been read retrospectively into *Watt.* The protagonist's anguish has been viewed as a variant on Sartre's *nausée,*[8] Mr. Knott's house has been described as the place where "there are no more questions, orders, explanations," given that "life is rendered inanimate or scaled down from the human or animal to the vegetable level,"[9] and in an up-to-date Lacanian study, Thomas J. Cousineau declares:

[*Watt's*] portrayal of a rational individual humiliated by an absurd world is only a special case of a more fundamental concern; the true center of *Watt,* of which the concern with rationality is merely the visible trace, is the *suspicion, apparent in all of Beckett's fiction, that humans are inhabited by a false consciousness.* Their true subjectivity, the support of their capacity for authentic action, has been suppressed; in its place we find a surrogate self, distorted and made unreal by the alienating culture whose mark it bears.[10] (My emphasis)

What I find curious in such assessments of Beckett's fiction is that the "darkness of our time," as Wittgenstein calls it in the 1945 preface to the *Investigations,* is left largely unspecified. The "alienating culture" Cousineau speaks of is presumably the culture of late capitalism; the reduction of human beings to a vegetable state is presumably the human condition "after the catastrophe"—after Auschwitz, in Adorno's famous formulation.[11] But the world of *Watt,* and by extension of the *Trilogy,* is, I shall argue here, "dark" (and also "light") in a much more specific way than such readings would admit. Its characters are victims, not so much of the "human condition" or even of the "alienating culture" in which they find themselves, as of a crisis of *language,* a crisis that occurs when the very possibility of making connections between public and private discourse breaks down, as it did in the years leading up to and during the Second World War. In *Watt,* all the characters—Watt, Sam, Mr. Hackett, Mr. Spiro, Mrs. Nixon—seem to be suffering from what we might call, in Wittgensteinian terms, a use or context deficiency. They know what words like "key," "door," "bell," and "park bench" mean, but they don't understand how these words function in specific sentences—sentences that seem, for that matter, perfectly ordinary. If one is told, as Watt is, that Mr. Knott's leftovers are to be given to "the dog" (W 87), but there is no dog on the premises, how does one follow instructions? Knowing what a dog is, what leftovers are, and what the command "give" requires does not answer the question. "Language," as Wittgenstein says in the *Investigations,* "is a labyrinth of paths. You approach from *one* side and know your way about; you approach the same place from another side and no longer know your way about" (PI #203).

In his first published novel, *Murphy,* written in London between 1933 and 1935, Beckett's language, however whimsical, parodic, and punning, still assumes that words refer to the objects they name:

> It was after ten when Celia reached the mew. There was no light in his [Murphy's] window, but that did not trouble her, who knew how addicted he was to the dark. She had raised her hand to knock the knock that he knew, when the door flew open and a man smelling strongly of drink rattled past her down the steps. There was only one way out of the mew, and this he took after a brief hesitation. He spurned the ground behind him in a spring-heeled manner, as though he longed to run but did not dare. She entered the house, her mind still tingling with the clash of his leaden face and scarlet muffler, and switched on the light in the passage. In vain, the bulb had been taken away. She started to climb the stairs in the dark. On the landing she paused to give herself a last chance, Murphy and herself a last chance.[12]

Here, despite such burlesque locutions as "he spurned the ground behind him in a spring-heeled manner" and "she paused to give herself a last chance," the facts of Celia's entrance into Murphy's mews flat make good sense: she tries to turn on the light, it doesn't go on *because* there's no bulb in the socket, and so she must climb the stairs in the dark.

Compare this description to the following, on the first page of *Watt,* where a Mr. Hackett is seen approaching a street-corner bench that happens to be occupied:

> Mr. Hackett did not know whether he should go on, or whether he should turn back. Space was open on his right hand, and on his left hand, but he knew that he would never take advantage of this. (W 5)

The absurdity here is of a different order. Mr. Hackett ignores the obvious fact that an ambulatory person in a space not occupied by anyone else has room to go forward or turn around. The decision to "go on" or "turn back" thus has nothing to do with the available amount of "space." And the addendum "he knew that he would never take advantage of this" is doubly ridiculous, for in what sense can the human body "take advantage" of the air that surrounds it?

In Beckett's world, however, such basic facts of locomotion are always called into question. When, for example, a "gentleman and lady" (later identified as the Nixons) appear on the scene and move to sit down on the bench next to Hackett, we read that "He called in his arms and they˙sat down beside him" (W 8). Again, we laugh at this absurdity, but why? If dropping one's arms at one's sides is a voluntary action, why is it foolish to talk of "calling" them in?

Wittgenstein takes up this very question in the *Philosophical Investigations,* in his discussion of the nature of willing. "When I raise my arm 'voluntarily,' " he writes, "I have *not* wished it might go up. The voluntary action excludes this wish" (PI #616). And again, "I don't need to wait for my arm to go up—I can raise it" (#612). If, on the other hand, a physician is examining my sprained arm and says, "Try to raise your right arm" or "Try to straighten out your arm and drop it to your side," then talk of "calling in" one's arm might not be quite so silly. Or again, if the reference is to weapons on the battlefield, "calling in one's arms" makes perfectly good sense. It all depends, in other words, in what language game this particular group of words is being used.

Instinctively, of course, we know perfectly well how to use such simple phrases. We know, for example, when we read "Mr. Hackett did not know whether he should go on, or whether he should turn back," that the reference is to physical motion in space, and that "go on" means something different here than it does when someone is working on an algebra problem and suddenly sighs with relief and says, "Now I know how to go on" (PI #179). In the same vein, when Beckett's Unnamable declares, "you must go on, I can't go on, I'll go on," we know that he isn't talking about an algebra problem.

All these instances illustrate the Wittgensteinian dictum that "The meaning of a word is its use in the language" (PI #43). But in *Watt,* and indeed in the fiction and drama that follow, the ability to exercise this basic use-function seems to have been lost. Consider the following conversation (W 21), which takes place when Mr. Hackett asks Mr. Nixon how he first met Watt:

I met him one day in the street. One of his feet was bare. I forget which. He drew me to one side and said he was in need of five shillings to buy himself a boot. I could not refuse him.

> But one does not buy a boot, exclaimed Mr. Hackett.
>
> Perhaps he knew where he could have it made to measure, said Mrs. Nixon.

This wonderfully absurd conversation, in which all three characters raise issues that are entirely beside the point (e.g., which of Watt's feet was the bare one? Why did Watt need money since one can't buy just one boot? How does one acquire one, rather than two, boots?) may be glossed by a telling comment Wittgenstein made in his 1931 Lectures:

> "Arbitrary" as we normally use it always has reference to some practical end: e.g. if I want to make an efficient boiler I *must* fulfil certain specifications, but it is quite arbitrary what colour I paint it. . . .
>
> It has no sense to say that language is "important" or "necessary" to communicate our meaning. But it may be important for building bridges and doing similar things. (LEC1 60–61)

It is this basic discrimination that the Beckettian subject cannot seem to make. Hackett, Nixon, and Mrs. Nixon know perfectly well what a "boot" or a "foot" is but they haven't learned how these words are used in sentences. In the words of the *Investigations,* "It is as if one were to believe that a written order for a cow which someone is to hand over to me always had to be accompanied by an image of a cow, if the order was not to lose its meaning" (PI #449).

But why should the characters in *Watt* have so much difficulty with language—a language, after all, that every child learns to handle quite adequately for its needs? In 1937, Beckett wrote a long letter to a German friend, Axel Kaun, who had asked him to do some poetry translations:

> It is indeed becoming more and more difficult, even senseless, for me to write an official English. And more and more my own language appears to me like a veil that must be torn apart in order to get at things (or the Nothingness) behind it. Grammar and style. To me they seem to have become as irrelevant as a Victorian bathing suit or the imperturbability of a true gentleman. A mask. Let us hope the time will come, thank God that in certain circles it has already come, when language is most efficiently used where it is being most efficiently misused.[13]

That time was indeed to come and sooner than Beckett had anticipated. "Is there any reason," he asks Kaun, "why that terrible materiality of the word surface should not be capable of being dissolved?" and notes that "With such a program, in my opinion, the latest work of Joyce has nothing whatever to do. There it seems rather to be a matter of an apotheosis of the word." He adds, "Perhaps the logographs of Gertrude Stein are nearer to what I have in mind. At least the texture of language has become porous" (DMW 172–73).

This is a difficult statement to unpack. Beckett is evidently horrified by the cliché mongering everywhere around him, the conventions and niceties that are associated with conscious literary stylization. But how can this "terrible materiality of the word surface" be "dissolved"? Not, Beckett confides to Kaun, by worshiping the Word in all its figural and aural properties (the Joycean way). Rather, Beckett turns to the "logographs of Gertrude Stein," which have made language "porous." What Beckett means here, I think, is that "official English"—what we would now call the dominant discourse—can only be dismantled if language is "efficiently misused," if, that is, the "unword" (the unpoetic, ungainly, ordinary, everyday word, phrase, and sentence, as well as the unanticipated pause, the odd silence) is allowed to intrude on the text, to disrupt the sound surface. In Stein's "logographs," as we saw in chapter 3, the grammar is "porous," allowing for the widest variety of interpretation of the seemingly ordinary, as in "Roast potatoes for." Beckett's "porosity" of language is rather different. A Stein sentence—"Helen Furr was quite a pleasant woman"—tends to foreground the status of specific words: what, the reader wonders, can "pleasant" mean in this sentence and in its subsequent complex modulations? A Beckett sentence, on the other hand—say, "Watt was surprised to find the back door, so lately locked, now open" or "The lock was of a kind that Watt could not pick"—raises narrative rather than semantic questions: how is it, one asks, that the back door is open? Or again, what kind of lock *could* Watt have picked?

In 1937, when he wrote the letter to Kaun, Beckett admitted that he had not yet found a way of producing the "literature of the unword, which is so desirable to me. . . . An assault against words in the name of beauty." "In the meantime," he confessed to his friend, he was "doing nothing at all" (DMW 173). Peggy Guggenheim, with whom Beckett had an affair in 1938, confirms that this was indeed the case: she calls him

Oblomov, after Goncharov's "strange inactive hero who finally did not even have the willpower to get out of bed."[14] Yet, within a few years, this Beckett-Oblomov was to become a committed activist. The dramatic change was brought on by the outbreak of World War II and especially the German occupation of Paris in June 1940. Within months of this event, Beckett had joined the Resistance and taken up work as a transmitter of coded messages.

Just as Wittgenstein, who had suffered a spiritual and emotional crisis in 1937 in Norway and felt he could no longer bear to be a Cambridge don, brought Part I of the *Philosophical Investigations* to completion during the war when he was working, first as a dispensary porter and then as a pharmacy technician, at Guy's Hospital in London (see RM, 373–400, 431–57), so Beckett ironically found his vocation in the war years in response to his "official" work in espionage—work that involved the use of a language very different from the literary one he had thus far mastered.[15] As the first fruit of this new preoccupation with the ways that words *mean*, *Watt* is a key work in the Beckett canon—indeed, in the postmodern canon.

"The Last Stuttering in English"

Let me begin with a chronological sketch. In a letter to his friend George Reavey (May 1947), Beckett wrote of *Watt:* "It is an unsatisfactory book, written in dribs and drabs, first on the run, then of an evening, after the clodhopping, during the occupation. But it has its place in the series, as will perhaps appear in time" (CL 75). According to Carlton Lake, the first notebook of the autograph manuscript (there are six notebooks in all, written in ink and colored crayon) bears the note "Begun evening of Tuesday. 11/2/41." The first page of the second notebook is dated "3/12/41"; the third, "5.5.41"; the fourth is marked "Poor Johnny / Watt / Roussillon" and dated "Roussillon, October 4th 1943." On the cover of Notebook 5 Beckett wrote, "Watt V / Suite et-fin / 18. 2. 45 / Paris."[16] The writing of *Watt* thus coincides almost precisely with the five-year period

from Beckett's joining of the Resistance (October 1940), to his escape from
the Gestapo to the Vaucluse in the summer of 1942, to his return to Paris
some eight months after the May 1945 Armistice.

Like most of his French friends, Beckett had taken part in the June
1940 exodus from Paris in flight from the advance of the invading Ger-
man army. He stayed with the Joyces, who were at Vichy, continued on
to the south on foot, hiding in trucks and sleeping on benches until he
reached Arcachon, where his American friend Mary Reynolds put him
up. In October he returned to Paris and, horrified by the arrest of such
Jewish friends as Paul Léon, joined the Resistance, at the urging of his
old friend Alfred Péron. As a neutral Irishman who spoke perfect
French, Beckett was in great demand; his cell, *Gloria,* headed by Jeannine
Picabia (the daughter of Francis and Gabrielle Buffet-Picabia) was a *ré-
seau de renseignement,* or information network, whose main job was to
translate documents about Axis troop movements and relay them to Al-
lied headquarters in London. At first, the information in question was
written out on plain sheets of paper and collected by a secret courier;
later, the preferred conduit was microfilm, which could be hidden by
the couriers in the bottom of matchboxes. Beckett also traveled to the
Normandy seaports and to the unoccupied zone at Chalons to obtain in-
formation.[17]

The coding of the messages in question has interesting implications.
In his archival study of the British SOE (Special Operations Executive)
in France between 1940 and 1944, M. R. D. Foot describes the "cut-out,"
the "nearest thing to a safe device in underground warfare . . . a means
of establishing contact between two agents which, if it works properly,
affords the minimum for the enemy security services to bite on." And
Foot gives this example:

One agent passes a message in a simple code to a cut-out; it might be to a bookseller,
saying 'I have two volumes of Anatole France that need binding; can you arrange it
for me?' The cut-out holds the message till approached by the next agent down the
line, who rings up to ask, 'Have you any Anatole France in stock?', and will infer
from the answer 'Yes, two volumes have just come in' that there are two escapers to

be collected from the circuit's safe house in the Boulevard Anatole France; while the reply, 'Sorry, Mademoiselle, we're right out of stock' means there are no passengers that day.[18]

Another feature of the cut-out system was the series of rendezvous, which divided each "line" into watertight compartments:

> Passengers would be taken from one section of the line by a guide who would leave them at a prearranged spot, usually a park bench, and go away. A quarter of an hour later a guide from the next section would arrive and collect them, never meeting her predecessor, whom the passengers would take care not to describe. . . . An adequate cut-out system ensured that most individual members of the line knew at most only two telephone numbers or rendezvous, one at each end of their stretch of it; and even if the enemy raided these, they could get little out of them unless they happened to have the luck to arrive when passengers were present. Telephone subscribers might give away under pressure what form the next code message took, but could not say—because they did not know—from whom it came. (SOE 94–95)

We will see later what role such "cut-out" systems play in the novel begun in the months when Beckett's "daytime" writing consisted of encoding-transmission-reception-decoding of what were often crucially important messages. For the moment, let us note a few other features of the information system. "Passwords were always very simple, so that they could easily be memorised; at the simplest, dropping a couple of words—'black stone,' for instance—into a conversation. More often, there was a short catch-sentence to be used as an introduction, to which the contact would make a prearranged reply: 'I come from—Victor.' 'You mean—Hugo?' This guaranteed to each side the good faith of the other" (SOE 96). Members were known and referred to only by their pseudonyms, Beckett's being "Sam" or "*l'Irlandais*" (DB 311). And further, "Verbal messages between Informant and Organizer through couriers were always given in veiled language which couriers could not understand" (SOE 97). A concomitant rule, one that anticipated our own computer discourse, was that "Passwords had to be given, word perfect, otherwise they would not be accepted" (SOE 97). Letter and word sequence and grammar thus take precedence over the individual word. Indeed, one particular code called the "worked-out key" was based on a phrase, usually a line from a poem, chosen by the agent because it could easily be remembered (SOE 105). But such a line couldn't be too obvious; otherwise, the enemy would immediately suspect something.

Despite all these precautions, the Resistance cells were repeatedly threatened by double agents. *Gloria* was eventually destroyed by a former priest turned informer, the abbé Robert Alesch. When, in August of 1942, Alfred Péron was arrested by the Gestapo, Beckett and his companion, Suzanne Deschevaux-Dumesnil, knew they had to flee. In the two months that followed, Beckett hid in such places as the crawl space beneath the attic in Nathalie Sarraute's house (Beckett was shut up for ten days in this suffocating space, together with Sarraute's aged and ill father); he spent a terrifying night in a tall tree in the woods outside Paris, while below him the Germans made periodic patrols with dogs and guns; and later, he and Suzanne hid in a series of barns, sheds, and haystacks on the way to the south, walking only at night when they were relatively safe. When they finally arrived at the village of Roussillon, where they were to spend the next two and a half years, they were in a state of physical and mental exhaustion.

At Roussillon, Beckett and Dusmenil lived first in the village's only hotel, run by the widow of the great chef Escoffier, and then in their own little house.[19] Beckett worked sporadically for a farmer named Bonnelli (to be mentioned in *Godot*)[20] in exchange for wine and later for another peasant named Aude, for whom he cut wood and helped harvest potatoes. Bair recounts that in 1943 Beckett seems to have suffered a protracted nervous breakdown, which he tried to alleviate by working on *Watt* in the evenings, and later working for the local Resistance group, the *Maquis,* now less concerned with information gathering than with direct acts of sabotage. On August 24, 1944, the first American soldiers came to Roussillon; after the Armistice (8 May 1945), Beckett went to Ireland to visit his mother and settle his affairs. In August, longing to return to Paris but finding it difficult to do so, given the chaotic circumstances of demobilization, Beckett joined an Irish Red Cross unit that left for war-ravaged St. Lô in Normandy. Here he served as interpreter and storekeeper for the local field hospital. By winter he was back in his Paris apartment. *Watt* was finished; in the course of the next five years, he was to write his great French works: *Godot, Molloy, Malone meurt, L'Inno-mable.*

Watt is usually regarded as a quest novel: much has been made of its "pilgrimage in search of meaning," its Heideggerian search for Being, or again its portrayal of the rationalist's journey into an irrational universe.[21] But what makes the journeys in *Watt* so peculiar is that their destination is usually a place as carefully chosen in advance as it is unknown to the traveler (e.g., Watt's journey to Mr. Knott's house). Moreover, meetings take place between persons about whom one knows nothing other than their names (which may not be their real names), and there are repeated arrivals and departures according to a fixed schedule (e.g., Watt replaces Erskine downstairs exactly when Erskine replaces Arsene upstairs, and so on), whose raison d'être is never made clear. Indeed, the narrative of *Watt* involves a series of missed opportunities and failed connections: for example, Watt's arrival at the station after the last train has left and his spending the night in the locked waiting room.

All these "events" raise unanswerable questions. Why does Watt get off at the tram stop where Hackett and the Nixons are sitting? How does he find Mr. Knott's house? Has he been there before? How does Arsene know Watt is the expected new arrival? Why has he been hired to work for Knott? Why, at some later date, is Watt transferred to "another pavilion" (W 149) of "the asylum" and what sort of asylum is it? Who is Sam? Most important: where does the Watt of the final chapter go when the "six-four" leaves without him?

Each "meeting" in the novel (between Hackett and the Nixons, between Watt and Spiro, between Watt and Arsene, and so on) takes place between people who are talking at cross-purposes or are saying things whose subtext may be quite different from what we are actually given. What's worse: when Watt is alone, he talks to himself at cross-purposes. And it is this talk which is central to Beckett's world. Plot counts for very little, one event never logically leading to another and interruption (in the form of poems, songs, lists, and charts) occurring frequently. Nor is the story complete when it ends, the Addenda furnishing us, as we shall see, with any number of narrative possibilities. Again, "character" is a concept alien to *Watt,* whose people behave in largely interchangeable ways and put forward the same conundrums. Watt is at the center, but his point of view is not normally distinguishable from the narrator's. And then Sam, introduced in Chapter III, seems to *be* the narrator. Or is he?

No character, no plot, "no symbols," as Beckett famously put it, "where none intended" (W 255). Rather, a book about the problematic of language use in the ordinary transmission of information. For life in the war zone, Beckett implies, heightens, but does not really alter, what happens in everyday life. In the underground, that is, someone's survival may literally hang on the thread of what X tells Y, who in turn tells Z. But how Y and Z *understand* X's words is a perennial problem. Consider the following example from the *Philosophical Investigations*.

If one says "Moses did not exist," this may mean various things. It may mean: the Israelites did not have a *single* leader when they withdrew from Egypt—or: their leader was not called Moses—or: there cannot have been anyone who accomplished all that the Bible relates of Moses. . . . We may say, following [Bertrand] Russell: the name "Moses" can be defined by means of various descriptions. For example, as "the man who led the Israelites through the wilderness," "the man who lived at that time and place and was then called 'Moses'," "the man who as a child was taken out of the Nile by Pharaoh's daughter" and so on. And according as we assume one definition or another the proposition "Moses did not exist" acquires a different sense, and so does every other proposition about Moses. . . .

But when I make a statement about Moses,—am I always ready to substitute some *one* of these descriptions for "Moses"? (PI #79)

Now, if "Moses did not exist" were a specific code sentence of the type used in an SOE operation (e.g., "Two volumes of Anatole France have just come in"), the transmitter might simply "translate" it and then follow directions. But ordinary language, as Wittgenstein repeatedly shows us, cannot be "translated." None of the descriptions of Moses given above has a "fixed and unequivocal use"; only the actual circumstance in which "Moses did not exist" is used can determine its particular meaning.

"A main source of our failure to understand," says Wittgenstein, "is that we do not *command a clear view* of the use of our words.—Our grammar is lacking in this sort of perspicuity. A perspicuous representation produces just that understanding which consists in 'seeing connexions' "

(PI #122). It is this failure to see connections, to command a clear view of the use of our words, that Beckett dissects in *Watt*. Consider the well-known meeting with the piano tuners, which occurs shortly after Watt has come to live at Mr. Knott's.

> On only one occasion, during Watt's period of service on the ground-floor, was the threshold crossed by a stranger, by other feet that is than Mr. Knott's, or Erskine's, or Watt's, for all were strangers to Mr. Knott's establishment, as far as Watt could see, with the exception of Mr. Knott himself, and his personnel at any given moment.
>
> This fugitive penetration took place shortly after Watt's arrival. On his answering the door, as his habit was, when there was a knock at the door, he found standing before it, or so he realized later, arm in arm, an old man and a middle-aged man. The latter said:
>
> We are the Galls, father and son, and we are come, what is more, all the way from town, to choon the piano.
>
> They were two, and they stood, arm in arm, in this way, because the father was blind, like so many members of his profession. For if the father had not been blind, then he would not have needed his son to hold his arm, and guide him on his rounds, no, but he would have set his son free, to go about his own business. So Watt supposed, though there was nothing in the father's face to show that he was blind, nor in his attitude either, except that he leaned on his son in a way expressive of a great need of support. But he might have done this, if he had been halt, or merely tired, on account of his great age. There was no family likeness between the two, as far as Watt could make out, and nevertheless he knew that he was in the presence of a father and son, for had he not just been told so. Or were they not perhaps merely stepfather and stepson. We are the Galls, stepfather and stepson—those were perhaps the words that should have been spoken. But it was natural to prefer the others. Not that they could not very well be a true father and son, without resembling each other in the very least, for they could. (W 67)

Watt takes the Galls to the music room and leaves them there but then wonders if "he had done right," given that they are strangers. But "in the absence of precise instructions to the contrary" (W 68), he decides to be the good servant and brings the piano tuners a tray of refreshments. Much to his surprise, he finds that it is Mr. Gall Junior rather than Mr. Gall

Senior who is tuning the piano. This is puzzling enough, given the younger's probable apprentice status, and Watt is speculating on its possible meaning when Gall Jr., evidently finished with the tuning, puts his tools back in their bag and the following dialogue ensues:

> The mice have returned, he said.
>
> The elder said nothing. Watt wondered if he had heard.
>
> Nine dampers remain, said the younger, and an equal number of hammers.
>
> Not corresponding, I hope, said the elder.
>
> In one case, said the younger.
>
> The elder had nothing to say to this.
>
> The strings are in flitters, said the younger.
>
> The elder had nothing to say to this either.
>
> The piano is doomed, in my opinion, said the younger.
>
> The piano tuner also, said the elder.
>
> The pianist also, said the younger.
>
> This was perhaps the principal incident of Watt's early days in Mr. Knott's house.
>
> In a sense it resembled all the incidents of note proposed to Watt during his stay in Mr. Knott's house, and of which a certain number will be recorded in this place, without addition, or subtraction, and in a sense not.
>
> It resembled them in the sense that it was not ended, when it was past, but continued to unfold, in Watt's head, from beginning to end, over and over again, the complex connexions of its lights and shadows, the passing from silence to sound and from sound to silence, the stillness before the movement and the stillness after. . . . It resembled them in the vigour with which it developed a purely plastic content, and gradually lost, in the nice processes of its light, its sound, its impacts and its rhythm, all meaning, even the most literal. . . .
>
> This fragility of the outer meaning had a bad effect on Watt, for it caused him to seek for another, for some meaning of what had passed, in the image of how it had passed. (W 68–69)

The Gall incident is generally read as Beckett's playful demolition of Watt's narrow Cartesianism, his obsessive rationalism and inability to resolve the mind/body dualism.[22] But to talk of Watt's interpretation as a failure is to imply that there is a correct or at least better way to behave, and it is not clear that the novel poses such an alternative. When Watt thinks about the piano-tuning incident later, it "seem[s] . . . to belong to some story heard long before, an instant in the life of another, ill-told, ill-heard, and more than half forgotten" (W 71). Indeed, "Watt did not know what had happened. He did not care, to do him justice, what had happened. But he felt the need to think that such and such a thing had happened then." And "This need remained with Watt. . . . For the incident of the Galls father and son was followed by others of a similar kind, incidents that is to say of great formal brilliance and indeterminable purport" (W 71).

This last description could be said to apply to the entire novel: a work of great formal brilliance and indeterminable purport. Let us consider how the paradigmatic Gall incident works. "We are the Galls, father and son, and we are come, what is more, all the way from town, to choon the piano." On a literal level, this is hardly a remarkable announcement. The use of "choon" for "tune" conveys the authenticity of recorded speech patterns; otherwise, Gall Junior is merely conveying the facts. But Watt now draws a series of odd surmises: (1) that the father must be blind and hence brings his son with him for support; (2) that the father must be blind, otherwise his son would strike out on his own career; (3) that they may not be father and son at all because they don't look alike; (4) that Gall Senior, not Gall Junior, will be doing the tuning, since seniority means responsibility, and Gall Jr. is only assisting and learning the ropes; and (5) that piano tuners tune pianos and don't engage in elliptical conversation.

All of these suppositions are, of course, easily refutable. (1) In the piano-tuning game, the son often inherits his father's trade; the support he gives his father may well be no more than the courtesy due to the older, more infirm man. (2) Gall Jr. may in fact take pride in his trade and have no intention of going elsewhere. (3) Gall Sr. *is* Gall Jr.'s father, otherwise why say so? (4) Gall Jr. is in his prime and hence does the bulk of the work, his father serving in the capacity of seasoned advisor. And (5) the dialogue between the Galls actually makes perfectly good sense. "The mice have returned": evidently, the mice are eating into the piano and have destroyed all but nine of the dampers and nine of the hammers.

Gall Senior asks whether these are corresponding keys (after all, they needn't be the same nine!) and learns that "in one case" they are. The younger Gall says that the "strings are in flitters"—that is to say, in shreds, in little fragments. "The piano," in short, "is doomed." " 'The piano tuner also,' said the elder": quite true, in that if there's no piano, he'll be out of a job. The riposte from the younger, "The pianist also," follows from this: no piano, no instrument for the pianist to play.

How, then, could such ordinary dialogue constitute "the principal incident of Watt's early days in Mr. Knott's house"? Because—and this is the "bewitchment" of language Wittgenstein talks about—"Everything we see could also be otherwise" (T #5.634). To begin with—and here Beckett may well be thinking of his own situation in occupied Paris— two strangers knock on the protagonist's door and Watt answers the door "as his habit was, when there was a knock at the door." Why is this redundant explanation proffered if not to suggest that knocks on the door are not necessarily to be answered? As indeed they weren't for the Beckett of the Rue des Favorites in 1941. But "in the absence of precise instructions to the contrary" (and perhaps the knock is coded), Watt invites the Galls in and even offers them "refreshments" of an unspecified kind. However, they pay no attention to him, talking to one another in a "code" he cannot understand.

Now since no one has told Watt to expect piano tuners, he is naturally suspicious. They might, after all, be criminals. One is old, one middle-aged: what proof is there that they are really father and son? That they are piano tuners? That they haven't been sent by the enemy as spies? What is the import of the parenthetical "what is more" (with a pun on "Watt") in Gall Jr.'s opening statement? What does the name "Galls" signify? Is it a pun on "Gauls" and hence a reference to possible invaders? On "gall," meaning impudence, nerve, bitterness of feeling? Or, as Michel Beausang posits, is the name Gall an allusion to Franz Joseph Gall, the father of phrenology, the first (c. 1813) to insist on the localization of brain functions and a student of the aphasia and ataraxia resulting from specific brain lesions?[23] And further: why does the older man lean on the younger? Why is it the younger who tunes the piano? And if the piano is in such bad shape, why does Mr. Knott pay to have it tuned?

Consider also the actual scene in the music room. "A *picture*," we read in the *Philosophical Investigations,* "held us captive. And we could not get outside it, for it lay in our language and language seemed to repeat it to us inexorably" (PI #115). Just so, Watt is held captive by the following image:

> The music-room was a large bare white room. The piano was in the window. The head, and neck, in plaster, very white of Buxtehude, was on the mantelpiece. A ravanastron hung, on the wall, from a nail, like a plover. (W 68)

What do these details signify? For *l'Irlandais,* decoding messages of German battle operations, they might be purely allegorical. The "ravanastron"[24] hanging from the wall on a nail connotes blackness and death. The "head, and neck, in plaster, very white"—how does Watt know that it is a bust of the organist Buxtehude?—looks ominously ahead to Winnie in *Happy Days.* Emptiness, whiteness, death: so much for Mr. Knott's music room.

In this context, the verbal exchange between "father" and "son" is the last straw. Since the dampers and hammers come in pairs, why the peculiar question, "Not corresponding, I hope," and the even more implausible answer, "in one case"? And why the ominous references to doom, not only of the piano but of the piano tuner and pianist? What, the suspicious onlooker wonders, are the two *really* saying? Is theirs a code used in plotting a crime? Are they really here for an entirely different reason? Are they spies? Thieves? The plaster cast of Buxtehude is on the mantelpiece, so evidently the so-called Galls have not had the gall to steal it. But should Watt in fact have let them into the music room at all? Is it enough to argue that there were no "precise instructions to the contrary"?

"Watt's problem," writes Jennie Skerl, "is that his language is totally unrelated to reality and neither *says* nor *shows* anything true" (JSK 485). But this is to assume that there *is* a "reality" *out there,* if only Watt could "see" it. Yet none of the characters in *Watt,* nor, for that matter, the novel's narrator, seem to penetrate "the fragility of the outer meaning," for what the conversations and incidents in *Watt* reveal is that the exchange of information (which is continuous, intense, and seemingly fraught with important consequences) does not ensure the transmission of any sort of knowledge. It is the split between the two that makes *Watt* such a hilariously funny, if also a very painful, book.

"We cannot," Beckett told Tom Driver in a 1961 interview, "listen to a conversation for five minutes without being acutely aware of the confusion. It is all around us and our only chance now is to let it in. The only chance of renovation is to open our eyes and see the mess. It is not a mess you can make sense of."[25] The "mess," Beckett adds, is not the same thing as "darkness": " 'If life and death did not both present themselves to us, there would be no inscrutability. If there were only darkness, all would be clear. It is because there is not only darkness but also light that our situation becomes inexplicable' " (LG 220). Such inexplicability must be accepted for what it is: "We feel," says Wittgenstein in a similar passage from the *Tractatus,* "that even if *all possible* scientific questions be answered, the problems of life have still not been touched at all. Of course there is then no question left, and just this is the answer" (T #6.52).

Is This Foot My Foot?

I have been suggesting that *Watt* is to be read as a Wittgensteinian novel, but it remains to look at the possible connections more fully. Jacqueline Hoefer, in a much cited essay on *Watt* (1959),[26] was the first to suggest that the discarded ladder mentioned in Arsene's monologue alludes to Wittgenstein's ladder metaphor, on the last page of the *Tractatus:*

> My propositions are elucidatory in this way: he who understands me finally recognizes them as senseless, when he has climbed out through them, on them, over them. (He must so to speak throw away the ladder, after he has climbed up on it.) (T #6.54)

But is this the source of Arsene's metaphor? Mr. Knott's upstairs man is recounting the epiphanic moment when he realized he could no longer rely on the "ladder" of logic as an explanatory mechanism. As he was sitting one Tuesday afternoon in the warm sun, smoking, suddenly "Something slipped":

But in what did the change *consist?* What was changed, and how? What was changed, if my information is correct, was the sentiment that a change, other than a change of degree, had taken place. What was changed was existence off the ladder. Do not come down the ladder, Ifor, I haf taken it away. (W 42)

Hoefer posits that this is a direct allusion to Wittgenstein's statement cited above. Even the mock-German accent ("I haf taken it away"), she suggests, alludes to Wittgenstein, whereas the name Ifor ("if-or") "describes the kind of ladder which has been climbed." "Wittgenstein," she concludes, "means, possibly, that in order to construct the principles of the ideal 'language,' he himself has had to make metaphysical statements. Once the system has been mastered, metaphysical statements must be abandoned" (JH 75).

But this is an oddly misleading reading of the conclusion of the *Tractatus*. Wittgenstein's "ladder" is not to be construed so narrowly. For, as I have suggested in chapter 1, the *Tractatus* moves toward the recognition that there is no ideal language, no "system" to be "mastered," that indeed, "The world is independent of my will" (#6.373). To follow the complex mental processes whereby Wittgenstein gradually comes to this recognition, to the understanding that "There is indeed the inexpressible. This *shows* itself; it is the mystical" (#6.522), is to come to the point where one no longer needs to proceed step by step up a ladder and can, on the contrary, throw it away. "He must surmount these propositions; then he sees the world rightly" (#6.54).

According to John Fletcher and others, Beckett vehemently denied that his ladder image owed anything to Wittgenstein. "Mr. Beckett told me in 1961," says Fletcher, "that the 'ladder' is a reference to 'a Welsh joke' (but he did not specify which), making the pronunciation not German but Welsh, and that he had only read the works of Wittgenstein 'within the last two years' "—in other words, about fifteen years after *Watt* was written, and long after the composition of *Godot* and the *Trilogy* as well.[27] But the Welsh joke may well be on Beckett's critics. It may be that Beckett really hadn't read the *Tractatus* when he wrote *Watt*—and of course, he could not have been familiar with the later, then yet-to-be published *Investigations,* which is, in fact, much more germane to his outlook—but it may also be that Beckett is expressing his irritation at readers like Hoefer, who misconstrue not only the *Tractatus* but his own work. The notion that Wittgenstein was a logical positivist, that there was no difference between his philosophy and Fritz Mauthner's (whose work Beckett *had* read), and the repeated references to the systematic philosophy Wittgenstein was supposedly articulating, may well have prompted Beckett to distance himself from the whole discussion.[28] Consider the following exchange with Tom Driver:

> I suggested that one must let [the mess] in because it is the truth, but Beckett did not take to the word truth.
> "What is more true than anything else? To swim is true, and to sink is true. One is not more true than the other. One cannot speak anymore of being, one must speak only of the mess. When Heidegger and Sartre speak of a contrast between being and existence, they may be right, I don't know, but their language is too philosophical for me. I am not a philosopher. One can only speak of what is in front of him, and that now is simply the mess." (LG 219)

The one "philosopher" who would have totally agreed with this disclaimer is, of course, Wittgenstein—the Wittgenstein who repeatedly insists that "We must do away with all *explanation* and description alone must take its place" (PI #109), who declares in a note of 1940, "How hard I find it to see what is *right in front of my eyes!*" (CV 39e). The issue here is less one of influence than of a peculiar symbiosis between the Austrian philosopher and the Irish writer. The Rumanian critic E. M. Cioran, who knew Beckett in Paris, put it this way:

Two mysterious apparitions, two phenomena that please one by being so baffling, so inscrutable. In both, one and the other, the same distance from beings and things, the same inflexibility, the same temptation to silence, to a final repudiation of words, the same desire to collide with boundaries never sensed before. In another time, they would have been drawn to the Desert. We now know that Wittgenstein had, at one time, considered entering a monastery. As for Beckett, one can very easily imagine him, a few centuries back, in a bare cell unsullied by any decoration, not even a crucifix.[29]

What Cioran sees is that the brand of asceticism we find in both Witt-genstein and Beckett attaches itself in both cases to the problematic of language. And here the scene in the so-called asylum in *Watt* is espe-cially important.

The episode is narrated by one Sam, a character whose thought pro-cesses are very much like Watt's: for example, Sam marvels at such "para-doxes" as that "though we could not converse without meeting, we could, and often did, meet without conversing" (W 149), and obsessively tries to determine what has caused the giant holes in the fences between the gar-dens: "numberless winds, numberless rains . . . a boar, or . . . a bull, flying, pursuing, a wild boar, a wild bull, blind with fear, blind with rage, or who knows perhaps with carnal desire, crashing at this point, through the fence, weakened by numberless winds, numberless rains" (158). Spec-ulation on the creation of these holes goes on for pages, for example: "Nor was it likely that the bull, or boar, after the bursting of the first hole, had withdrawn to a point from which, proceeding as before, he might acquire the impetus necessary to the bursting of the second hole, via the first hole" (259).

Sam and Watt are staying in two separate "pavilions" or "mansions," where their lives seem to be quite solitary: they have "No truck with the . . . scum, cluttering up the passage-ways, the hallways, grossly loud, blatantly morose, playing at ball, always playing at ball" (W 150–51). "Weather permitting"—Sam loves sun, Watt loves wind, but Sam toler-ates wind if there is sun and vice-versa—they meet one another in "the garden," which is actually a large wooded tract of "ten or fifteen acres" (151), a garden only in the sense that it (or they—for it is not clear whether there is one garden or a number of gardens) is fenced in. As such, it seems more a prison than a garden. Into this very odd "garden" the two men don't always dare to venture, each one regularly making the "hollow vow, never to leave his mansion again" (149). And the unspecified fear of meeting in the asylum garden is characterized by Sam as a form of "resistance":

So we knew resistance too, resistance to the call of the kind of weather we liked, but seldom simultaneously. Not that our resisting simultaneously had any bearing on our meeting, our conversing, for it had not. For when we both resisted we no more met, no more conversed, than when the one resisted, the other yielded. (W149)

Does the word *resistance,* appearing here with its cognates five times in three short sentences, point to the Resistance itself? Beckett wrote this particular section of *Watt* after the disbanding of the Gloria cell, when he was living in hiding at Roussillon, which was indeed a prison of the sort described here—that is, it was "open" country, heavily wooded, which might as well have been fenced in because the escapees from Paris, forced to hide, couldn't leave, no matter how "wild the grass" and thick the "great pale aspens" and "yews ever dark" (151), the "thickets [that] rose at every turn, brakes of impenetrable density, and towering masses of brambles, of a beehive form" (153). The furtive meetings between Sam and Watt—two men who are not really friends and yet "yield" in order to meet and "perhaps converse in the little garden" (149), which is really a large wooded tract of land—recall the meetings on park benches and similar locales where the "cut-outs" exchanged coded information.

The language of Sam's narrative, moreover, is marked by a curious formalism, a sort of pseudoarchaic English:

... I, when illuminated by rays of appropriate splendour, could forgive a wind which, while strong, might with advantage have been stronger. It is thus evident that the occasions were few and far between on which, walking and perhaps talking in the little garden, we walked there and perhaps talked with equal enjoyment. For when on Sam the sun shone bright, then in a vacuum panted Watt, and when Watt like a leaf was tossed, then stumbled Sam in deepest night. (W 151)

Note that the last sentence is phrased as a poem:

> For when on Sam the sun shone bright
> then in a vacuum panted Watt,
> and when Watt like a leaf was tossed,
> then stumbled Sam in deepest night.

Is this little jingle an example of what was called a "worked-out key," a lyric password? The language of Resistance must be one of extreme deviousness—a language game, in fact, "understood" only by the players, but perhaps not even by them.

This deviousness of tone becomes even more marked in Sam's account of the birds and beasts in this dystopic Garden of Eden:

> Birds of every kind abounded, and these it was our delight to pursue with stones and clods of earth. Robins, in particular, thanks to their confidingness, we destroyed in great numbers. And larks' nests, laden with eggs still warm from the mother's breast, we ground into fragments, under our feet, with peculiar satisfaction, at the appropriate season, of the year. (W153)

Killing, destruction, torture—these have become (as in fact they had become in 1942) par for the course—indeed, a mode of survival.

> But our particular friends were the rats, that dwelt by the stream. They were long and black. We brought them such tidbits from our ordinary as rinds of cheese, and morsels of gristle, and we brought them also birds' eggs, and frogs, and fledgelings. Sensible of these attentions, they would come flocking round us at our approach, with every sign of confidence and affection, and glide up our trouser-legs, and hang upon our breasts. And then we would sit down in the midst of them, and give them to eat, out of our hands, of a nice fat frog, or a baby thrush. Or seizing suddenly a plump young rat, resting in our bosom, after its repast, we would feed it to its mother, or its father, or its brother, or its sister, or to some less fortunate relative.
>
> It was on these occasions, we agreed, after an exchange of views, that we came nearest to God. (W 153)

The grotesque image of the cannibal rats and the pleasure Watt and Sam take in them seems a far cry from the comic opening of *Watt,* in which Hackett and the Nixons try to figure out why Watt has gotten off at the tram stop in question, or indeed from the many hilarious scenes at Mr. Knott's house, when Watt himself is trying to determine what it is that is happening. In the "garden" episode, the emphasis on the survival of the fittest (rats devouring frogs and thrushes, finally big rats devouring smaller ones) is, after all, part of the wartime picture: one Frenchman betraying another, fathers betraying their sons, and so on. But "rat" was also the designation applied to Nazi collaborators; in this sense, if the rats devour one another, they will be eliminated.

"It was on these occasions . . . that we came nearest to God." "God," it would seem, "is the term for the mystery about which we cannot speak, about which we must be silent"—the source of both destruction and cleansing. We recall the comment Beckett made to Tom Driver: "If there were only darkness, all would be clear. It is because there is not only darkness but also light that our situation becomes inexplicable" (LG 220). "God," as Wittgenstein says in the *Tractatus,* "does not reveal himself *in* the world" (T #6.432). It is, in any case, after the recounting of this episode that Watt's language breaks down. In Wittgensteinian terms, Watt begins as an Augustinian: he speaks "with scant regard for grammar, for syntax, for pronunciation, for enunciation, and very likely, if the truth were known, for spelling too" (154). The latter comment is, of course, absurd since speech does not necessarily reveal correct or incorrect spelling. "Proper names, however, both of places and of persons, such as Knott, Christ, Gomorrah, Cork, he articulated with great deliberation." The suggestion is that Watt originally believes that names (which he puts together in a characteristically Joycean jumble) are the names of things, that they point to their referents. But the next time he and Sam meet, Watt is walking backwards and it is at this point (157) that he begins to reverse the words in the phrases and sentences he speaks: "Not it is, yes," and "Wonder I . . . panky-hanky me lend you could, blood away wipe" (i.e., "Yes is it not," and "I wonder, could you lend me [your] handkerchief ["hanky-panky"], [to] wipe away [the] blood"). This "reversal of discourse" becomes more and more acute: Watt begins "to invert, no longer the order of the words in the sentence, but that of the letters in the word" (163). "To one, such as me," Sam reports, "desirous above all of information, the change was not a little disconcerting" (163). And he reproduces the following speech:

> *Otbro, lap rulb, krad klub. Ot murd, wol fup, wol fup. Ot niks, sorg sam, sorg sam. Ot lems, lats lems, lats lems. Ot gnut, trat stews, trat stews.*

"These were sounds," Sam recalls "that at first, though we walked breast to breast, made little or no sense to me." But "soon I grew used to these sounds, and then I understood as well as before."

How is it that Sam comes to understand the sounds in question? For if we follow the ostensible rule he has just given us, and merely reverse the letters in each word, we have the following:

Orbto, pal blur, dark bulk. To drum, low puf, low puf. To skin, gros mas, gros mas. To smel, stal smel. To tung, tart swets, tart swets.

Some slight orthographic and word boundary changes give us the words "orb to," "pale blur," "low puff," "gross mass," "stale smell," "tongue," "tart sweats." But the five short sentences still don't make sense. Moreover, the reversal rule is not applied consistently, "sorg sam," repeated twice, evidently referring to the sorrow (*Sorge* in German) of Sam; and "club," "murd[-er]," and "wol fup (wolf up)" making more sense in the original (letter-reversed) passage than in its "translation."

What is it, then, that Sam has gradually "understood"? Here Beckett seems to be referring precisely to the way passwords and coded messages were relayed from "passenger" A to "passenger" B along the transmission chain, neither having the information that would precede or follow a given statement. Note that Sam is "desirous above all of information"; and later, when his hearing begins to fail, he reports "conversations [to which] we are indebted for the following information" (167). Words, Beckett suggests throughout this passage, far from naming things as Watt originally thought, function only in larger sequences, and, even then, everything depends on how they are used. "Sorg sam" means one thing to someone who knows German and is relating "sam" to the Sam who is narrating the story at this point as well as to Sam Beckett. It would mean quite another to someone who had been taught to apply the reversal code and translate "stews" into "swe[a]ts." On the other hand, in the "word perfect" game of information retrieval, "swets" remains "swets"; the code allows for no variation.

Beckett's treatment of word and letter reversal, in any case, has an interesting analogue in the *Philosophical Investigations,* in the long section on the meaning of the word *reading,* which begins in #156. "The use of this word in the ordinary circumstances of our life," Wittgenstein posits, "is of course extremely familiar to us. But the part the word plays in our life, and therewith the language-game in which we employ it, would be difficult to describe even in rough outline." And he proceeds to show in what varying context we say that someone is reading. In #160 we read:

Suppose that a man who is under the influence of a certain drug is presented with a series of characters (which need not belong to any existing alphabet). He utters words corresponding to the number of the characters, as if they were letters, and does so with all the outward signs, and with the sensations, of reading. . . . In such a case some people would be inclined to say the man was *reading* those marks. Others, that he was not.—Suppose he has in this way read (or interpreted) a set of five marks as *A B O V E*—and now we shew him the same marks in the reverse order and he reads *E V O B A;* and in further texts he always retains the same interpretation of the marks; here we should certainly be inclined to say he was making up an alphabet for himself *ad hoc* and then reading accordingly.[30]

Does "reading" then mean to "*derive* the reproduction from the original" (#162)? Someone might, for example, "always write *b* for *A, c* for *B, d* for *C,* and so on, and *a* for *Z*—Surely we should call this too a derivation by means of the table" (#163). But now take this example of *derive:*

Suppose, however, that he does not stick to a *single* method of transcribing, but alters his method according to a simple rule: if he has once written *n* for *A,* then he writes *o* for the next *A, p* for the next, and so on.—But where is the dividing line between this procedure and a random one?

But does this mean that the word "to derive" really has no meaning, since the meaning seems to disintegrate when we follow it up?

"To derive," Wittgenstein shows step by step, does not mean one thing, even as "we also use the word 'to read' for a family of cases" (#164). Similarly, Watt comes to learn that the lists of proper names (e.g., "Knott, Christ, Gomorrah, Cork") he once took so seriously don't designate fixed entities, that there is, to go back to the 1937 letter to Axel Kaun, no way to tear apart the "veil" of language "in order to get at the things (or the Nothingness) behind it." For one set of words—"sorg sam sorg sam"— is not necessarily more or less "real" than another ("gros mas gros mas"); it all depends on what we want to do with the words in question.

Does Watt's so-called quest end in failure? Beckett never answers this question, and the mysterious Addenda leave it wide open. The ninth

Addendum begins, "*Watt learned to accept* etc. Use to explain poverty of Part III" (W 248). But what did Watt learn to accept? In the "descant heard by Watt on way to station (IV)," the key words are "heart," "breathe," and "exile," culminating in the lines:

> *Sop.* darkly awhile the exile air
> *Alt.* the — ex — ile — air —
> *Ten.* ile — — — air — — —
> *Bas.* ile — — — air — — —
>
> (W 254)

And, having once again described Watt as "looking as though nearing injections of sterile pus," Beckett drops a short phrase from Dante's *Inferno, 7,* 60: "parole non ci appulcro" ("I will add no more words to embellish it"). This is followed by "Threne heard by Watt in ditch on way from station. The soprano sang": and the rest of the page is left blank until we come to "no symbols where none intended," another blank, and then the signature "*Paris, 1945.*"

When we turn from the Addenda to the end of the novel itself, we note that Watt buys a ticket for "the end of the line," and when asked "Which end?" reflects a moment and says, "The nearer end," only to correct himself and say, "I beg your pardon . . . I mean the farther end," to which Mr. Nolan responds, "What you want is a free pass" (W 244). The train now pulls in but "It did not take up a single passenger, in the absence of Mrs. Pim" (245). We never know, therefore, where Watt ("the long wet dream with the hat and bags," as Nolan scathingly calls him) has disappeared.

The usual assumption is that Watt has gone to the asylum, where Sam later recounts his story. But this is to take the first half of Chapter III as somehow normative, the source of the entire narrative, whereas there is no indication that Sam and the novel's narrator are one and the same. The only thing we can know for sure is that Watt's "exile" begins *in ditch on way from station*—a situation about which Watt's creator refuses to say anything at all: "Parole non ci appulcro / no symbols where none intended." The characters in the novel are never quite cured of their

"use-disorder," their inability to find appropriate contexts for their state-
ments. Watt, for one, may well continue to search for the "true name"
of the pot he is contemplating, even though the "true name had ceased,
suddenly, or gradually, to be the true name for Watt" (W 78–79). But
Beckett himself, having given up the naming game of his youth, the
search for the Reality behind the veil, now has a "free pass" to create a
language that *resists,* a language that is not, as Wittgenstein put it, "*contig-
uous* to anything else" (LEC1 112). Or again:

The honourable thing to do is to put a lock on the door which will be noticed
only by those who can open it, not by the rest. (CV 7)

—Nothing could be more remarkable than seeing a man who thinks he is unobserved performing some quite simple everyday activity. Let us imagine a theatre; the curtain goes up and we see a man alone in a room, walking up and down, lighting a cigarette, sitting down, etc. so that suddenly we are observing a human being from outside in a way that ordinarily we can never observe ourselves; it would be like watching a chapter of biography with our own eyes. . . . We should be observing something more wonderful than anything a playwright could arrange to be acted or spoken on the stage: life itself.—But then we do see this every day without it making the slightest impression on us! True enough, but we do not see it from that point of view.

—Wittgenstein, *Culture and Value*

five

Border Games: The Wittgenstein Fictions of Thomas Bernhard and Ingeborg Bachmann

Two friends or acquaintances who meet in the "garden" between their respective "pavilions" in what seems to be a mental hospital: it is the setting, as we have seen, for the strange encounter of Sam and the protagonist in Chapter III of Beckett's *Watt*. In a novel (or is it an autobiographical memoir?) written some forty years later by the Austrian writer Thomas Bernhard, this paradigm recurs.[1] The narrator is a patient in the Hermann Pavilion for lung patients; across the way, as part of the same hospital complex on the Wilhelminenberg outside Vienna, is the Ludwig Pavilion for mental patients, where the narrator's friend Paul Wittgenstein, the nephew of the philosopher, is a resident. *Wittgenstein's Nephew* (1982) is the story of the relationship between Thomas Bernhard and Paul Wittgenstein, between those who are pulmonary patients and those who are mental patients, between the Hermann Pavilion and the Ludwig Pavilion, both of which turn out to be part of the same diseased society that is, in Bernhard's lexicon, post–World War II Vienna.

Wittgenstein's Nephew, the last in a series of what we might call Bernhard's Wittgenstein fictions, takes a more despairing view of language than do the fictions of Beckett or Stein. The famous proposition "*The limits of my language* mean the limits of my world" ("*Die Grenzen meiner*

Sprache bedeuten die Grenzen meiner Welt," T #5.6) is read by Bernhard (as it is by Ingeborg Bachmann, who cites it admiringly a number of times), not, in the usual way, as the assertion that one has no access to the world independent of one's language,[2] but rather (and somewhat eccentrically) as a statement about human limits, those limits (*Grenzen*) that ultimately lead to the inability to say anything—that is, to silence. This twist is not surprising when one remembers that postwar Austrians like Bernhard and Bachmann had good reason to be sensitive about *Die Grenzen,* given that warning signs bearing the word *Grenze* were an everyday sight, designating the border between inside and outside, between the safe and *gemütlich* Austria where one was at home and the feared and alien Ost-Europa just a hundred miles or so to the north (Czechoslovakia), east (Hungary), and southeast (Yugoslavia). The encirclement of Austria by the Soviet empire was also a reminder of Austria's shame in the Hitler years, its enthusiastic response to Nazi annexation in March 1938. In this context, the "limits of language" easily came to mean the limits of the German language, specifically the language of the great German lyric from Goethe and Hölderlin to Rilke and Trakl.

The evolution of both Bernhard's and Bachmann's poetics must be understood in terms of this particular limit situation.[3] Both were brought up in provincial Austria (Bachmann in Klagenfurt, Bernhard in Traunstein and the Salzkammergut). Both were, in one sense or another, fatherless (Bachmann because she rejected her Nazi father, Bernhard because he never knew the man, a local farmer, who had impregnated the village girl who was his mother).[4] Both left home in order to pursue an advanced degree (Bachmann in philosophy at the University of Vienna, where she wrote a doctoral dissertation called "The Critical Reception of Martin Heidegger's Existential Philosophy," a dissertation, she later explained, written not in veneration of but *against* Heidegger;[5] Bernhard in theatre and music at the Salzburg Mozarteum, where he wrote a thesis on Brecht and Artaud). Both began their careers as journalists, writing poetry on the side. Both were highly successful and yet felt increasingly allergic to the hypocrisies of postwar Viennese culture, a culture so thoroughly in denial that it seemed, in Bachmann's words, to have "fallen out of history" (IBGI 63–64). Bachmann settled in Rome and began work on a projected trilogy of novels called *Todesarten* (*Ways of Death*), of which only the first, *Malina* (1971), was completed. Bernhard made his home on a remote farm in Upper Austria and produced dozens of novels as well as plays, whose performances—especially of his last drama *Heldenplatz*— were the subject of heated political controversy.[6] Finally, both died in mid-career and quite unexpectedly: Bachmann in 1973 at the age of forty-six, of burns caused by a smoking accident (or was it a suicide?); Bernhard in 1989, at the age of fifty-eight, of the pulmonary disease that had plagued him since early childhood.

But perhaps the most curious linkage between the two is that both began as lyric poets, viewing the production of lyric as the highest calling a writer might hope for, yet both were to renounce the writing of lyric in less than a decade. Bernhard and Bachmann published their first volumes of poems in the mid-fifties (she in 1953, he in 1957), shifted to fiction and drama in the early sixties, and effectively ceased to write new poems after 1963. Or, more accurately, they ceased to write texts that are convention-ally designated as poems. For their novels are hardly novels, their plays (or, in Bachmann's case, *Hörspiele*) hardly plays, but rather are hybrid works built on elaborate forms of verbal and phrasal repetition, highly stylized forms one associates with poetry rather than prose.

For both authors, repetition seems to be closely linked to the question of nominal function, especially of the proper name, as Wittgenstein exam-ines it in the *Philosophical Investigations*. For Bernhard, as we shall see, proper names deconstruct themselves by the pressure of hyperrepetition; for Bachmann, the urge is to undercut the power of the nominal by subor-dinating it to the "lesser" parts of speech, used in everyday "language games." I shall turn, in a moment, to the poem-fictions in which this happens. But first, we must try to determine why lyric *qua* lyric proved to be inadequate for the particular poeticity of both writers.

JE EST UN AUTRE

The concept of lyric subjectivity inherited by the poetry circle in which Bernhard and Bachmann moved is, roughly speaking, that of the early

Rimbaud as filtered through the poetry of Georg Trakl—the "I" as visionary other, as the inner voice that speaks through the poet, in a series of concrete, often hallucinatory images that convey sensations and feelings untranslatable into "normal" prose. Hence, the "I" speaks primarily in the present tense, its utterances short and gnomic, its syntax paratactic and cumulative.

Consider Bachmann's short poem called "Im Gewitter der Rosen" ("In the Storm of Roses"), from her first collection, *Die Gestundete Zeit (Mortgaged Time)*, of 1953:

> Wohin wir uns wenden im Gewitter der Rosen,
> ist die Nacht von Dornen erhellt, und der Donner
> des Laubs, das so leise war, in den Büschen,
> folgt uns jetzt auf dem Fuss.
>
> Wherever we turn in the storm of roses,
> thorns illuminate the night. And the thunder
> of a thousand leaves, once so quiet in the bushes,
> is right at our heels.[7]

The "storm of roses" and "thunder" of leaves that seem to pursue the speaker wherever she turns are familiar romantic images: one thinks, for example, of the "huge cliff," ominously striding after the guilty boy who has stolen the boat at Ullswater in Wordsworth's *Prelude*.[8] But in Bachmann's dark dreamscape, the night is illuminated not by lightning flashes signaling the impending storm but by "thorns." Indeed, the "storm of roses" generally associated with sexual love points here to the Passion (the crown of thorns); Bachmann's is a world of suffering, whose cause is never explained and that occurs outside a specified context. It merely is.

Like Trakl's visionary lyric, Bachmann's has an outward formality that belies its indeterminacy: three four-stress lines followed by a foreshortened three-stress one, this last line made up of six ominous monosyllables. "*W*ohin *wi*r uns *w*enden *i*m Ge*wi*tter der Rosen"—four *w*'s and four short *i*'s as well as the internal rhyme on feminine endings ("wend-*en*"/"Ros*en*")—this pattern of alliteration and assonance is kept up throughout. In line 2, the consonance of "Dornen"/"Donner"; in line 3, the alliteration of *l*'s; and in line 4, the foregrounding of the emphatic *f* phoneme ("*f*olgt," "*F*uss")—all these are markers of poeticity; they testify to the faith in a language that distinguishes itself from ordinary discourse.

Phonemic density coupled with semantic openness: in Bachmann's early lyric, nature imagery functions as the objective correlative of complex and inexpressible emotional states; again and again, the poet is presented as a subject who reads meanings into "clouds, mist and beyond," into "sea breeze and oak leaf," who watches "the land of my soul succumb" and the "mortgaged time" of the title poem "take shape on the horizon" (ISR 31, 43). Like Paul Celan, to whom she has been compared, Bachmann relies on the power of concrete images, images presented without authorial intrusion, as the locus of meaning. Take a second short poem, this time from *Invocation of the Great Bear:*

> **Schatten Rosen Schatten**
> Unter einen fremden Himmel
> Schatten Rosen
> Schatten
> auf einer fremden Erde
> zwischen Rosen und Schatten
> in einem fremden Wasser
> mein Schatten

> **Shadow Roses Shadow**
> Under an alien sky
> shadow roses
> shadow
> on an alien earth
> between roses and shadows
> in alien waters
> my shadow

(PF 213)

The key word here is "fremden" ("alien" or "foreign"), which appears three times in the space of the poem's twenty-one words.[9] First, "shadow" applies to the roses themselves—"shadow roses" may refer to a particular species of rose; or again the reference may be to the roses' appearance in a particular light. But then the roses themselves cast a shadow "on an alien earth," and, in the final epiphany, it is "between roses and shadows" and "in alien waters" that the poet sees her own shadow. No matter how foreign the setting (Bachmann wrote this poem shortly after having taken up residence in Rome), there seems to be no escape from the shadow self. One is reminded of Celan's:

> Stehen im Schattendes Wundenmals in der Luft.
>
> Für-niemand-und-nichts-Stehn.
> Unerkannt,
> für dich
> allein.
>
> Mit allem, was darin Raum hat,
> auch ohne
> Sprache.

> To stand in the shadow
> of the scar up in the air.
>
> To stand-for-no-one-and-nothing
> Unrecognized,
> for you,
> alone.
>
> With all there is room for in that,
> even without
> language.[10]

But whereas Celan's interrogation of poetic convention led to the writing of an ever sparer, more rigidly compressed, more gnomic and dense lyric, Bachmann's led to the writing of "prose." Between 1959 and 1964, she wrote only a handful of poems, mostly about the difficulties of writing poems, and her last poem, "Keine Delikatessen" ("No Delicacies") was framed as a farewell to poetry. By this time, she had already turned to the writing of radio plays (e.g., "The Good God of Manhattan") and short stories, and in the last decade of her life she wrote only prose fiction.

Why did Bachmann, whose early lyric was favorably compared to that of Rilke, Eliot, and Celan, stop writing "poetry," or rather, verse?[11] Why, even in the years of enormous poetic success, did she express doubts about poetry? "I think," Bachmann tells one interviewer in 1956, "that we cannot, indeed that we may not, use the old images, the way, say, Mörike or Goethe used them, because they would sound insincere coming from our mouths. We must find true sentences, which are worthy of our own zone of consciousness and of our changed world" (IBGI 19). And in a 1961 interview, Bachmann explains that the poem "Ihr Worte" ("You Words") was written after a five-year hiatus, during which she promised herself to stop writing poetry:

I have nothing against poems, but you must try to understand that there are moments when suddenly, one has everything against them, against every metaphor, every sound, every rule for putting words together, against the absolutely inspired arrival of words and images. . . . I still know little about poems, but I do know that suspicion is important. Be sufficiently suspicious, suspect the words, the language, I have often told myself, heighten this suspicion—so that someday, maybe, something New can come into being. . . . (IBGI 25)

What Bachmann is referring to here is the need to rethink the traditional subject position, which, in German lyric, was almost invariably masculine; indeed, she herself had adopted this position in her poetry. In "Dunkles zu sagen" ("To Speak Darkness"), for example, the poet speaks as Orpheus, playing "death on the strings of life"; in the title poem of *Mortgaged Time,* the "I" is a chaser of hounds, *his* beloved "sinks in the sand, / It climbs around *her* waving hair, / it breaks into *her* words";[12] and in "Bohemia Lies by the Sea," a reworking of the question Antigonus puts to the mariner in *The Winter's Tale,* III,iii ("Thou art perfect then our ship hath touched upon / The deserts of Bohemia?"), the speaker describes himself as "a man from Bohemia, a vagrant, a player / who holds nothing and whom nothing holds, / granted only, by a questionable sea, to gaze at the land of my choice" (ISR 179). Even the late poem "Exil"

("Exile"), which deals with the poet's ambivalence about her "German" identity, especially "the German language / this cloud about me / that holds me like a house," oddly presents the exiled "I" as male:

> Ein Toter bin ich der wandelt
> gemeldet nirgends mehr
> unbekannt im Reich des Präfekten
> überzählig in den goldenen Städten
> und im grünenden Land
>
> (IBW, vol. 1, p. 153)

> A dead man am I who wanders
> no longer registered anywhere
> unknown in the empire of the prefect
> superfluous in the golden cities
> and the greening countryside.

"I had only known," Bachmann was to admit a decade later, "how to tell a story from a masculine position. But I have often asked myself: why, really? I have not understood it, not even in the case of the short stories, why I so often had to adopt the voice of the masculine 'I' " (IBGI 99–100).

The authority of that masculine "I"—an authority to which even a radical woman poet of the 1950s like Bachmann deferred—had the further problem of the political uses to which it had been put in recent German culture. As Paul Celan observed in 1958:

The German lyric . . . cannot, despite all its invocation of the tradition to which it belongs, speak the language which many a sympathetic ear continues to expect from it. Its language has become soberer, plainer; it mistrusts the "beautiful," it tries to be true. It is, then . . . so to speak, a "grayer" language, a language which, among other things, wants to see its "musicality" settled in a different place, a place where it no longer has anything in common with that "harmony" which sounded more or less unchallenged, side by side with the *most dreadful.*[13]

How to write poetry or, for that matter, prose in the language of the *most dreadful,* the language so recently associated with endless sloganeering for *Volk* and *Reich?* For Bachmann this became a pressing question, as it did even more fully for Thomas Bernhard. Interestingly, Bernhard, like Bachmann, began as a neoromantic lyric poet: her imagery of roses and shadows, of foreign waters and the "thunder of the foliage," is matched, in his youthful poetic efforts, by Baudelairean (or, for that matter, Goethean) correspondences between the natural and the spiritual. Here is an early poem called "Unten liegt die Stadt" ("Below Lies the Town"):

> Unten liegt die Stadt,
>   du brauchst nicht wiederkommen,
> denn ihr Leichnam ist von Blüten übersät.
>
> Morgen spricht der Fluß.
>   Die Berge sind verschwommen,
> doch der Frühling kommt zu spät.
>
> Unten liegt die Stadt.
>   Du merkst dir nicht die Namen.
> Aus den Wäldern fließt der schwarze Wein.
>
> Und die Nacht verstummt.
>   Die kranken Vögel kamen.
> Und du kehrst nur mehr in Trauer ein.[14]

> Below lies the town,
>   you need not return,
> for her corpse is buried under blossoms.
>
> At dawn the river speaks.
>   The mountains are hazy,
> but spring comes too late.
>
> Below lies the town.
>   You don't remember the names.
> From the forests flows the black wine.
>
> And the night grows silent.
>   The sick birds came.
> And you return only in mourning.

The mournful tone, the mysterious identity of the lost loved one, and especially the pathetic fallacy—mountains shrouded in mist, delayed spring, the "black wine" (blood) coming from the forests, diseased birds, early nightfall—all these are standard romantic devices, as are the variably stressed, rhyming (*abcdbc*) tercets, with their flowing assonantal lines. The "I" who addresses himself in the second person is archetypally sensitive, attentive, aware, soft-spoken—the ubiquitous elegiac "I" of the 1950s and '60s, who confronts death, loss, and inner emptiness. Consider the following:

> Ich sterbe vor der Sonne und
> vor dem Wind und vor den Kindern,
> die sich um den Hund streiten, ich sterbe
> an einem Morgen, derzu keinem
> Gedicht werden kann; nur traurig und grün und endlos
> ist dieser Morgen ("Qual," GG 64)

> I am dying in the face of the sun and
> in the face of the wind and in
> the face of the children, who quarrel over the dog, I am
> dying
> on a morning that can turn into no poem; only sad and green and
> endless
> is this morning ("Torment")

> Die Nacht bebt vor dem Fenster, sie will durch mein Herz stoßen
> und die Namen rufen, die ich geschändet habe. ("Die Nacht," GG 66)

> The night trembles outside the window, it wants to push through my
> heart
> and call up the names that I have defamed. ("The Night")

Note that one never learns why the night is so threatening, the sun so alarming; such conventional valuations are simply put before us like stage props we expect to see. Indeed, Bernhard's lyric remains curiously ungrounded, relating less to any conceivable personal or social situation than to literary convention. Even the titles of these early collections—*Auf der Erde und in der Hölle* (*On Earth and in Hell,* 1957) and *Die Rosen der Einöde* (*The Roses of Solitude,* 1959)—point to the residual romanticism of this phase of Bernhard's development.

Nature, as in Bachmann's case, always wears the colors of the spirit. "Hinter dem schwarzen Wald/," we read in "In Hora Mortis" (1958), "verbrenne ich dieses Feuer meiner Seele" ("Behind the black forest / I burn this fire of my soul"; GG 181). The narrator, who feels the black night pierce his heart, who knows he is dying in the presence of the sun, which burns his fiery soul, assumes that the "I" can encounter himself as a subject. This sense of self-presence became increasingly problematic for Bernhard. Much more congenial, it seems, was the proposition from the *Tractatus* (#5.631), a proposition with which Bernhard was quite familiar: "The thinking, conceptualizing subject; there is no such thing" ("Das denkende, vorstellende, Subjekt gibt es nicht").[15] And again, "The subject does not belong to the world but is a limit (*eine Grenze*) of the world" (T #5.6331). This notion of liminality, which I want to explore below, evidently suggested new possibilities for writing in the first person. In the autobiographical fictions to which Bernhard and Bachmann now turned, the "I" is as ubiquitous as ever, but, as David Pears explains the 5.63 series of propositions in the *Tractatus,* "if 'I' is the subject, it cannot exist as an identifiable object within the subject's world. No language, in other words, is able to mention the point of view from which it can be understood" (DP 178). Rather, "The I occurs in philosophy through the fact that the 'world is my world.' The philosophical I is not the man, not the human body or the human soul of which psychology treats, but the *metaphysical subject, the limit — not a part of the world*" (T #5.641, my italics). This distinction between the "human soul" and the "metaphysical" subject proved to be decisive.

The Liminal I/Eye

In 1971 the Austrian novelist Hilde Spiel asked Thomas Bernhard why he didn't write something about Wittgenstein, whose thinking was obviously so important to him. Bernhard replied that he felt too close to Wittgenstein's philosophy (or rather, to his "poetry") to write about it:

> It's as if I would have to write something (propositions!) about myself, and that won't work. . . . The question is not: do I write about Wittgenstein for even a *single* moment without disturbing him (W.) or myself (B.). . . . Wittgenstein is a question that can't be answered. . . . so I don't write about Wittgenstein *because I can't,* but because *I can't answer.*[16]

One solution, it turned out, was not to write directly "about" Wittgenstein but to fictionalize him, as is the case in the novel *Correction* and in the play *Ritter, Dene, Voss.*[17] The other possibility was to incorporate the meanings and strategies of the *Tractatus* and the *Investigations* directly into the text. This is what happens in *Wittgenstein's Nephew.* Bernhard's autobiographical memoir opens as follows:

> In 1967, one of the indefatigable nursing sisters in the Hermann Pavilion on the Baumgartnerhöhe placed on my bed a copy of my newly published *Gargoyles,* which I had written a year earlier at 60 rue de la Croix in Brussels, but I had not the strength to pick it up, having just come round from a general anesthesia lasting several hours, during which the doctors had cut open my neck and removed a fist-sized tumor from my thorax. As I recall, it was at the time of the Six-Day War, and after undergoing a strenuous course of cortisone treatment, I developed a moonlike face, just as the doctors had intended.[18]

It reads like a flat, eyewitness account—date, place, context, specific event—an account, moreover, we can verify as accurate so far as Bernhard's actual history goes. But this careful documentation is soon called into question by the language itself. For one thing, the memoir, like almost all of Bernhard's fiction, is written as one continuous block of prose. There are no chapter divisions, no paragraphs, no dialogue set off from the text (in fact, all speech here is reported speech); indeed, the only visual variation in an otherwise uniform print block is produced by the use of italics to underscore the irony of this or that noxious statement or to foreground a particularly absurd valuation. Neither is there any plot to speak of. The narrator learns that his old friend Paul Wittgenstein is at the nearby Ludwig Pavilion for the mentally ill. The two men spend some time together at the Hermann Pavilion, but most of the story loops back to the past, to their first and subsequent meetings, and forward to Paul's death, narrative regularly giving way to seemingly unrelated anecdote, to speculation, and to commentary.

But if the hospital complex on the Wilheminenberg, with its division into Baumgartnerhöhe (for the lung patients) and Am Steinhof (for the mental patients), and further division into Hermann Pavilion and Ludwig Pavilion, is only the occasion for anecdotes, memories, jokes, and speculations—a kind of obsessional monologue—why are certain words, especially proper names, compulsively repeated? Consider the following passage, in which the narrator is trying to decide whether to venture over to the Ludwig Pavilion to visit Paul:

> The **Ludwig Pavilion** was now Paul's *residence.* And I suddenly hesitated, wondering whether it was really wise to establish a link between the **Ludwig Pavilion** and the **Hermann Pavilion,** whether it might not do both of us more harm than good. For who knows, I thought, what state he's really in? Perhaps he's in a state that can only be harmful to me, in which case I'd better not visit him for the time being. I won't establish a link between the **Hermann Pavilion** and the **Ludwig Pavilion.** And if I did make an appearance in the **Ludwig Pavilion,** I thought, especially a surprise appearance, it might have a devastating effect on my friend too. I was suddenly scared of seeing him, and I thought of letting our friend Irina decide whether or not it was advisable to make contact between the **Hermann Pavilion** and the **Ludwig Pavilion.** (WN 31, boldface added)

Here the language, unlike that of Bernhard's early lyric, seems perfectly ordinary until we stop to consider the effect produced by word repetition: five appearances each of "Hermann Pavilion" and "Ludwig Pavilion" in the space of ten lines, together with eight uses of "I" (as in "I thought"), and two uses each of the words "whether" and "state" and of the phrase "establish a link between."[19]

Why this odd repetition compulsion? From a Wittgensteinian perspective, there are two reasons. First, the attempt, which goes on throughout the narrative, to differentiate the Hermann Pavilion from the Ludwig Pavilion can be seen as the Augustinian attempt to find a specific meaning behind a given name (see PI #1). We can see how this works if we consider that the "Hermann Pavilion"/"Ludwig Pavilion" pair is part of a network that contains the following pairs, some of them repeated as much as thirty or forty times in the space of two or three pages:

"lung patients"/"mental patients"	*Lungenkranken/Geisteskranken*
"lung clinic"/"mental clinic"	*Lungenanstalt/Irrenanstalt*
"lung patients"/"madmen"	*Lungenkranken/Verrückte*
"philosophy"/"madness"	*Philosophie/Verrücktheit*
"sick person"/"healthy person"	*"Der Kranke"/"der Gesunde"*
"I"/"Paul"	*"Ich"/"Paul"*

The lengthy comparisons and distinctions made between these paired nouns always backfires: all diseases, it appears, are the same disease, the chest-patient Bernhard being no "sicker" or "healthier" than the mental patient Paul; again, "Paul the madman [is] just as philosophical as his uncle Ludwig, while Ludwig the philosopher [is] just as mad as his nephew Paul" (WN 26). A long passage near the beginning modulates the phrase "Wie der Paul," translated into English sometimes as "Like Paul," sometimes as "Just as Paul," comparing Paul's actions and character traits to the narrator's (e.g., "just as Paul's life had once again run into an impasse, so mine too had run into an impasse"; WN 19), but as repetition piles on repetition, the reader begins to sense that this "just as" or "like" is actually relating quite unlike elements. Take, for example, the following comparison, about three pages into the "Just as" passage: "Just as Paul became increasingly ruthless toward his madness, so I became increasingly ruthless toward my lung disease and my madness, and as our ruthlessness toward our diseases increased, so did our ruthlessness toward the world around us, which naturally became increasingly ruthless toward us" (WN 22). But no sooner are these links established than Paul is differentiated from the narrator by a reference to the huge Wittgenstein fortune, culminating in the sentence "We were alike and yet completely different" (WN 23), which now sets us off on an "Unlike Paul . . ." sequence.

All such exercises in analogy ("As X, so Y"), Bernhard posits, are doomed to failure, for the real "madness" in *Wittgenstein's Nephew*—the madness that brings together Paul, Ludwig, and the narrator himself in a hopeless triangle—is the madness of definition. Facticity, the narrative implies, has its value: the proper name acts as pointer, specifying someone or something. But the significance of that nominalization remains incommensurate. "The sense of the world," as the *Tractatus* puts it, "must lie outside the world. In the world everything is as it is and happens as it does happen. *In* it there is no value—and if there were, it would be of no value" (T #6.41). And again, "there can be no ethical propositions. Propositions cannot express anything higher" (T #6.42). Or, to turn it around:

> When philosophers use a word—"knowledge," "being," "object," "I," "proposition," "name"—and try to grasp the *essence* of the thing, one must ask oneself: is the word ever actually used in this way in the language-game which is its original home?—
>
> What *we* do is to bring words back from their metaphysical to their everyday use. (PI #116)

In this connection, one of the funniest, most sardonic passages in *Wittgenstein's Nephew* is the account of the narrator's quest for a copy of the *Neue Zürcher Zeitung,* "because I wanted to read an article about Mozart's *Zaïde* that was due to appear in it" (WN 53):

> Believing that I could obtain a copy in Salzburg, I drove the fifty miles to this so-called *world-famous* festival city ["die sogennante *weltberühmte* Festspielstadt"], with Paul and a woman friend of ours in her car. But the *Neue Zürcher Zeitung* was not to be had in Salzburg. Then I had the idea of getting a copy at Bad Reichenhall, and so we drove to this *world-famous* spa. But the *Neue Zürcher Zeitung* was not to be had there either, and so we drove back to Nathal, somewhat disappointed. Just outside Nathal, Paul suddenly proposed that we drive to Bad Hall, another *world-famous* spa, where we would be sure to get the *Neue Zürcher Zeitung* and so be able to read the article on *Zaïde*. (WN 54–55)

So it goes through a series of "world-famous" spas in the Salzkammergut in search of the renowned Swiss newspaper that, unlike the Austrian ones, carries news of cultural events. The narrator reflects that "Had we not been totally exhausted . . . we would have thought nothing of simply driving to Zurich to buy the *Neue Zürcher Zeitung,* for in Zurich, I fancy, we would have been certain to get a copy." And he concludes, "To think that I can get the *Neue Zürcher Zeitung* all the year round in Spain and Portugal and Morocco, even in the smallest town boasting only one drafty hotel—but not in this country! . . . We should live only in a place where we can at least get the *Neue Zürcher Zeitung,* I said, and Paul wholeheartedly agreed" (WN 55).

This is the other side of the naming game. Bernhard cannot give us a definition of what he takes to be Austrian hypocrisy and cultural pretension in the postwar world. But by bringing the words *Neue Zürcher Zeitung* back to their everyday use—by permutating, that is to say, the basic sentence "I wanted to get a copy of the *Neue Zürcher Zeitung,*" he can *show* us a series of actions that convey the ethos of the "world-famous" culture in which he and his friend Paul (like Paul's Uncle Ludwig) stand out as somehow "mad." Indeed, the paradox is that this highly political elegiac fiction makes no overt political comment of any sort. "The subject," in Wittgenstein's formulation, "does not belong to the world but it is a limit of the world" (T #5.632). The "I," in other words, is not an object ("Das ich ist kein Gegenstand") to be dissected but a limit from which the institutions of a belated Vienna—its "musical" evenings at Irina's apartment in the Blumenstockgasse and "intellectual" afternoons on the terrace of the Sacher Hotel, its prizewinning ceremonies at the Academy of Sciences and matinees at the Opera—can be exposed.

Toward the end of *Wittgenstein's Nephew,* the narrator tells us that "throughout my friendship with Paul I accustomed myself to the lifesaving rhythm of constantly switching between the city and the country, a rhythm that I intend to maintain for the rest of my life—going to Vienna at least every other week, and at least every other week to the country" (WN 76). And an elaborate comparison follows:

The mind cannot develop in the **country;** it can develop only in the **city,** yet today everyone flees from the **city** to the **country** because people are basically too indolent to use their minds, on which the **city** makes the greatest demands, and so they choose to perish surrounded by nature, admiring it without knowing it, instead of seizing upon all the benefits the **city** has to offer, which have increased and multiplied quite miraculously over the years, and never more so than in recent years. I know how *deadly* the **country** is, and whenever possible I flee from it to some big **city**—no matter what it is called or how ugly it is—which always does me a hundred times more good than the **country**. I have always cursed my unhealthy lungs, which prevent me from spending all my time in the **city**, which is what I would most like to do. . . . It occurs to me how lucky my friend Paul was to have good lungs and not have to live in the **country** merely to survive. He could afford what I regard as the greatest boon—to spend all his time in the **city**. (WN 76–77, my emphasis)

Here Bernhard takes the most familiar of questions—"Which do you prefer, the city or the country?"—and turns it into an ironic game. For Paul's "luck" in having "good lungs" is of course no luck at all, any more than is the narrator's luck at having a "good" mind. Terms like "city" and "country" thus have no fixed meaning; they only function in specific sentences. Indeed, the irony is that, in the period memorialized in *Wittgenstein's Nephew,* both Paul and the narrator are living neither in the country nor in the city, but on the limit (*Grenze*) between the two, the Baumgartnerhöhe, on the edge of Vienna. And further: this is the limit where the surface limits are undone: the Ludwig Pavilion (with its reference to Wittgenstein's uncompromising asceticism as a form of madness) and the Hermann Pavilion, with its anagram on Thomas Bernhard's own name, turn out to be the same space: "In fact *he* often shamed me by putting me right in precisely those fields which were properly mine and in which I was convinced I was at home. Very often I would think: *He's* the philosopher, not me, *he's* the mathematician, not me, *he's* the expert, not me" (WN 57). The disclaimer, repeated again and again, inevitably inverts itself: if "he" has all "my" attributes, then of course "he" *is* "me." And it is toward this recognition that Bernhard's elegiac memoir has been moving all along.

THE LIMITS OF MY LANGUAGE

Having given up lyric, Bernhard paradoxically becomes a master of a key lyric genre—elegy. One of his fictional memoirs is a short piece called "Auslöschung" ("Extinction"), in which "Maria" (Ingeborg Bachmann), who has come to stay with the author and his friends in an Alpine village, gradually reveals the despair that will lead to her suicide.[20] That despair is inscribed in *Malina,* a triangle love story that ends with a murder—the narrator's own. The three principals are presented on the opening page as "The Cast":

Ivan: Born 1935 in Pécs (formerly Fünfkirchen), Hungary. Has lived for a number of years in Vienna and pursues a well-organized line of work, in a building on the Kärntnerring. So as not to compromise Ivan and his future with unnecessary complications, this building shall be designated as an Institute for Extremely Urgent Affairs, since its business is money. It is not the Credit Union.
Béla
András: The children, ages 7 and 5

Malina: Age impossible to determine from his appearance, has turned forty today, author of an "Apocrypha" that is no longer available in the bookshops, and of which only a few copies were sold in the late fifties. For the sake of anonymity, Civil Servant Class A, employed by the Austrian Army Museum, where advanced degrees in history (his major subject) and art history (his minor) made it possible for him to find employment and move into a good position, where he is regularly advancing without making a move, without ever calling attention to himself by interfering, displaying ambition, making demands or petty suggestions for the improvement of the procedures and written transactions between the Ministry of Defense on the Franz-Josefs Quai and the Museum of the Arsenal, which, without being especially conspicuous, belongs to the greatest curiosities of our city.

I [*Ich*] Austrian passport, issued by the Ministry of the Interior. Official Austrian I. D. Eyes—br., Hair—bl., born in Klagenfurt; some dates follow and a profession, crossed out twice and written over, addresses, crossed out three times, and above them written clearly: residence, Ungargasse 6, Vienna III.
Time: Today
Place: Vienna[21]

But neither "triangle love story" nor "murder story" (Bachmann does use many of the devices of detective fiction) accurately describes this novel's strange plot. To begin with, the narrator and Malina, who live together, are never presented as lovers; rather, their relationship seems to be that of brother and sister, but a brother and sister whose fates are curiously intertwined, Malina being more accurately the narrator's male alter ego or animus. Malina is never jealous of Ivan; he pays no attention to his comings and goings and is oddly self-sufficient throughout the story. When, in the third chapter ("Last Things"), he comes to the narrator's aid, it is only to make her see what has been inside her all along. For that matter, there is yet another man, not listed in the cast of characters, who furnishes the title for the second chapter, namely, "The Third Man," who is the narrator's father—both her real father and her nightmare version of the Father as Patriarch, Nazi officer, Victimizer, Torturer.

Such a synopsis makes the novel sound histrionic,[22] but Bachmann avoids melodrama by grounding her narrative firmly in the social and political realities of postwar, postimperial Vienna. In this "cultural capital," no one ever talks of the recent war, but that only makes its presence more real. As Bachmann put it in the poem "Every Day" ("Alle Tage"): "War is no longer declared, / only continued. The monstrous has become everyday" (ISR 53). The "today" of *Malina* is the end product of the so-called seven German years, as postwar Viennese society was given to calling the period 1938–45, when Austria belonged to the Third Reich. The reference to seven years is of course an egregious evasion of the reality that Austria was not so much "occupied" by Hitler as readily absorbed and that even the Nazis were welcomed with open arms by a large part of the population. At war's end the country was accorded the status of "occupied nation," along with Hungary, Czechoslovakia, Poland, and Yugoslavia, but when the Iron Curtain was drawn across Central Europe, Austria, briefly occupied by the four Allied powers (the U.S., Britain, France, the Soviet Union), was given to the West. As a formerly occupied nation, it never underwent the de-Nazification that marked the postwar years in West Germany. On the contrary, Austrian society tried to resume its prewar way of life: to restore its opera house and symphony, its museums and architectural monuments, as if nothing had really happened, as if the "seven German years" had been some sort of mistake. It is this mindset—a mindset we now know only too well from the Kurt Waldheim affair—that Bachmann satirizes in her account of summer vacation life on the Wolfgangsee, as it is experienced by families like the Altenwyls and Wantchuras.

In this context, it is significant that Ivan is Hungarian, whereas Malina, who comes from the Yugoslavian border, has a Slavic name. The novel, as Mark Anderson points out in his afterword to the Boehm translation, "is a fictional microcosm of the House of Austria with its Germanic, Hungarian and Slavic components" (M 230). Ivan speaks Hungarian to his two young children, who live with their mother in Budapest and come to visit on weekends; the narrator and Malina sometimes speak to each other in Slovenian dialect (e.g., "Jaz in ti. In ti in jaz" ["Me and you. You and me"]). Only the narrator herself is of "pure" Austro-German descent; only she, it seems, is consumed by war guilt and has dreams about Nazi troops and concentration camps, in which her father seems to figure largely.

The three principals live in a street called the Ungargasse, Ivan at #9, the narrator and Malina at #6 (hence mirror images). The Ungargasse lies just outside the Ring, or inner city, in a quarter neither elegant nor shabby—a quarter fairly nondescript that is nevertheless adored by the narrator as her "Ungargassenland." The appeal of the street seems to be its anonymity, an anonymity in which the Germanic features of the Vienna inside the Ring give way to the possibilities of a more nondescript, less culpable Hungary, as represented by Ivan. Indeed, the narrator's obsessive passion for Ivan—a passion that grows and grows and that cannot be satiated by their rendezvous or telephone conversations—reflects the narrator's consuming desire to be not German-speaking, not a woman, not an intellectual, not a writer—not, in short, Ingeborg Bachmann herself. If the scholarly, detached, highly professional, oddly androgynous Malina (significantly, he and the narrator first meet when he is lecturing on the Benjaminian title "Art in the Age of Technology") is the narrator's intellectual alter ego, Ivan represents the opposite pole—utter normalcy, uncomplicatedness, a happy-go-lucky response to everyday life, a predilection for trivial pursuits and entertainments, the "ability to make me laugh again" (MA 34).

Ironically, however, Ivan and Malina are more alike than either of them is like the woman narrator. For both, life is something that can be dealt with readily enough: one takes it one day at a time without too much concern. Both go to their offices and work regular hours without asking too many questions. The woman, on the other hand, even though she is neither wife nor mother but a writer, spends her days at home alone, waiting for Ivan to phone or Malina to come home. Sometimes her secretary, Fräulein Jellinek, is present; sometimes the maid Lina. For the "I," nothing is ever simple or uncomplicated. The slightest household task—boiling water, clearing the table, opening the window—becomes problematic; the present is always haunted by a terrifying but unknown past. "When I say 'today,' " she says early in the novel, "my breathing becomes irregular, an arrhythmia sets in, which can already be detected on an electrocardiogram" (MA 9).

Malina makes no overt ideological statements; it provides no commentary about the "plight of the woman writer"; it contains no manifesto for a better future. But having given up the authoritative and largely male voice that characterized her earlier lyric, Bachmann is able to articulate, for the first time in her career, a feminist poetic. One of her stylistic signatures in *Malina* is the dialogue that isn't really a dialogue but a "conversation," recorded as a set of truncated (and hence indeterminate) sentences, whereby the fiction's meanings are created. It is a form that owes a great deal to Wittgenstein's concept of the language game, as outlined in *The Blue Book* and in the *Philosophical Investigations.*

Here we should note that Wittgenstein had been central to Bachmann's thought from the time that she was a philosophy student in Vienna.[23] Indeed, she wrote one of the first critical essays in German on Wittgenstein, published in a scholarly journal in 1953.[24] Here, as in those subsequent interviews in which she is questioned about her particular interest in Wittgenstein, Bachmann refers the reader to the *Tractatus*'s "question of language," specifically, the key proposition (T #5.6): "*The limits of my language* mean the limits of my world":

> What merits our renewed and endlessly renewable consideration are not [Wittgenstein's] clarifying, negative propositions, which limit philosophy to a logical analysis of scientific language and restrict the analysis of the real world to specialized scientific fields; but rather his despairing attempt to chart the limits of linguistic expression, which provides the *Tractatus* with its inner tension, a tension into which he eventually disappears. (IBW, vol. 4, p. 13; trans. in ISR 12)

"What I really learned [from Wittgenstein]," she tells an interviewer in 1973, ". . . is how to think with enormous exactitude and clear expression" (IBGI 136). And she cites the "beautiful" conclusion to the *Tractatus:* "Wovon man nicht sprechen kann, darüber muss man schweigen" ("Whereof one cannot speak, thereof one must be silent"). If "the limits of my language are the limits of my world," the writer's task is to *unwrite* (*zerschreiben*) the phrasemaking of our ordinary, everyday discourse, the "prefabricated sentences" by means of which business-as-usual is conducted.[25] And, with what is evidently a reference to *Philosophical Investigations* #116 (see above), she cautions that the writer must stay away from the Big Words of the public sphere—words like Democracy, Economy, Capitalism, or Socialism—the aim of *writing* being, so Bachmann insists, not to *tell* but to *represent* (IBGI 91).

Consider how these notions are put into practice in the opening chapter of *Malina*, "Glücklich mit Ivan" ("Happy with Ivan"), which can be read as an ironized version of Wittgenstein's enigmatic proposition in the *Tractatus:* "The world of the happy [*Die Welt des Glücklichen*] is a different world from that of the unhappy [*des Unglücklichen*]" (T #6.43). The chapter begins as follows:

> Smoked again and drank again, counted the cigarettes, the glasses, saved another two cigarettes for today, because between today and Monday, there are three days without Ivan. Sixty cigarettes later, however, Ivan is back in Vienna, first he'll call "Time" to check his watch, then the wake-up service oo, which returns his call right away, immediately afterwards he'll fall asleep as instantly as only Ivan can, awaken to his wake-up call, in a grumpy mood, which he expresses differently each time, with sighs, curses, tantrums, complaints. Next he's forgotten all about being grumpy and has raced into the bathroom to brush his teeth, shower, and shave. He'll turn on the transistor and listen to the morning news. Austria I.APA. Here are the headlines: Washington . . . (MA 25; ellipsis in original)

Here is the beginning of obsession. The narrator has recently begun an affair with this total stranger, whose path she happened to cross in front of a neighborhood flower shop. The projection into Ivan's routine (we never know, of course, what he is really thinking or doing or even what his last name is) takes on a surreal air: the cigarettes, the glasses, the wake-up calls—all these pave the way for the set of telephone sentences, which becomes Bachmann's new poetic mode. As the "I" explains:

Nonetheless we have managed to conquer our first few sets of sentences, wayward sentence beginnings, half-sentences, sentence endings, surrounded by the halo of mutual consideration, and up to now, most of the sentences may be found in the category telephone sentences. We practice them over and over, since Ivan calls once from his office on the Kärntnerring, or a second time late in the afternoon, or in the evening from home.

> Hello. Hello?
> It's me, who else?
> Oh right, of course, excuse
> How I? And you?
> I don't know. This evening?
> I can barely understand you
> Barely? What? So you can
> I can barely hear you, can you
> What? Is anything?
> No, nothing, later on you can
> Of course, I'd better call later
> I, I was supposed to go with friends
> Of course, if you can't then
> I didn't say that, only if you don't
> In any case, let's talk later
> OK, but around six, because
> But that's too late for me
> Yes, actually for me too, but
> Today maybe it makes no sense
> Has someone come in?
> No, only now Fraülein Jellinek is
> Oh, I see, you're no longer alone
> But please later, please, definitely!
> (MA 36)

This could hardly be more ordinary, or could it? The lovers say just exactly what any X would say when he/she calls Y to make a date: "What are you doing tonight?" "Can you make it by six?" "Call me later," and so on. But there are two marked oddities. First, Bachmann's sentences have no proper beginnings or endings. It's often not clear to what a sentence is responding, and since its ending is truncated, we have to guess what's really going on. Thus, the fourth line above is evidently a response to the question "How are you?" and the fifth, "I don't know," responds not to the "And you?" above it but to a missing suggestion such as "Do you want to get together tonight?" Again, line 9, "What? Is anything?" has to be completed by a word like "wrong" or a phrase like "going on."

Thus, although the language could hardly be flatter and although we all talk to our intimates this way, leaving sentences hanging and assuming the person at the other end of the line gets the drift of what is said, communication in *Malina* is always already occluded. Misunderstanding is the order of the day, as in "Of course, if you can't then," with its response, "I didn't say that, only if you don't." Partly it's the nature of the telephone situation—a situation in which the verbal response may or may not match facial expression and gesture. And further: telephone sentences, like the smoking sentences or chess sentences or scolding sentences used later in the novel, are deceptive in their formulaic quality.

Indeed, that reliance on formula makes it difficult to tell who is speaking, the "I" or Ivan. Which *I* is which? In this particular example, the only clues come at the beginning and the end. Ivan is the one who calls, so presumably he says, "It's me, who else?" Toward the end (line 21), Fraülein Jellinek's presence is mentioned, so the speaker of that line is presumably the woman who employs Jellinek as her secretary. But who is it who says, "I really should see these"? In the prose that follows the dialogue, the narrator tells us that "Ivan and I both have friends and also acquaintances, but only very seldom someone of whom the other one has heard or knows what their names are. With these friends and other people, we have to take turns going out to dinner, or at least meet them at a café, or we have to take foreigners sightseeing, without knowing what to do with them, and most of the time we must also wait for a phone call" (MA 36).

One might conclude that such doubling (the sentence sets don't really constitute a dialogue because there are not two distinct characters) is designed to suggest that the lovers are perfectly in sync, that they speak the same language and know each other's needs implicitly. But that isn't quite the way this paradigmatic language game works. Consider the following set of smoking sentences:

> Now I just have to get the ashtray
> Just a minute, OK, me too
> Have you lit one too?
> There. Now. No, it's not working
> Don't you have any matches?
> The last one I, no, now on the candle
> Do you hear that too? Hey, get off the line
> This phone has its little tics
> What? someone is constantly cutting in. What sticks?
> I said "tics," it's not important, "tics" with a hard "t"
> I don't understand that stuff about sticks?
> Sorry, it was the wrong word for it
> Why wrong, what do you mean?
> Nothing, just that when you repeat a word so often[26]

The breakdown of communication between the lovers takes place on a number of levels. There is first the obvious noise in the channel, the noise from a crossed wire that interrupts their dialogue with someone else's conversation. But even without this intrusion, the conversation is extremely odd. The smoking ritual becomes a substitute sexual ritual, the lighting of the cigarette designed, so to speak, to turn the other one on. Hence the double entendre of being "out of matches" and needing to use a candle. But because the particular language game being played restricts the area of discussion to that which is actually happening or about to happen, there is soon nothing further to say. The "word" that one repeats "so often" is not the word the "I" wants to speak or to hear. And why is this conversation occurring at all, when Ivan could simply drop everything (as could the narrator) and cross the street so as to join the other?

What, in this context, is the meaning of the cigarette ritual? Is it an erotic rite or a talking game that functions as an escape from eroticism? For that matter, are the two lovers playing the same language game? And does each understand the other's game?

At the end of the dialogue above, the narrator thinks: "But even if four people are talking at once, I can still make out Ivan's voice, and as long as I hear him and know that he hears me, I'm alive. So long as the telephone, even if we have to interrupt the conversation, rings again, screams, buzzes, raves, sometimes with a tone too loud or several tones too soft, if you add the refrigerator, the record player or turn on the water in the tub" (MA 40). But what are *his* thoughts about the phone call? Does he have thoughts about it at all? Or is a phone call just a phone call, in which case the narrator is merely deluding herself?

"We have a lot of head-sentences," says the "I" a little later, referring to sentences such as "Who put this nonsense in your head." "Piles of them, just like the telephone sentences, the chess sentences or the sentences about life in general, but we're still missing a lot of sentence sets. About feelings, we don't have a single sentence, because Ivan won't pronounce one, because I don't dare to make up the first sentence of this set" (MA 46). This is a markedly Wittgensteinian motif: if the narrator cannot choose the sentence set to "play," Ivan will force her to play the game of his choice, a game in which she can do nothing but follow his stated rules. "One learns the game by watching how others play" (PI #54). Or, in the words of the *Tractatus:*

> For an answer which cannot be expressed the question too cannot be expressed.
> *The riddle* does not exist.
> If a question can be put at all, then it *can* also be answered.
> (T #6.5)

Which means, in practice, that the narrator never asks Ivan about anything that really matters to her, for she knows that, given the ground rules he has laid down, she cannot receive a satisfactory answer. Consequently, the lovers only ask questions that *can* be answered (e.g., "This evening?") or give answers to possible questions ("maybe later I can").

How do these language games relate to Bachmann's earlier lyrics? The elaborate images, metaphors, and allusions of the poems are replaced by the smallest of function words—*yes, no, now, well, and, but, then, oh*— and especially *I* and *you*, where, as in *Wittgenstein's Nephew,* the *I* and *you* become increasingly blurred. Indeed, the rigidly restricted register of this phrasal poetry paradoxically allows for a greater range of meanings than does a poem like "Exile." In one of the narrator's happiest moments with Ivan, when they are driving back into Vienna from an outing in the country and he has turned the car radio way up, there is the following exchange:

> Auprès de ma blonde
> I'm
> What are you?
> I'm
> What?
> I'm happy
> Qu'il fait bon
> What are you saying?
> I didn't say anything
> Fait bon, fait bon
> I'll say it to you later
> What do you want later?
> I'll never say it
> Qu'il fait bon
> Go ahead and say it
> It's too loud, I can't say it any louder
> What do you want to say?
> I can't say it any louder
> Qu'il fait bon dormir
> Say it, you have to say it today
> Qu'il fait bon fait bon
> That I've been resurrected

> Because I've survived the winter
> Because I am so happy
> Because I already see the Stadtpark
> Fait bon, fait bon
> Because Ivan exists
> Because Ivan and I
> Qu'il fait bon dormir!

(MA 58–59)

Here the French song refrain ("Auprès de ma blonde / qu'il fait bon, fait bon, fait bon") frames a series of sentences about *saying,* sentences that pose the question, What does it mean to say anything or not to say it? And again, when does one "say" it and to whom? The question remains open, even though "say" and its cognates appear nine times in the twenty-nine-line passage. The impossibility of "saying" yields to the anaphoric series of the last eight lines, which finally reveal little. If the narrator is happy because Ivan has entered her life, Ivan is evidently happy because he already sees the Stadtpark (i.e., we're almost home). If she says or thinks "Because Ivan and I," the loud refrain drowns her out with the final "Qu'il fait bon dormir!"—suggesting that Ivan hasn't been listening to her anyway. And in the night scene that follows this line, Ivan asks her, "why is there only a Wailing Wall, why hasn't anyone ever built a Wall of Joy?"

Bachmann's structure of repetitions and permutations can be linked to that of Bernhard or, for that matter, to that of Beckett, whose *Molloy* Bachmann regarded as the model of first-person narration (IBGI 57). But hers differs from theirs in that verbal or phrasal repetition does not work to undercut the certainties of the "I," but rather to undermine the difference between her language and that of her interlocutor, communication thus becoming impossible. "Sagen" ("to say") means something different to Ivan than it does to the narrator, and even then it takes on a slightly different edge every time she herself uses it, as does the word "glücklich" ("happy")[27] and the "qu'il fait bon" refrain. And the set of sentences and sentence fragments never constitutes a coherent paragraph. The incompleteness of statement, surrounded as the statements are by white space, conveys the ever increasing inability of the lovers to *say*.

In Chapter 3 ("Last Things"), the narrator, sensing she has lost Ivan and the happiness his normalcy represents for her, turns more and more to her alter ego Malina. The dialogues between "I" and "Malina" are just that—dialogues, with occasional stage directions such as "I (*leggermente*)" or "I (*con fuoco*)," operatic conventions, used to heighten the melodrama. For example:

Malina: Stop falling down all the time. Get up. Go out, have fun, neglect me, do
  something, anything!
I: (*dolcissimo*) I do something? Abandon you? Leave you? (MA 321)

Between these arias for two clearly distinct voices, arias in which Malina gradually gets the "I" to confess to her deepest feelings and fears, even as the intervening prose paragraphs present us with her more private medi- tations, Bachmann introduces one final telephone conversation between "I" and "Ivan." It follows the narrator's sad reflection that she and Ivan don't have time to play chess anymore: "we play less and less . . . the chess sentences are lying barren, other sentence sets are also suffering some loss" (MA 266–67).

> Unfortunately I have, my time is
> Of course if you're under so much time pressure
> It's just that today I have especially little time
> Naturally, if you have no time now
> Later, when I have more time again
> In time, we will be, it's just that now
> Then we'll be able to, once when you have time
> Just at this time, when things straighten out
> Your time must be a little less
> If only I could at the right time
> But where has the time gone, not too late
> I still have so little time, that unfortunately
> Later, when you have more time again, perhaps
> Later, I'll have more time again!

This sentence set has fourteen lines and may be read as a postmodern sonnet on time, a parodic version, perhaps, of a Shakespeare sonnet (e.g., "When I have seen by Time's fell hand defaced / The rich proud cost of outward buried age"). The word "time" appears once (but only once) in every line; in the German, the repetition of the emphatic noun "Zeit" is even more noticeable, both aurally and visually, the capital *Z* dominating the poem's layout and culminating in its columnar appearance in:

> Wenn du dann wieder mehr Zeit hast, vielleicht
> Später werde ich dann mehr Zeit haben!
>
> (MA 266–67)

Perhaps the main difference between this phrasal poetry of repetition and Bachmann's earlier lyric of "mortgaged time" is that the "poem" is no longer self-sufficient. It lacks a frame. Indeed, after the fourteenth line above, we read, in the prose passage that follows, "Every day, sometimes even cheerfully, Malina and I brood about the horrible things that might still happen tonight in Vienna." Between the crimes and murders reported in the paper, and the "murder" the heroine of *Malina* is about to undergo because of Ivan's desertion, there are, of course, endless metonymic connections. The embedded "poem" thus becomes part of a larger context—a context, in the case of *Malina,* made up of prose narrative, found text, mock interview, the fairy tale of the *Princess of Kagran,* the Malina dialogues, and so on.

The second chapter, "The Third Man," is a series of surrealistic dream sequences in which memories of childhood sexual abuse on the part of the father (sexual abuse that is part of the larger political oppression) unfold like so many film shots. Ironically, the prose of the dream sequences is much more conventionally "poetic" than the lineated language games we have been looking at. Bachmann thus reverses the time-honored romantic opposition between *prose* as that which signals the ordinary, mundane, and *verse* as that which embodies higher truth, transcendence. For the "ordinariness" of Bachmann's prose is gradually seen to present a world at war, a war that, as Bachmann repeatedly points out, is just as ubiquitous at times of ostensible peace.

On the novel's last page, in which the narrator's "death" and removal from the scene via the crack in the wall is recounted, the phone rings once more (MA 355–56):

> Excuse me?
> No?
> Then I didn't express myself clearly.
> It must be a mistake.
> The number is 723144.
> Yes, Ungargasse 6.
> No, there isn't.
> There's no woman here.
> I'm telling you, there was never anyone here by that name.
> There's no one else here.
> My number is 723144.
> My name?
> Malina.

Death is the absence of all conversation, the end of the language game. "Death is not an event of life. Death is not lived through" (T #6.4311). In the series of thirteen (note the unlucky number) sentence units above, there is only one speaker, and he is identifed as Malina. If, that is to say, the narrator has "died" ("There's no woman here"), then Ivan no longer exists either. His words are no longer represented, and all the evasions on the phone ("there was never anyone here by that name") are Malina's. The address and phone number are now solely his. More important: each sentence now ends with a period, in contrast to the complex stychomythia of the earlier lyric segments, in which the phrases and clauses were always left open. The sentence series culminates in a short paragraph describing Malina's receding footsteps: "death"—the death of the narrator—is not an event in *his* life. Hence the terrible flatness of the final complete sentence, "It was murder." The conclusion is pure prose.

The irony of this prose conclusion is further heightened when we consider that Ivan—solid, bourgeois, ordinary, unpoetic Ivan—is regularly linked to the traditional poem. "He has come," the narrator says at the beginning of "Happy with Ivan," "to make consonants constant and comprehensible ["*fest und fasslich*"] again, to open up the vowels so that they can sound fully, to let the words come through my lips again, to restore those first connections that had been disrupted" (MA 29). Ivan is, in other words, the maker of meters, of rhythmic regularity, even as Malina regularly speaks the "plain truth" of prose. What the "I" learns in the course of the novel is that the constancy and comprehensibility of consonants and the "full sound" of vowels are suspect, that the "connections," once disrupted, can't be reestablished so readily, that the "problems" can't simply be "solved" by electing to play a different language game.

Here the middle term posed by Chapter 2 is especially interesting. This chapter, "The Third Man," is in many ways the novel's most conventional—a series of gothic, hallucinatory dream- or memory-images in which the "I" is abused, punished, and tortured by the Father:

> My father has brought me to a tall building, there's even a garden above, he lets me plant flowers and little trees in it to pass the time, he makes jokes about the many Christmas trees I'm cultivating, they are from the Christmases of my childhood, but so long as he's making jokes it's all right, there are silver balls and it's blooming violet and yellow, only they aren't the right flowers. I also plant and sow in many ceramic pots; always the flowers that come up have the opposite, unwanted colors, I'm dissatisfied and my father says: "Who do you think you are, a princess? Who do you take yourself for, anyway, someone superior? You'll get over it, you'll be cured of it, and this, this—he points to my plants—this will soon have an end, what is this insane occupation, this green stuff?" I hold the garden hose in my hand, I could aim a blast of water right in his face, so that he would stop insulting me. . . . (MA 212)

The highly concrete, imagistic prose of this passage somewhat melodramatically sets the sensitive young girl against her brutal and bullying "father." But in the context of the whole text, we can sense something else happening. If Chapter 1, "Happy with Ivan," can be read as a rebuttal of the "meter-making argument" of traditional lyric, then "The Third Man" is a rejection of phanopoeia, of the Poundian notion that it is only the Image that "gives that sense of sudden liberation; that sense of freedom from time limits and space limits . . . which we experience in the presence of the greatest works of art" and that, accordingly, we should "Go in fear of abstractions."[28] In "The Third Man," to the contrary, the Image as "radiant node or cluster" is regularly associated with deception and false appearances; its immediacy and concreteness become cloying and oppressive, belonging as they do to the surreal landscape of dream in which one refuses to come to terms with the way words are actually used.

The poetry of the future, as Bachmann envisions it in her language games, is more literal and spare—a poetry that uses ordinary language although, to cite Wittgenstein, that language is "not used in the language-game of giving information" (Z #160)—not, at least, until the very end of the novel, when the complete sentences are closed by periods. Until that point, Bachmann's prose, like that of Bernhard's *Wittgenstein's Nephew,* is structured *poetically,* although rhetorical figures—repetition, parallelism, antithesis, anaphora—become more important than the tropes of synesthesia and symbolism that characterized their earlier work. Toward the end of *Malina,* the narrator makes one last attempt to call 726893, Ivan's number, a number she can dial in the dark:

> Yes, it's me
> No, only I
> No, really?
> Yes, about to leave
> I'll call you later
> Yes, much later
> I'll call you even later!

> (MA 310–11)

"We do the most various things with our sentences," says Wittgenstein, and he gives the example of such exclamations as "Water!" "Away!" "Help!" and "Fine!" (PI #27). To see what Bachmann is up to in the above exchange, consider what happens when we substitute "soon" or "sooner" for "later":

> I'll call you soon!
> Yes, much sooner!
> I'll call you even sooner!

This would be an appropriate conversation between friends or lovers, between the narrator and Ivan of Part I. But when the antonym is substituted, the construction becomes absurd. For in what context would one tell someone, "I'll call you even later!," unless one wanted to be openly insulting? And further: compare this final conversation with Ivan to the first in the novel (see p. 167 above), where "later" is embedded in suggestive phrases ("No, nothing, later on you can") and promises ("In any case, let's call each other later"), culminating in the eager anticipation of "But please later, please, definitely!"

The narrative of *Malina* moves from this sexually charged "But please **later,** please, definitely!" (MA 36), to the noncommittal "I'll say it to you **later**" (59), to the apologetic "**Later,** I'll have more time again" (267), to that final "I'll call you even **later.**" "The meaning of a word is its use in the language" (PI #43). In the context, "I'll call you even later" tells us, without the shadow of a doubt, that the end of the affair has come. Indeed, *later* opens up the space between #6 and #9 Ungargasse, a space finally absorbed into a phone number we meet for the first time on the novel's final page: 723144. There are no 6s or 9s here. And now it is only Malina's number, even as the novel we have just read bears only his name. But the crack in the wall into which the "I" disappears is the crack of writing, and it is the woman "murdered" who is the author of the book we have just finished reading. **Later:** the game of "love sentences" will begin somewhere else, but with new rules.

—It is wrong to say that in philosophy we consider an ideal language as opposed to our ordinary one. For this makes it appear as though we could improve on ordinary language. **But ordinary language is all right.** Whenever we make up "ideal languages" it is not in order to replace our ordinary language by them; but just to remove some trouble caused in someone's mind by thinking that he has got hold of the exact use of a common word. That is also why our method is not merely to enumerate actual usages of words, but rather deliberately to invent new ones, some of them because of their absurd appearance.

—Wittgenstein, *The Blue and Brown Books*

(my emphasis)

six

"Running Against the Walls of Our Cage": Toward a Wittgensteinian Poetics

"After Wittgenstein," writes Jean-François Lyotard, "the first task is that of overcoming [the] humanist obstacle to the analysis of phrase regimes, to make philosophy inhuman." For Wittgenstein, Lyotard argues, "still had empiricist notions of language use"; he took it as a given that "people make use of language," whereas we now know that "Humanity is not the user of language, nor even its guardian; there is no more one subject than there is one language. Phrases situate names and pronouns (or their equivalent) in the universes they present." And he concludes:

> ... the implications of this inhumanity for the question of the "social bond" remain to be analyzed. It should be understood that the principal difficulty is neither that of the state nor of "civil society," as is often thought, but consists in the functioning of capital, which is a regime of linking phrases far more supple and far more "inhuman" (oppressive, if you will) than any political or social regime. Wages, profits, funds for payment and credit, investment, growth and recession, the money market: it would indeed be interesting to analyze these objects as moves or rules proceeding from various language games. And what if capital were a multiform way of dominating time, of linking?[1]

This argument, representative of the deconstructionist climate of the early eighties in which it was advanced, already has a curiously dated ring. For the notion that "humanity" is wholly at the mercy of an "inhuman" discourse, whether of capital or some other hidden, "oppressive" force, now seems a signal instance of the essentialist model that deconstruction has so steadily opposed. "We never," counters Wittgenstein, "arrive at fundamental propositions in the course of our investigation; we get to the boundary of language which stops us from asking further questions" (LEC1 34). In the endlessly overlapping language games that constitute our individual and collective experience, there is no theory, no explanatory mechanism (e.g., "Humanity is not the user of language") that is universally applicable. "Propositions cannot express anything higher" (T #6.42).

Does such repudiation of theory make Wittgenstein the empiricist Lyotard takes him to be? Hardly. "Empirical reality," Wittgenstein insists in the *Tractatus* (and there is no reason to think he ever changed his mind on this issue), "is limited by the totality of objects. The boundary appears again in the totality of elementary propositions" (T #5.5561). As for "the sense of the world," in Wittgenstein's scheme of things, it "must lie outside the world.... If there is a value which is of value, it must lie outside all happening and being so" (T #6.41). For Wittgenstein, *contra* Lyotard, "There is indeed the inexpressible. This *shows* itself; it is the mystical" (T #6.522).

It is, as I have argued in earlier chapters, the curious collision of the "mystical" with the close and commonsensical study of actual language practices that makes Wittgenstein such a natural ally for the poets and artists of our time. For Lyotard's assertion that "Humanity is not the user of language, nor even its guardian," Wittgenstein substitutes a series of seemingly endless "poetic" questions as to how "humanity" in fact *does* use language, given the recognition that the language we use is, in Ian Hacking's words, "first of all public and firmly rooted in what we do together," that "shared practices, actions, reactions, and interactions among people provide the foothold upon which . . . self-description of our mental life must rest."[2]

Traditionally, the lyric has been held to be the literary genre in which language expresses the private experiences, sensations, and thoughts of the individual poet. As great a modern literary theorist as Mikhail Bakhtin, whose radical analysis of fiction and related discourses we are still trying to process, could declare that "Even when speaking of alien things, the poet speaks his own language. To shed light on an alien world, he never resorts to an alien language, even though it might in fact be more adequate to that world." And he explains:

In poetic genres, artistic consciousness—understood as a unity of all the author's semantic and expressive intentions—fully realizes itself within its own language; in them alone is such consciousness fully immanent, expressing itself in it directly and without mediation, without conditions and without distance. The language of the poet is *his* language, he is utterly immersed in it, inseparable from it, he makes use of each form, each word, each expression according to its unmediated power to assign meaning . . . as a pure and direct expression of his own intention.[3]

The resultant creation of a special "poetic language" makes lyric tend toward "authoritarian" form, "sealing itself off from the influence of extraliterary social dialects" (DI 287). We might note that it is this sealing off, this *monoglossia,* that seems to have turned writers like Ingeborg Bachmann and Thomas Bernhard or, for that matter, Samuel Beckett away from "poetry" toward the world of prose fiction and drama.[4] And it is true that, even today, mainstream poetry often seems to be trapped in an oppressive circle of self-presence, the "cry of the heart" designed to convey some sort of unique personal essence.[5]

But in recent years, especially in the U.S., the "priestly language" (DI 287), as Bakhtin somewhat scornfully labeled the language of lyric poetry, has begun to give way to a poetics that does accommodate the "extraliterary social dialects" Bakhtin took to be the exclusive province of prose fiction, a poetics, for that matter, that has made "ordinary" language its locus of attention. As the "great divide" (Andreas Huyssen's term)[6] between high and low culture has given way to all sorts of crossings, the notion of a "separate" language for poetry has become increasingly suspect. And here Wittgenstein has unwittingly played a central role.

Suppose we reconsider the aphorism from *Culture and Value* that was discussed at the beginning of this study: "Philosophy ought really to be written only as a *form of poetry* (CV 24). Presumably the converse would be equally valid: "Poetry ought really to be written only as a *form of philosophy.*" What this proposition implies is that poetry is not, as is commonly thought (and as Wittgenstein himself seems to have thought of it when he commented directly on specific poems), the *expression* or externalization of inner feeling; it is, more accurately, the critique of that expression. A poetics of everyday life is thus not simply the empirical record of the actual words of this or that person—a record whose interest would be minimal—but what Henri Lefebvre called, in his book by that title, the *critique of everyday life.*

In the foreword to the second edition (1958) of this monumental work, Lefebvre discusses the dialectical image of Charlie Chaplin, the alienated little tramp in the bowler hat, walking stick, and trousers of London's petty bourgeoisie, whose mannerisms Charlie assiduously apes, much to the comic delectation of his audience:

> ... on the one hand, "modern times" (with everything they entail: bourgeoisie, capitalism, techniques and technicity, etc.), and on the other, the Tramp. The relation between them is not a simple one. In a fiction truer than reality as it is immediately given, they go on producing and destroying one another ceaselessly. In this way the comical produces the tragic, the tragic destroys the comical, and vice-versa; cruelty is never absent from the clowning.

This duality, Lefebvre posits, is at the heart of modern urban life:

> The most extraordinary things are also the most everyday; the strangest things are often the most trivial.... Once separated from its context ... once presented in all its triviality, i.e., in all that makes it trivial, suffocating, oppressive—the trivial becomes extraordinary, and the habitual becomes "mythical."[7]

Lefebvre is, of course, referring to the everyday *event* rather than to everyday language, but his discussion of the separation from context is applicable here. For the comparable strangeness of everyday words—the verb "give," the noun "pain," the pronoun "I" ("The word 'I' does not have a central place in grammar, but is a word like any other")[8]—depends precisely on such decontextualization. "When Wittgenstein asks us to think hard about the philosophical implications of saying 'I *have* a pain,'" observes Guy Davenport, "... he is being a dramatist at a primal level, trying to get us to wake up in the midst of dreaming."[9] Do I *have* a pain in the same sense that I have a book? And if you tell me that you think I have a pain, how does that compare to my saying it about myself?

Notice that the above examples contain no metaphor, no arresting symbol or allegorical image—indeed, none of the figuration that Bakhtin associated with the "priestly language" of poetry. Wittgenstein's "book" is neither the symbolic "Book of Life" nor a pun on the verb "book," nor is "pain" a homonym for "pane." It thus paves the way for a poetry of denotation, but, as we shall see, denotative meaning has its own mysteries and aporias. "Do not forget," we read in *Zettel,* "that a poem, even though it is composed in the language of information, is not used in the language-game of giving information" (Z #160). And again, "Why don't I call cooking rules arbitrary, and why am I tempted to call the rules of grammar arbitrary? Because 'cooking' is defined by its end (*Zweck*), whereas 'speaking' is not. That is why the use of language is in a certain sense autonomous, whereas cooking and washing are not" (Z #320).[10]

"Autonomous" in what sense and why? Perhaps the obsession with the uses of ordinary language—an obsession Wittgenstein has bequeathed to poets and artists today—has to do with the increasing production, within a given national literature, of poetry, fiction, drama, and film by those who are not that nation's native speakers. The great nineteenth-century British writers, from Austen and Wordsworth to Ruskin and Arnold, Newman and Pater, were, after all, English writers; by the time of Conrad and James, Yeats and Eliot, the hegemony of "native" English had dissolved, even as the "native" French of Baudelaire and Mallarmé gave way to the polyglot idiom of the Swiss Blaise Cendrars and the Polish-Italian Guillaume Apollinaire. In the United States, Charles Bernstein reminds us in "Time Out of Motion," Gertrude Stein, William Carlos Williams, and Louis Zukofsky all learned English as a second language.[11] And by the late twentieth century, such "second language" writing may well have become the norm rather than the exception, at least in the Western nations, even as, paradoxically, the media-speak within each national culture (and cross-culturally via CNN and related networks) has become a fixed and authoritarian lingua franca.

This gulf between, say, Standard American English (SAE) and the actual idiolects of immigrant or minority citizens of the United States surely produces a good deal of confusion, as it must have for the Wittgenstein who couldn't quite "hear" when it was and was not appropriate to use the word "Baloney!" or to call someone "Old Bean." Indeed, Wittgenstein himself, as his personal letters testify, never really mastered the language he dissected so mercilessly. As late as 1950, having lived for twenty years in England (not counting the years of study before World War I), he was given to constructions like the following, typical of his letters from Vienna to Georg von Wright:

> I don't yet feel acclimatized at all.
> I enjoyed what talks we had and I liked to see Kreisel again. I hope you still saw him after I left.
> I did some work, though not good work, for quite some time.
> We had excellent weather the whole time and were surrounded by the greatest kindness. (PO 476–78)

If these sound like literal translations from German to English (e.g., "I liked to see Kreisel again" is "Ich freute mich Kreisel wieder zu sehen"), the translations of Wittgenstein's writings into English are even more awkward. I have remarked on this problem in chapter 2, but it is worth repeating here that the English version of a given aphorism often has little in common with the idiomatic German of the original. In *Zettel,* for example, we read, "A poet's words can pierce us" (#155) as the translation of "Worte eines Dichters können uns durch und durch gehen." Literally: "The words of a poet can penetrate us through and through." In rendering "durch und durch gehen" with the one verb "pierce," the translator (G. E. M. Anscombe) overdramatizes the effect "words" have on us on the one hand and, at the same time, misses the inflection of the original. And such transpositions occur quite regularly.

But the irony is that the aspects of language that interest Wittgenstein are those that such translation (or mistranslation) affects least. When, for example, Wittgenstein posits in the *Philosophical Investigations* (#558), "What does it mean to say that the 'is' in 'The rose is red' has a different meaning from the 'is' in 'twice two is four'?" ("Was heißt es, daß im Satze 'Die Rose ist rot' das 'ist' eine andere Bedeutung hat als in 'zwei mal zwei ist vier'?"), he is raising a question that transcends the specific language, a question about the way language works at its most elemental grammatical level. What, to take another example, does it mean to *try* to do something? "When I raise my arm I do not usually *try* to raise it" ("Wenn ich meinen Arm hebe, *versuche* ich meistens nicht, ihn zu heben"; PI #622). Again, the question cannot be confined to a single language and the issue in question is not one of connotation, nuance, or metaphor.

This preoccupation with the bedrock of grammatical structure has important implications for the current situation in poetry. On the one hand, the poet, as I have argued in *Radical Artifice,* now dwells in a world of media-speak, oppressively uniform in its locutions, idiom, phraseology, word choice, even its accent.[12] On the other hand, the poetry establishment (especially the official verse-culture of the university writing programs) still posits a situation in which the aspiring poet can—indeed must—discover his or her own unique *voice,* a voice that somehow differs from all others. But in what exactly does this uniqueness consist, given the ongoing commodification of language in our culture? How much more "sensitive-than-thou" can the individual artist be?

Or perhaps poetic "uniqueness" in our postromantic age is less a matter of authenticity of individual *expression* than of sensitivity to the language pool on which the poet draws in re-creating and redefining the world as he or she has found it. It is in this context that Wittgenstein himself may be considered a poet. English idiom, after all, has changed a great deal since he wrote the *Philosophical Investigations,* and yet we know, just as "instinctively" as did his contemporaries, that it is absurd to talk about the right hand giving the left hand money or to ask whether a particular dog is waiting for his master to come on Wednesday. The "poetic" thus functions as a heightened form of social and cultural critique, a way of defamiliarizing not so much what is seen, as was the case in modernist poetry, as what is known and actually done. Hence a "denotative" poetry that may look improperly "poetic," even as it fulfills Pound's famous dictum that "Poetry is news that stays news" or, for that matter,

Wittgenstein's own dictum that "A poet's words can pierce us" ("uns durch und durch gehen"). In what follows, I want to look at some examples of this new Wittgensteinian poetics.

"That Insistent Distance": Robert Creeley's *Away*

"One can own a mirror [*Spiegel*]; does one then own the reflection [*Spiegelbild*] that can be seen in it?" This question, posed by Wittgenstein in *Zettel* (#670), is the epigraph of Robert Creeley's *Away* (1976), one of the poet's later lyric sequences, illustrated by a series of grainy black-and-white monoprints by his then wife Bobbie. The title may also be an allusion to Wittgenstein:

> If I hear someone say "Away!" with a gesture of repulsion, do I have an "experience" of meaning *here* as I do in the game where I pronounce that to myself meaning it now in one sense, now in another?—For he could also have said, "Get away from me!" and then perhaps I'd have experienced the whole phrase in such-and-such a way—but the single word? Perhaps it was the supplementary words that made the impression on me. (Z #31)

Away: what does that single word mean when isolated from any context and placed by itself on a book's title page? And how can one "own" a reflection in a mirror one happens to "own"? These are the sort of conundrums that interest Creeley. Here is the opening of the title poem:

> Yourself walked in the room tonight
> and it wasn't you. Your way of
> being here isn't another's way.
> It's all the same somewhere maybe,
> and the same old thing isn't you.
> All the negatives in existence
> don't change anything anyway.
>
> The people tell me a sad story sometimes,
> and I tend to tell it back to them.

Come home. It's where you are anyway.
Anyway, I wish you weren't home.
Where is home anyway without me.[13]

What are we to make of these ungainly stanzas, these halting lines that
sound as if their speaker were all but incapable of articulate speech? Not
only is the poem's diction abstract, but the abstractions lack conceptual
force, being indefinite nouns, pronouns, and adverbs: "anyway" (four
times), "home" (three times), "way" (twice), "where" (twice), "same"
(twice), "all" (twice), "anything," "another," "sometimes," "here,"
"maybe," "without." The personal pronoun "you" and its cognates appear
five times, "I" or "me" four times, and "it" four times. The predominant
verb form is the copula followed by a negative contraction: "wasn't,"
"weren't," "isn't" (twice). The only transitive verbs in these twelve lines
are "change" and "tell," but here nothing "changes anything anyway,"
and the "sad story" the "people tell me," and which the poet tells "back
to them," is a blank.

   If Creeley's sound patterning and word choice are intentionally
"awkward," so is his sentence structure. The opening line contains a
grammatical error: it should be "You walked in the room tonight," not
"Yourself walked." Creeley evidently introduces this obvious "error" so
as to stress the *selfhood* of the woman who isn't there, the woman he longs
for to whom the poem is addressed. But his rhythms break down: lines 2
and 3 are almost impossible to scan. They sputter along haltingly, the
sound grinding and spinning its wheels rather than flowing:

and it wásn't / yoú. // Yoúr wáy of
béing / hére / ísn't / ànóther's / wáy.
It's áll the sáme / sómewhère / máybè.... [14]

What, many readers have asked, makes this poetry? When, six lines fur-
ther into the poem, we read, "Home, / wherever, is where the heart is,"
we begin to think we are reading some sort of Hallmark "friendship"
card that bears the message "I miss you," "I love you," "I'm lonely,"
"Come back!" For that matter, it also invokes birthday cards:

Your birthday is here
without you, that day
you were born to be here.

And the last stanza recalls popular song:

Only the same time,
your birthday. You and me
at the same time in
the same place, always.

(A 13)

Critics have often expressed exasperation with these "primitive" language-games. "This dogged, obsessive plainness," writes Robert Pinsky of an earlier poem, "works its way . . . practically to the point of inarticulateness. . . . Creeley's language [is] so chastened that it seems to aspire toward some kind of non-language."[15] John Perreault, reviewing Creeley's earlier collection, *Words,* declares: "The same subjects remain: personalized versions of love, pain, sex and death, but whittled down to 'breath units' of often breathless banality." And the anonymous *Times Literary Supplement* reviewer of *Poems 1950–1965* complains that "the effect [of Creeley's "numb repetition of colourless words"] is that of wading interminably through some unfamiliar shorthand or of listening to a glazed monotone."[16] Helen Vendler does not include Creeley in *The Harvard Book of Contemporary American Poetry* (1985), nor is his name on Harold Bloom's recent list of canonical contemporary poets, a list that does include such younger poets as Edward Hirsch, Alfred Corn, and J. D. McClatchy.[17]

Yet, despite these reservations and omissions, Creeley has been not only a very popular poet (in Germany his *Collected Poems* made the bestseller list!) but, interestingly, a poet's poet, whose work has commanded the attention not only of his own Black Mountain and Beat contemporaries (Charles Olson, Robert Duncan, Denise Levertov, Ed Dorn, Allen Ginsberg, Gilbert Sorrentino) but of the later poets we associate with the Language movement, for example, Charles Bernstein, Ron Silliman, Lyn

Hejinian, Michael Palmer, Susan Howe, Nathaniel Mackey, Bob Perelman, Michael Davidson. For these writers, Creeley's minimalism can be understood as a new kind of realism, a tacit understanding that, in Wittgenstein's words, *"Ordinary language is all right."* Not ordinary language in Wordsworth's sense of a "selection of the language really used by men," or in Yeats's sense of "passionate normal speech" (for, like Wittgenstein, Creeley doesn't put much stock in *heightening*), but rather, language in those "primitive" forms that allow us to contemplate the puzzles and mysteries of ordinary communication. In a lecture called "The Creative" (1972), Creeley remarks:

> To say of someone, that their appearance is *pleasant,* or *ugly*—each are creative acts. A "world" in each case occurs in which that person takes place, whether or no his or her agreement is given. . . . For years I have been intrigued by a quotation of Louis Zukofsky's from Wittgenstein: "A point in space is a [the?] place for an argument . . . " Think of it. Is that the point? What point? What has come to it? Who is present and realizes that to be the case? When? Is there the possibility of agreement in any such situation?[18]

Creeley cites this particular Wittgenstein sentence (T #2.0131) again and again and has referred to it as his "motto."[19] Not that he is particularly interested in the larger argument of this section of the *Tractatus,* that is, the distinction Wittgenstein is making between "simples" and "complexes." Rather, Creeley gives Wittgenstein's terse aphorism his own interpretation, reading it to mean that, in language, "a problematic aura," as Hugh Kenner puts it, "attends the simplest utterances."[20] "I believe," says Creeley in *A Quick Graph,* "in a poetry determined by the language of which it is made. . . . I look to words and nothing else, for my own redemption."[21] But he also recognizes that, as he had suggested in the headnote to *Words* (1967), "Words will not say anything more than they do, and my various purposes will not understand more than what they say" (RCCP 261).

Thus, on the opening page of *Away,* Creeley modulates the words *way, away,* and *anyway* in the most intricate of *ways.* What is Bobbie's "way" that isn't "another's way"? Is the poet's pain the result of her being "away" or of trying to drive the thought of her "away"? And "anyway," what does it all matter? Unlike the confessional poets of the seventies, Creeley gives us no image of his wife or of himself; we learn nothing about their past, the course of their marriage, how many children they have, what they have done for a living—we don't even know where "home" is located,[22] and Bobbie Creeley's blurred, semiabstract, enigmatic photographs (see figs. 4 and 5) don't make the location any clearer. The vocabulary is purposely restricted so as to focus on nothing but the vagaries of what we call despair. For example:

> For hours I didn't think of you
> And then I did and can't stop.
>
> Your birthday is here
> without you, that day
> you were born to be here.

These seemingly banal lines recall the following passage in *Zettel,* Creeley's favorite Wittgenstein text:

> Imagine someone saying: "Man hopes." How should this general phenomenon of natural history be described?—One might observe a child and wait until one day he manifests hope; and then one could say "Today he hoped for the first time." But surely that sounds queer! Although it would be quite natural to say "Today he said 'I hope' for the first time." (Z #469)

"For hours I didn't think of you" sounds ordinary enough until we stop to think why someone would say it. The sentence only makes sense in a situation in which the speaker means "The truth is that I think of you all the time." And if this is the case, the respite can't last: "And then I did and can't stop." Similarly, the sentence "Your birthday is here / without you" more accurately means that it is here "without *me.*" Her birthday, after all, belongs to her and no one else. But so obsessed is the speaker that he further declares her birthday to be "that day / you were born to be here," where "here" is patently absurd: it is the poet who can't have her "here." Indeed, the one specific memory of her that is given, "The loveliest day I saw you / buying your first car / with such a lovely presence, of mind," only adds to the pathos: the association of "lovely" with

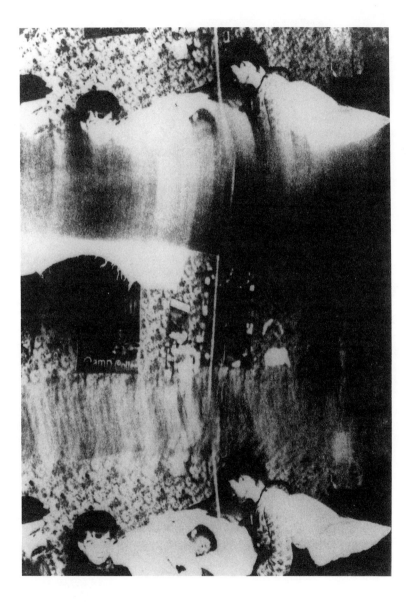

4. Bobbie Creeley, Untitled photograph, in Robert Creeley, *Away*, p. 30. Santa Barbara: Black Sparrow Press, 1976.

5. Bobbie Creeley, Untitled photograph, in Robert Creeley, *Away*, p. 51.

"buying" a car puts an odd spin on the relationship between man and wife, a spin that depends upon the smallest of discriminations:

> It doesn't work without you.
> I do, it doesn't . . .
>
> I'll be home, all ways—
> you name it. I'll put a ribbon
> on it. You're my love.

What is this "it" which is his birthday present for her? Her "way," another "way," "away," "anyway" now modulates into "all ways" (with the pun on "always") that the difficult husband evidently exhibits, all those ways that seem to have driven her away. Before the poem ends, the pop song routines ("You and me / at the same time in / the same place, always") have turned surprisingly sour.

Now let's come back to the epigraph: "One can own a mirror; does one then own the reflection that can be seen in it?" The entire series called *Away* plays with this notion. The poet owns or wants to own it all: his wife's body, his daughter's childhood, the memory of his mother Genevieve (see A 23–27). One very minimal poem, roughly halfway through the sequence, is called "Shot" (A 45):

> The bubble breaking
> of reflecting mirrors.
> Water

where the title refers to a snapshot as well as a shot in the arm or perhaps a death by water. In the next poem, the speaker is "Falling from grace— / umpteenth time / rain's hit my head / generous water," and from then on, the vocabulary of flood, wave, and water suggests that he is renouncing the absurd and impossible ownership of others' reflections. "Where I am, / is alone here, / on the sand / Water out in front of me / crashes on" (A 55). And then in the next lyric, he notes: "Woods, water, / all you / are." The culminating poem is "Water," which begins:

As much to know you,
love, to witness this changing surface
from so constant a place.

I'll never get it right enough
will never stop trying.

Old one-eye,
fish head,
wants his water back.

Dear friend,
bring bucket
and shovel.

Truly see you,
surfacing, all
slippery, wetness,
at home.

                              (A 56)

By now we know that the "changing surface" of "water" is the form
of the woman who went "away"; "Old one-eye" (Creeley literally has only
one eye because of a childhood injury) "wants his water back," asks for
"bucket" / and shovel" so as to "Truly see you, / surfacing, all / slippery,
wetness, / at home." "Home" is a startling word in this context, re-
minding us, as it does, that the "wetness" images are not metaphoric—
not some excursus into a mermaid tale—but the body itself, to be brought
back with "bucket / and shovel." And now the mirror image comes to
the fore:

If I wanted
to know myself,
I'd look at you.

Having "loved / what I was, / it was that reflection" (A 57), he now recog-
nizes he has to let go of hers: "Love's watery condition / waits only for

you." But that recognition does not necessarily produce resolution: the
final poem, "Up in the Air," concludes:

> The right one.
> The wrong one.
> The other one.
>
>   .
>
> Heavy time moves
> imponderably present
>
>   .
>
> Let her
> sing it
> for herself
>
>   .
>
> Keep a distance
> recovers space.
>
>   (A 78)

Which is the "other one": the "right one," or the "wrong one"? we always
try to reason out such things, even when there is no solution. Here, in any
case, separation has occurred: the "yourself" of the opening line of the
first poem in the sequence has become "herself." "Keep a distance" may
be either an imperative, an admonition to himself, or a fragment of a
larger sentence such as "I have learned to keep a distance." And interest-
ingly, the verb form doesn't match "recovers" (first person singular, pres-
ent tense) in the final line. Perhaps she "recovers space" as a result of the
decision to "keep a distance" (*post hoc, ergo propter hoc*), or perhaps not.

   What John Perreault refers to as Creeley's "breathless banality" is
thus an intricate exercise in what we might call word replacement. And
of course the lineation, Creeley's special signature, plays a major role in
this process. Units like "Let her / sing it / for herself" ("for" meaning "by"
or "for the sake of"?) force the reader to put weight on every single word.
The most ordinary pronouns and prepositions take on a curious charge.
Consider the nine-line, twenty-one-word lyric "Here":

> No one
> else in the room
> except you.
>
>   .
>
> Mind's a form
> of taking
> it all.
>
>   .
>
> And the room
> opens
> and closes.
>
>   (A 17)

The "no one" of line 1 becomes, as we move past the line break, "No one / else"—in other words, "someone." But the second stanza suggests that the presence of that someone is all in the mind. And then in stanza 3, where we might expect "you" to either come in or go out, it is oddly the "room" rather than the door that "opens / and closes." "Here" thus functions as empty space, the room opening and closing without any change. And now we realize something very odd: nine of the poem's twenty-one words have an empty "o" at the center: "No" "one," "room" "you," "form," "of," "room" "opens," "closes." In this context, the "all" "tak[en]" in line 6 can only mean "nothing," and the poem's opening line turns out to be right after all. Who is there "Here"? "No one."

Creeleyan lyric depends upon such minute discriminations between words, morphemes—even phonemes. When he begins a poem ("Sitting Here") with the stanza

> Roof's peak is eye,
> sky's grey, tree's
> a stack of lines. . . .
>
>   (A 70)

he is using "simple" language (eleven monosyllables) to produce an elaborate paragram, to wit, "my eye is like the roof's peak, surveying what's below," or "the roof's peak am I," or "the roofs peak (noun + verb) where my eye is." Then "eye"—sky's"—"grey" produce further paragrammatic play: "eye" is contained in "grey" and rhymes with "sky," recalling the phrase "pie in the sky." "Tree's" follows "Roof's" grammatically, but whereas "Roof's" can be heard as possessive or plural noun, "tree's" has nothing to modify, and the absent noun is compared to "a stack of lines"—bare trees line a line of telephone poles, perhaps, but also the stack of lines in the poem.

"The limits of language," Wittgenstein writes in a notebook entry, "is shown by its being impossible to describe the fact which corresponds to (is the translation of) a sentence, without simply repeating the sentence" (CV 10). He might have added that poetry is the "form of life" that shows this limitation most startlingly. In the above passage, Creeley isn't conveying a set of prior ideas that could be said in a number of ways; rather, the saying itself, words and their syntax, *is* the poem. "There are no gaps in grammar," as Wittgenstein puts it, "grammar is always complete" (LEC1 16).

THE POETRY OF GRAMMAR, THE GRAMMAR OF POETRY

As a "grammarian," Wittgenstein paved the way for such later twentieth-century movements as *Oulipo* and Language Poetry. Not that he would have been interested in these "experiments." But, ironically, his self-positioning outside all literary and artistic circles in Cambridge, London, and Vienna made it possible for Wittgenstein to see how misguided those efforts were that tried simply to carry on the poetic or musical traditions of previous centuries. Mozart, for example, was, for Wittgenstein, the greatest of composers, but to imitate his work in the post–World War I era, as certain composers tried to do, was obviously an exercise in futility. In a sketch for the foreword to *Philosophical Remarks* (1930), Wittgenstein admits that the spirit of contemporary civilization is "alien and uncongenial" to him, that, for example (CV 6), he regards "what is called modern music with the greatest suspicion (though without understanding its language)." But, he remarks, the decline of "high culture" may well be countered by something else, something outside the arts as we have known them. "The disappearance of a culture does not signify the disappearance of human value, but simply of certain means of expressing this value." And, even though Wittgenstein quickly adds the disclaimer "yet the fact remains that I have no sympathy for the current of European civilization and do not understand its goals, if it has any" (CV 6), for our purposes what is remarkable about his statement is that, unlike, say, Lyotard, Wittgenstein refuses to equate cultural change with the loss of "value," arguing that, on the contrary, value simply takes new forms—forms, he admits, he himself cannot fathom.

There is, in other words, no nostalgia in Wittgenstein's response to his culture, no trace of the romanticism that haunted the work of the Cambridge and Oxford poets who were his contemporaries. "A crack is showing in the work of art's organic unity and one tries to stuff it with straw," he once remarked acidly, "but to quieten one's conscience [*das Gewissen zu beruhigen*] one uses only the *best* straw" (CV 4). But why "straw" to begin with and why the need for "organic unity"? Wittgenstein himself, after all, concluded that his own composition could only take the form of what he modestly called "philosophical remarks," "short paragraphs, of which there is sometimes a fairly long chain about the same subject, while I sometimes make a sudden change, jumping from one topic to another" (PI p. v). In the poetic composition of the 1980s and '90s, such "remarks" have increasingly provided poets with lyric paradigms. I turn now to some recent exemplars, in which the Wittgensteinian poetic, only implicit in the poetry and fiction I have discussed thus far, becomes increasingly overt, even as it also becomes the occasion for parody and play.

THE AGE OF HUTS

In his manifesto-essay "The New Sentence," Ron Silliman envisions a paragraph that might organize sentences even as a stanza organizes lines: it would function as "a unit of quantity, not logic or argument," the sentences within its "frame" relating to one another not by normal continuity but by a complex system of polysemic and syllogistic relationships.[23] In this scheme of things, individual units (at the sentence or phrase level) that seem to make no sense may take on meaning by contiguity. And Silliman quotes the "Bring me sugar" passage from the *Philosophical Investigations,* which I have cited more fully in chapter 3 with reference to Gertrude Stein:

498. When I say that the orders "Bring me sugar" and "Bring me milk" make sense, but not the combination "Milk me sugar," that does not mean that the utterance of this combination has no effect. And if its effect is that the other person stares at me and gapes, I don't on that account call it the order to stare and gape, even if that was precisely the effect I wanted to produce.

499. To say "This combination of words makes no sense" excludes it from the sphere of language and thereby bounds the domain of language. But when one draws a boundary it may be for various kinds of reasons. If I surround an area with a fence or a line or otherwise, the purpose may be to prevent someone from getting in or out; but it may also be part of a game and the players be supposed, say, to jump over the boundary; or it may shew where the property of one man ends and that of another begins and so on. So if I draw a boundary line that is not yet to say what it is for. (Cited in NS 70)

It is not surprising that this passage appeals to Silliman, whose own poetry, whether in verse or prose, has been committed to testing the boundary between the "sense" of "Bring me sugar" and the "non-sense" of "Milk me sugar." "The Chinese Notebook," which appears in *The Age of Huts* (1986) is a sequence of 223 aphorisms, most of them on questions of language and poetics, that sometimes echo, sometimes gently spoof, the method of the *Philosophical Investigations.* For example:

29.   Mallard, drake—if the words change, does the bird change?

35.   What now? What new? All these words turning in on themselves like the concentric layers of an onion.

60.   Is it language that creates categories? As if each apple were a proposed definition of a certain term.

94.   What makes me think that form exists? [24]

And so on. The poet Alan Davies, who is a friend of Silliman's, recalls that "one morning . . . I received from Ron a lovely chinese notebook. . . . I read the text enthusiastically. I was impressed by the number of interrogatives in the work. My own tendency has often been to suppress questions and, where they did occur, to end them with a period. I knew that I would make my most considered response to the text by answering each of the questions in it."[25] Here are Davies's responses, appearing in the text "?s to .s: for Ron Silliman and for The Chinese Notebook," in *Signage* (1987):

> 29.   Ask the bird.
> 35.   Unpeel the onion a layer at a time; at center, the still point.
> 60.   Categories create categories; language gets used, again, again.
> 94.   Having the thought that form exists, you have the fact that it does. This operation, seeming to prove itself, *supports* itself.[26]

The question-answer format (unanticipated by Silliman when he wrote "The Chinese Notebook") generates a witty homage to Wittgenstein, Davies's text depending on Silliman's even as Silliman's is most effective when read against Wittgenstein's. But *The Age of Huts* contains another text that is perhaps more genuinely Wittgensteinian than "The Chinese Notebook"—namely, "Sunset Debris," a thirty-page text made up entirely of questions. In a 1985 interview with Tom Beckett, Silliman explains:

> My idea with *Sunset Debris* was to explore the social contract between writer and reader. As sender and receiver do not exist in vacuums, any communication involves a relationship, an important dimension of which is always power. In writing as elsewhere, this relationship is asymmetrical—the author gets to do the talking. The reader can shut the book, or consciously reject its thesis, but an actual response is not normally available. As advertisers have known for decades, the process of consuming information is an act of submission. To have read these words is to have had these thoughts, which were not your own.
>
> . . . It was this aspect of intersubjectivity which caused me to introduce so much explicitly sexual language. . . . Every sentence is supposed to remind the reader of her or his inability to respond. (DRS 45)

Every poem is, of course, a "social contract between writer and reader," but what makes "Sunset Debris" distinctive is that, in Wittgensteinian terms, the "psychological I" is replaced by the "metaphysical subject, the limit—not a part of the world" (T #5.641), the limits of the poet's language becoming the limits of his constructed world. In Wittgenstein's words, "solipsism strictly carried out coincides with pure realism" (T #5.64). Consider the prose poem's first forty-four questions:

Can you feel it? Does it hurt? Is this too soft? Do you like it? Is this how you like it? Is it alright? Is he there? Is he breathing? Is it him? Is it near? Is it hard? Is it cold? Does it weigh much? Is it heavy? Do you have to carry it far? Are those hills? Is this where we get off? Which one are you? Are we there yet? Do we need to bring sweaters? Where is the border between blue and green? Has the mail come? Have you come yet? Is it perfect bound? Do you prefer ballpoints? Do you know which insect you most resemble? Is it the red one? Is that your hand? Want to go out? What about dinner? What does it cost? Do you speak English? Has he found his voice yet? Is this anise or is it fennel? Are you high yet? Is your throat sore? Can't you tell dill weed when you see it? Do you smell something burning? Do you hear a ringing sound? Do you hear something whimpering, mewing, crying? Do we get there from here? (AH 11)

"In the language of everyday life," says Wittgenstein in the *Tractatus*, "it very often happens that the same word signifies in two different ways ... or that two words, which signify in different ways, are apparently applied in the same way in the proposition" (T #3.323). "Sunset Debris" seems to carry this process to its furthest possible limit. The first question—"Can you feel it?"—normally refers to a sensation: can you feel the cold? the pain? the touch of something? The second question, "Does it hurt?" would seem to support that view. But we have no way of knowing what "it" is or whom the poet is addressing as "you," and so, when "it" changes to "this" and we have the sequence:

Do you like it?
Do you like this?
Is this how you like it?

the simple shift from "what" to "how" and the predication relating "this" to "it" produces an erotically charged sexual reference, reinforced by "Is it alright?"

One of the central subjects of the *Tractatus* is the question of identity, the verb "to be" being endlessly ambiguous. "The word 'is,' " writes Wittgenstein, "appears as the copula, as the sign of equality, and as the expression of existence" (T #3.323). And in the later writings, Wittgenstein poses again and again the question of how it is we know that the "is" in "The rose is red" is different from the "is" in "twice two is four" (see PI #558–561). This conundrum is expressed in the opening passage of "Sunset Debris," in the triad

> Is he there?
> Is he breathing?
> Is it him?

where the seemingly similar constructions signify quite differently: the first demands simple information, the second requires judgment on someone's part, while the third is one of identification—who is "he"?

Throughout the passage, indeed throughout the poem, such syntactic indeterminacy plays with the reader's expectations and forces him/her into submission. Consider the pairs "Has the mail come? Have you come yet?" or "Do you prefer ballpoints? Do you know which insect you most resemble?," where a neutral question suddenly gives way to a very personal and, in the second case, nasty one. Or again, the triad

> Do you smell something burning?
> Do you hear a ringing sound?
> Do you hear something whimpering, mewing, crying?

where the questions are deceptively parallel: the first doesn't necessarily implicate the "you" at all, the second implies that there's something wrong with "you" (i.e., "you hear things!"), and the third implies that someone—you?—is failing to show concern for a lost cat, or a cat in distress.

So far as I can tell, not one of the approximately three thousand questions of "Sunset Debris" is repeated, except for the penultimate one—"Can you feel it?"—which takes us back to the beginning. Silliman's prose poem is an extraordinary tour de force: it takes ordinary language and everyday events—eating, working, talking, making love—and, by means of the seemingly simple rhetorical device of turning statement into question, creates a verbal vortex that becomes increasingly explosive as the reader becomes increasingly disoriented:

> Is it time to think time? Do the words time? How many times? Is it locatable? Has it a space? Does it have a secret? When will you tell it? Are you anxious? Are you ready? Is it simply because you do it? (AH 38)

Since the questions remain entirely uncontextualized, the "you" continually shifting from self to lover to friend to reader—a reader who cannot *know* what language game is being played. "How is it," asks the poet on the last page, "[that] with all this language there is still this thing so vast that we have no name for it, even if we sense it as a thing we have seen?" (AH 40). And neither he nor the reader can formulate an answer. There are, it seems, no more romantic sunsets, only "sunset debris." As for the poem's readers, "Is not communication an act of violence? Is not writing an act of privacy?" (AH 34).

THE REPRODUCTION OF PROFILES

Language, Rosmarie Waldrop observed in a recent interview, "is really the only transcendence that is available to us, that we can enter into.... It is like a sea. I often think of it as a space." And again, "we cannot get out of language. Only God can, and He doesn't exist. So there's the problem."[27]

The subject of this particular interview, conducted by Edward Foster, the editor of *Talisman,* is translation, specifically Waldrop's own remarkable translations of Edmund Jabès. But she might have been referring to her own book of Wittgensteinian meditations, or more accurately Wittgenstein parodies, *The Reproduction of Profiles,*[28] published in the same

year as Ron Silliman's *The Age of Huts.* Like Silliman, Waldrop is espe-
cially interested in the way meanings are created in everyday language
use, but writing as she does from a distinctively feminist perspective, she
raises questions about the "everyday" that Wittgenstein would not have
considered. "A main source of our failure to understand," we read in the
Philosophical Investigations, "is that we do not *command a clear view* of the
use of our words" (PI #122). To which Waldrop would add, yes, and men
and women further "fail to understand" one another because they are
likely to use the same words quite differently.

   The Reproduction of Profiles is written in short prose paragraphs that
recall those of the *Investigations,* although the overall structure of part
1 (thirty-nine paragraphs) is modeled on the *Tractatus,* the five sections
("Facts," "Thinkable Pictures," "Feverish Propositions," "If Words Are
Signs," and "Successive Applications") following the *Tractatus*'s develop-
ment from "The world is the totality of facts, not of things" (#1.1) to the
picture theory of language in section 2, to the discussion of different kinds
of propositions in section 3, and so on. But despite Waldrop's adaptation
of this structure, part 1 of *Profiles* is essentially a narrative, a love story of
sorts in which a man and a woman spar, on the whole good-naturedly,
about their divergent modes of perception and behavior. In part 2, "In-
serting the Mirror," there are thirty numbered paragraphs, the emphasis
being more speculative and abstract than the *Tractatus* section.

   Waldrop herself explains on the dust jacket: "I used Wittgenstein's
phrases in a free, unsystematic way, sometimes quoting, sometimes letting
them spark what they would, sometimes substituting different nouns
within a phrase (e.g., his famous anti-metaphysical statement that 'the
deepest questions are no questions at all' becomes 'You could prove to me
that the deepest rivers are, in fact, no rivers at all')." What Waldrop is too
modest to say, however, is that her knowledge of Wittgenstein's writ-
ings—not only the *Tractatus* and the *Philosophical Investigations* but the
minor writings as well—is remarkably thorough: the "profiles" here "re-
produced" allude to, among other things, the picture theory of language,
the discussion of the meaning of the word "red" in *Remarks on Colour,*
the communication of the word "pain" in the *Investigations,* and the prop-
osition that the *"limits of my language* mean the limits of my world" in

the *Tractatus* (#5.6). Consider the following paragraph from "Feverish Propositions":

> You told me, if something is not used it is meaningless, and took my temperature which I had thought to save for a more difficult day. In the mirror, every night, the same face, a bit more threadbare, a dress worn too long. The moon was out in the cold, along with the restless, dissatisfied wind that seemed to change the location of the sycamores. I expected reproaches because I had mentioned the word love, but you only accused me of stealing your pencil, and sadness disappeared with sense. You made a ceremony out of holding your head in your hands because, you said, it could not be contained in itself. (RP 23)

Here the first sentence plays on #43 of the *Investigations:* "the meaning of a word is its use in the language." By submitting this aphorism to false syllogistic reasoning (i.e., "The meaning of word X is its use, but X is not used, therefore X is meaningless) and having it reflect the opinion not of the "I" but of the "you," Waldrop gives Wittgenstein's theorem a sardonic twist. For what if "use" involves imposition? We know from the context that the "you" is a man—the poet's lover or husband—and that it is he who insists that "if something is not used it is meaningless" and then proceeds to "take" the woman's temperature. In the context, the ordinary idiom ("to take one's temperature") has overtones of "take away," especially since the poet refers to her "temperature" as something "which I had thought to save for a more difficult day."

"In the mirror, every night, the same face, a bit more threadbare, a dress worn too long." This might be a sentence from a Victorian novel, except for the peculiar use of "threadbare" as a transferred epithet (from dress to face) and the ambiguity of the construction "worn too long" (too long a time or is the dress literally too long?). The simplest phrases, Waldrop implies, have their difficulties. What, for instance, are we to make of the assertion, in the third sentence, that "The moon was out in the cold"? "The moon was out" is simple constatation of fact; "X was out in the cold" is a common idiom for being left out or rejected. But to say that "the moon was out in the cold" sounds absurd although it makes perfect literal sense: the moon is indeed out in the cold night sky. Further: the moon is now placed on the same spatial plane as the "restless, dissatisfied wind" romantically transforming the sycamores—the pathetic fallacy full-blown.

"I expected reproaches because I had mentioned the word love, but you only accused me of stealing your pencil." The language game here refers to sexual politics—the "I" is always ready to offer "love," while the "you" accuses her of stealing his pencil,[29] even as he wanted to "take" the temperature she wanted to "save." But perhaps the nameless "you" is just teasing the "I," perhaps his "accusations" are not to be taken seriously. The "I," in any case, is more or less placated: "sadness disappeared with sense." In the final sentence, Waldrop slyly draws upon the discussion of objects in Part II of the *Tractatus*. "Objects form the substance of the world. Therefore they cannot be compound" (#2.021); "In the atomic fact the objects are combined in a definite way" (#2.031). If a definable object, in this case the human head, is always found in combination, if it cannot be "contained in itself," then, it seems, we must invent "ceremon[ies]," in this case the "ceremony" of "holding your head in your hands." As if such actions would resolve personal differences!

Waldrop's "Feverish Proposition" thus shifts Wittgenstein's ground imperceptibly and ironically: if the *Investigations* demonstrates the inability of words to have precise meanings outside their particular language games, *Profiles* is more interested in the interactive deployment of these language games, in the way language games are related to gender and power. *He* takes her temperature but then accuses *her* of stealing his pencil. He makes a ceremony out of holding his head in his hands, while her face keeps getting a little bit more threadbare. He has both the first and the last word ("You told me," "you said"), while she "expect[s] reproaches."

In the course of *Profiles,* the identity of "you" begins to shift, the later sections involving primarily self-address, as in "It is best to stop as soon as you hear a word in a language you don't know" (RP 66). The male voice largely disappears. "As long as I wanted to be a man," we read in #18 of "Inserting the Mirror," "I considered thought as a keen blade cutting through the uncertain brambles in my path. Later, I let it rust under the stairs. The image was useless given the nature of my quest" (RP 74). The quest is to escape the imposition of someone else's logic, even someone as close to her own sensibility as is Wittgenstein. "I had inferred from pictures that the world was real and therefore paused" (RP 5). The picture theory of language of the *Tractatus,* which Wittgenstein himself was soon to repudiate, forces the language user into ridiculous positions, as when the poet says, "I thought I would die if my name didn't touch me" (RP 5), or as when, in poem after poem, we meet references to causality such as "because," "so," "therefore," or "in response to." Indeed, a mock causality determines Waldrop's syntax, which marks a notable departure from the syntactic norms of modernist and, for that matter, many postmodernist poetic sequences. From Whitman's *Song of Myself* to Pound's *Cantos* to Olson's *Maximus* and Ginsberg's *Howl,* to Ron Silliman's "Sunset Debris" and "The Chinese Notebook," the grammatical structure tends to be prominently paratactic rather than syntactic—the structure of "and . . . and . . . and then . . . and then also," a structure that, as we have seen in the case of Silliman, has elements that could easily be transposed and reversed. In contrast, *The Reproduction of Profiles* relies on the syntactic structures one associates with a more traditional poetry: structures of subordination rather than coordination, conditional and subjunctive verb forms, clauses beginning with "although" (or "though"), "because," "if only," or "despite." Here are some instances of "though":

Though a speck in the visual field must have some color, it need not be red. (RP 9)

The gulls stood still, though the light fell on their strained bodies. (RP 18)

My thoughts began to share the darkness of the river, though we were miles from the nearest reactor. (RP 48)

In these examples, the use of causal clauses is consistently parodic: of course, the presence of color doesn't guarantee that the color is red, any more than that the light falling on the gulls' bodies has a direct relationship to their standing still, or that the dark thoughts experienced on a walk along a river can only be produced by proximity to a reactor. "A proposition," as Waldrop puts it, "flaunts every logical scratch that follows from it" (RP 47). And this sentence is followed by the sentence "I felt sleepy, no doubt because I have a long past and don't speak foreign languages."

Syntaxis, the poems imply, can heighten the poet's sense of the absurd by providing contrast, the seemingly neat container refusing to contain. In a poem that begins with "Snowflakes float[ing] to the ground," for instance, we read that "A woman opened her window and overlooked the difference between the sexes" (RP 49), a wonderfully Wittgensteinian conundrum, *overlooking* having the two opposed meanings "to have a view of or over (a place) from above" and "to fail to observe or consider." But of course—and this is where language is so tricky—the second meaning is inherent in the first: to overlook a wide enough panorama from a great height is inevitably to overlook this or that detail.

Toward the end of *Profiles,* we read: "This is where grammatical terror opens a distance between you and yourself in order to insert the mirror" (RP 73). *Grammatical terror* characterizes the entire sequence, in which the insertion of the mirror into the poet's vagina (see RP 57) refers, like the insertion of the thermometer into her mouth, to the violation of her body and to the "lesions of language" that are her subject. For Waldrop, as for Silliman, the Keatsian life of sensations is always already mediated by language, the language pool becoming, so to speak, the poet's new Spiritus Mundi.

Thus, when Waldrop ends a prose poem with the sentence "Like old idols, you said, which we no longer adore and throw into the current to drift where they still" (RP 9), the words themselves are perfectly ordinary but their syntax makes no sense until we construe the sentence in relation to its intertext, Yeats's "The Wild Swans at Coole." The lines in question refer to the envy the speaker of that poem feels for the "natural" life of the swans: "Passion or conquest, wander where they will / Attend upon them still" (stanza 4), and the lines "But now they drift on the still water, / Mysterious, beautiful," in the final stanza.[30] "Still," as has often been remarked, is the key word in the poem, which begins with the "brimming water" that "Mirrors the still sky," and moves to the double entendre of "still" (silent)/"still" (without change). But whereas Yeats's swans are at home in the "cold / Companionable streams" of Coole, Waldrop's "old idols," whatever they may be, are "thrown into the current to drift where they still." Still what? Is "still" a transitive verb here? An adverb? We cannot know for sure; indeed, Yeats's flooded streams have given way, in the sentence that opens this prose poem, to a "Flooding with impulse [that] refracts the body and does not equal" (RP 9). And why should it, given the ambiguity of the verb "is" ("is" sometimes meaning "equals," sometimes not) Wittgenstein talks about?

"THE COMPOSITION OF THE CELL"

A related undermining of the equal sign has been brilliantly explored in the work of Lyn Hejinian. Her recent collection, *The Cold of Poetry* (1994), for example, contains a text called "The Composition of the Cell," which begins:

1.1   It is the writer's object to supply.

1.6   Rocks are emitted by sentences to the eye.

2.13   Circumstances rest between rocks.

2.14   The person of which I speak is between clocks.

3.1   Exploration takes extra words.

3.4   The words anticipate an immoderate time and place.

3.5   Reality circulates making objects appear as if they belong where they are.

4.2   Exactly!

5.8   The sky pours shape into intervals.

5.10   Those between seeing and believing.[31]

Here the number system and use of short aphoristic sentences immediately recalls the notation and visual layout of Wittgenstein's *Tractatus:* 1.1, 1.6, 2.13, and so on. But in fact, Hejinian's numbers have a specific referent: the sentences in "The Composition of the Cell" are culled from the much longer poetic sequence *The Cell,* published in book form two years earlier. Thus "1.1 It is the writer's object to supply" refers us back to line 1 of the first (unnumbered) poem in the sequence:

> It is the writer's object
>   to supply the hollow green
>   and yellow life of the
>   human I

and "1.6 Rocks are emitted by sentences to the eye" is a version, though not an exact one, of "Words are emitted by the rocks to the eye," which is line 6 of the same poem.[32] Or again "4.2 Exactly!" refers to line 2 of the fourth lyric in *The Cell:*

> Eyeball-to-eyeball, a small spot, and
> > its temporary moment-to-moment hoarding stasis
> Exactly! (CELL 11)

What is the point of this now-you-see-it, now-you-don't sentence game? Why does Hejinian want to produce a poem by writing through her own earlier poem and rearranging or recontextualizing its statements? What language game, in other words, is the poet playing in "The Composition of the Cell"? In an essay called "The Rejection of Closure," Hejinian takes up some of these questions. The use of "discrete intact units," units that have "sizable gaps" between them, she explains, may make it possible to create a genuinely "open" or "generative" poetic text, a text that "relinquishes total control and challenges authority as a principle and control as a motive." "In fact," she remarks, "I would like each sentence itself to be as nearly a complete poem as possible."[33]

Hejinian does not mention Wittgenstein in this essay but, she seems to have the *Investigations* in mind, as when, for example, she rejects "The *nomina sunt numina* [*sic*] position (i.e., that there is an essential identity between name and thing, that the real nature of a thing is immanent and present in its name ...)" in favor of the view that "Language discovers what one might know, which in turn is always less than what language might say" (RC 141, 138). And she explains:

Even words in storage, in the dictionary, seem frenetic with activity, as each individual entry attracts to itself other words as definition, example, and amplification. Thus, to open the dictionary at random, *mastoid* attracts *nipplelike, temporal, bone, ear,* and *behind.* Turning to *temporal* we find that the definition includes *time, space, life, world, transitory,* and *near the temples,* but, significantly, not *mastoid.* There is no entry for *nipplelike,* but the definition for *nipple* brings over *protuberance, breast, udder,* the *female, milk, discharge, mouthpiece,* and *nursing bottle,* and not *mastoid,* nor *temporal,* nor *time, bone, ear, space,* or *word.* It is relevant that the exchanges are incompletely reciprocal. (RC 140)

The absence of such reciprocity ("mastoid" attracts "temporal" but not vice versa) is a function of a revisionary notion of "The Person," as Hejinian calls a recent long poetic sequence.[34] There is, Hejinian has argued in a symposium on "The Poetics of Everyday Life," no "core reality at the heart of our sense of being," and the poem is not, as is usually thought, "an expression uttered in the artist's 'own voice,' issuing from an inner, fundamental, sincere, essential, irreducible, consistent self, an identity which is unique and separable from all other human identities."[35]

What, then, is a self? What is a "person"? "Certainly," says Hejinian in a Wittgensteinian locution, "I have an experience of being in position, at a time and place, and of being conscious of this, but this position is temporary, and beyond that, I have no experience of being except in position" (PEL 167). And again, "The person, in this view, is a mobile (or mobilized) reference point" (PEL 167). Like Silliman, then, Hejinian evidently accepts Wittgenstein's proposition that "The philosophical I is not the man, not the human body or the human soul of which psychology treats, but the metaphysical subject, the limit—not a part of the world" (T #5.641).

For Hejinian, "the person becomes a component in a poetics . . . [at] the point at which the person enters everyday life. The person is both the agent and the agency of the quotidian, doing things which are hardly notable, hardly noted":

Routinely it puts its right foot on the floor at a little distance from its left and slightly ahead of it; both heels are red, and it spits into the sink after brushing its upper teeth with eleven strokes starting on the left side and working across the teeth; it notices a sore area on the gum and doesn't know if the gum was sore yesterday.

Here the person has no opposite.

But the person acquires its opposites at the moment it writes this. (PEL 170)

Hejinian's examples of everyday life—putting one foot in front of the other, brushing one's teeth, spitting into the sink—are so ordinary that the reader almost fails to notice a tiny proposition buried at the center of the paragraph: "both heels are red." Grammatically and semantically, this is the simplest of sentences, except that we cannot determine what it means. Why should both heels (or, for that matter, either heel) be red? Are they chapped? Bruised? Or is the reference to the heels of the "person's" shoes? Is she wearing red shoes like the heroine of the ballet by that name or like Proust's Oriane, dressed inappropriately for the Guermantes soirée? The sentence functions as a kind of clinamen, a swerve away from the "normal" base of the familiar, reminding the reader not to take anything for granted. "Everything we see could also be otherwise" (T #5.634). And further: "We feel that even if *all possible* scientific questions be answered, the problems of life have still not been touched at all. Of course there is then no question left, and just this is the answer" (T #6.52).

Generically, "The Composition of the Cell" is probably best described as a commonplace book, but the "commonplaces" take the form of pseudodefinitions, nonanswers to hypothetical questions, and riddles that can't be solved. Take those first sentences again:

1.1	It is the writer's object to supply.
1.6	Rocks are emitted by sentences to the eye.
2.13	Circumstances rest between rocks.
2.14	The person of which I speak is between clocks.
3.1	Exploration takes extra words.

Note that the "poem" begins with two rhyming couplets; indeed, there is a nursery-rhyme element in these jingly lines that recalls such children's riddles as:

> —Why did the moron eat hay?
> —To feed his hoarse voice.

or

> —How do you get down from an elephant?
> —You don't, you get down from a goose.

"Children," says Hejinian, commenting on these riddles in "The Rejection of Closure," "objectify language when they render it their plaything in jokes, puns, and riddles, or in glossolaliac chants and rhymes" (RC 138). And her own version of such children's riddles gives us sentences like

I cannot separate lucidity from undressing. (70.1)

where the dictionary meaning of *lucidity* as "transparency of thought and expression" becomes a synonym for nakedness and hence "undressing."

Such reductio ad absurdum becomes especially marked when words or sentences are, as Hejinian wants them to be, separate, discrete units. The gap between 1.1 and 1.6 above is a case in point. True, the sentences are related by the reference to writing, but just when the reader has decided that "It is the writer's object to supply" new poetic subjects or information or whatever other direct object we wish to "supply" for the verb "supply," the poet inexplicably introduces "Rocks." Not a particular rocky landscape or rocks rising out of the ocean (as in "Scylla and Charybdis"), not the Rock of Ages or T. S. Eliot's "Come in under this red rock." Just plain, literal rocks, "emitted by sentences to the eye," rocks between which "Circumstances rest" (2.13).

The task of the reader is to construct a context that might make sense of these riddling references. Suppose X and Y are out sailing and X says to Y, who is steering the boat, "Watch out! We're about to hit some rocks!" In that case, "Rocks *are* emitted by sentences to the eye," which immediately starts to scan the visual field. And other stories might be invented to account for the same grammatical construction. In the same vein, "Circumstances rest between rocks"—the circumstances of survival, perhaps, or of easy passage between rocky islands. As for the rhyme "Rocks"/"clocks": the "person," designated ungrammatically as "which," not "whom," might be one of those little puppets that come out of fancy cuckoo clocks and wave their arms in both directions.

"Exploration," we see, certainly does "take extra words." Extra, not in the sense of "more," for Hejinian's sentences are very terse, but "extra" precise in defining the parameters of the exploration. "Reality," we read in 3.5, "circulates making objects appear as if they belong where they are," a sentence that gives a slightly surreal edge to Wittgenstein's proposition "In the world everything is as it is and happens as it does happen" (T #6.41). All one can do, then, is to track the "ordinariness" and watch it go up in smoke. So a phrase like Hejinian's 36.10, "Interposed between the public and the sun," looks odd until we start to think about it and imagine all the things that might be so interposed: airplanes, sequoia trees, skyscrapers, low clouds. "Everything," we read in 40.2, "is subject to visibility."

As in the writing of Gertrude Stein, who is one of Hejinian's central precursors, the ordinary turns out to be nothing if not strange. "For sight and cell" (43.8) substitutes for the expected "For sight and sound." "There are no matching dead" (116.3) plays on the pair "matching"/"missing"— as in the case of matching and missing socks. "Out comes a perfect tongue" (52.13) recalls such items in *Tender Buttons* as "Custard is this" or "Out of kindness comes redness." From where does this perfect tongue come? Out of the mouth? Out of the oven? And what would an imperfect tongue look like?

"The poem," we read in 69.1, "is a correct metonym"—correct in the sense that each sentence, however discrete, relates in intricate ways to its neighbors. As one goes through Hejinian's text, one becomes aware that she takes her title "The Composition of the Cell" quite seriously. The "cell" (hermit's cell, monk's cell, prison cell) is the poet's private room, even as it is the "ultimate element in organic structures" (OED). "The bone of communication [the cup-like cavity of the cell] is hollow" (68.1), until words start to interact and then "Someone must be feeling it" (94.14). But where is "the person" in all this? Subjectivity, Hejinian implies throughout, occurs only as a limit experience. In Wittgenstein's words:

> If I wrote a book "The world as I found it," I should also have to report on my body and say which limbs obey my will and which do not, etc. Namely, this would be a method of isolating the subject, or rather of showing that in an important sense there can be no subject: of it alone, namely, there could be *no* reference in this book.[36]

Does this mean, as Hejinian's detractors complain, that her poetry lacks edge and emotional resonance, that it suffers from an absence of individual "voice"? Not at all, when we observe how very particular Hejinian's signature is, how phrases like "Circumstances rest between rocks" or "I cannot separate lucidity from undressing" represent *her* world, even as Wittgenstein's propositions, embedded in other texts, immediately stand out as stylistically his. In Hejinian's case, the pecular conjunction of abstraction and concrete image ("circumstances" and "rocks"), the wry wit of "On *what* do the eyes finally come to rest?" (81.1), and the particular use of domestic imagery ("My portrait is a bowl and I tap it with a spoon"; 24.4) are quite distinct, not only from the harsher, more violent, more masculine "limits" of Ron Silliman's world, but also from the more sexually charged narrative of Rosmarie Waldrop. Yet in all three, it could be argued, "I is a word like any other." There is no "self" at center stage to which all else is subordinated.

"People," it seems, despite Lyotard's pessimistic conclusion (with which I began this chapter) that we are now in a posthuman age, "still make use of language." It is true that we are in large part constructed by our language, that, as Lyotard observes, "phrases situate words and pronouns ... in a universe they present." In Hejinian's own version of this notion, "One cannot introspect except with respect to something" (80.10). Or can one? In this very sentence, the poet alters standard phraseology by rhyming three of her eight words: "introspect," "except," "respect." Which is to say that "Someone must be feeling it" (94.14), that there is "someone in it" (93.14).

What Wittgenstein's own "philosophical remarks" suggest—and it is a lesson too often obscured today in the heated debates on agency and identity—is that the "personal" is not necessarily equivalent to the inward-looking gaze of the psychologically complex subject. Poised on the edge or limit of the "world as [she] found it," the poet's "private" linguistic construction of that world represents a complex negotiation with the language of her culture. "On *what*," asks the poet in the first line of poem 81 in *The Cell*, "do the eyes / finally come to rest[?]" The answer given reads as follows:

> Sentences that hang the face
> The eyes winching their things
> Quietly to *what*
> The body is bent to
>   speak of thoughts changing into
>   new forms

> Many thoughts are of no
>   things
>   (CELL 115)

In the "writing through" of this passage found in "The Composition of the Cell," even this response evidently struck the poet as excessive; now the unpunctuated question "On *what* do the eyes finally come to rest" (81.1) is followed by the sentence "A single body whose function is to represent the queen" (82.3). But what does such a "body" look like and how does it "represent"? Here we may turn to one of Wittgenstein's many propositions about chess:

> One has already to know (or be able to do) something in order to be capable of asking a thing's name. But what does one have to know?
>
>   When one shews someone the king in chess and says: "This is the king," this does not tell him the use of this piece—unless he already knows the rule of the game up to this last point: the shape of the king. You could imagine his having learnt the rules of the game without ever having been shewn an actual piece. (PI #30, 31)

It is no coincidence, surely, that Hejinian has switched the gender of the chess piece. She never tells us who or what "the queen" is, but presumably we would know how to use the noun in a given context. And that, Hejinian's lyric sequence implies, is the challenge of the poetry game: "Pleasure is stubborn, in retrospect, with nowhere to end" (83.16), and, what's more, "Maybe constructedness could take forever."

—Just don't pull the knot tight before being certain that you have got hold of the right end.

Wittgenstein, *Notebooks 1914–1916*

coda

"Writing Through" Wittgenstein with Joseph Kosuth

For the centennial of Wittgenstein's birth (1989), the conceptual artist Joseph Kosuth mounted a large art exhibition at the Secession museum in Vienna. Called *The Play of the Unsayable,* Kosuth's show brought together avant-gardists of the early part of the century—Marcel Duchamp, Giacomo Balla, El Lissitsky, Kasimir Malevich, René Magritte, François Picabia, and Man Ray—with such postmodernists as John Baldessari, Marcel Broodthaers, Gunther Förg, Jenny Holzer, Jasper Johns, Sherrie Levine, Bruce Nauman, Robert Rauschenberg, Gerhard Richter, Cindy Sherman, Robert Smithson, and Cy Twombly. In the preface to the catalogue, Kosuth observed:

> The work of art is essentially a *play* with the meaning system of art; it is *formed* as that *play* and cannot be separated from it—this also means, however, that a change in its formation/representation is meaningful only insofar as it effects its *play*. My point is that primary theory is *part* of that play, the two are inseparably linked. This is not a claim that the commentary of secondary theory can make. *Talking about art* is a parallel activity to making art, but without *feet*—it is providing meaning without an *event context* that socially commits subjective responsibility for consciousness produced (making a world). . . .

> One of the lessons for art which we can derive from the *Philosophical Investigations* is that I believe the later Wittgenstein attempted with his parables and language-games to construct theoretical *object-texts* which could make recognizable (*show*) aspects of language that, philosophically, he could not assert explicitly. This aspect of philosophy, *as a process to be shown,* resists the reification of the direct philosophical assertion.[1]

Here Kosuth probably has in mind the reference Wittgenstein makes in *Culture and Value* to "the queer resemblance between a philosophical investigation ... and an aesthetic one" (CV 25). Or again, "Philosophy ought really be written only as a *form of poetry*" (CV 24). But no longer a form of poetry or art as expressive model. For Wittgenstein, as Kosuth puts it earlier in the preface, "The *self* is grammatical—it punctuates. Thus it cannot be named because every attempt to do that would presume it. It can be shown, and, as art, it represents the limits of the world (culture, history) as a manifestation of it" (AAP 247).

A few years after producing this Wittgensteinian manifesto, Kosuth himself published a remarkable "artist's book" that illustrates some of these points. The book, called *Letters from Wittgenstein, Abridged in Ghent,* takes the bilingual edition of Paul Engelmann's *Letters from Ludwig Wittgenstein with a Memoir* (1967) and superimposes on the text, at twelve-page intervals and placed on facing pages (German on the left, English on the right), thirteen pairs of black-and-white 5 inch by 7 inch photographs of urban street scenes and building sites. The pages themselves have a parchment-like thickness, but the print has been made so faint one must strain to read what is otherwise an exact replica of the original Blackwell edition.[2] The glossy photographs are tipped in at their top horizontal margins and can be lifted up like flaps, so that one can read almost all of the text underneath. Each pair has identical captions, but the one on the right adds a date, 1992, which is uniform throughout. In the center of the book's gray matte front cover (a cover quite unprepossessing, like that of a manual, with the name of the author and work barely visible in lighter gray letters) is a small photograph of an old building covered by scaffolding, evidently in the process of being renovated.

What possible purpose can there be in thus "treating" an edition of letters? Why Ghent rather than Wittgenstein's Vienna, and why these dreary, nondescript images of warehouses and apartment buildings, of old bridges and parking lots? Here we must reconsider the relationship between Wittgenstein and Paul Engelmann, especially with respect to the house on Kundmanngasse that Engelmann was commissioned to build for Wittgenstein's sister Margarete ("Gretl") Stonborough—a house whose design and building Wittgenstein was to complete.

In 1916 Wittgenstein, on leave from his regiment, was attending artillery school in Olmütz, an old cathedral city in what was then Moravia. He had an introduction to Paul Engelmann, whose family lived in Olmütz, from the eminent Viennese architect Adolf Loos, whose acquaintance he had made, before the war, through Karl Krauss and Ludwig Von Ficker (the editor of *Der Brenner*). Engelmann, who had studied architecture with Loos, had been drafted soon after the outbreak of the war but was discharged from the army because of illness. The Engelmanns were a cultured family and Wittgenstein became a frequent visitor to their house, discussing literature, philosophy, and especially religion with Paul and his friends.[3] The letters Wittgenstein wrote to Engelmann from the front and, after the war, from Vienna and then Otterthal, where he was teaching primary school in the early twenties, give us some of the most intimate glimpses we have of Wittgenstein's mental state in these years. The memoir that follows fills in some of the blanks in these letters, although Engelmann admits he never really understood the *Tractatus* and found Wittgenstein's views on religion and mysticism puzzling.

The letters, in any case, break off late in 1925; only a single subsequent letter (dated 21.6.37) is included.[4] "From the autumn of 1926," writes Engelmann in the memoir, "Wittgenstein was in Vienna engaged on the building of the house in the Kundmanngasse for his sister, Mrs. Margaret Stonborough" (PE 147). He makes no allusion here to what actually transpired between himself and Wittgenstein, and even Ray Monk has assumed that the execution of the Kundmanngasse project was a real partnership.[5]

But as Paul Wijdeveld's recent *Ludwig Wittgenstein, Architect* reveals, Wittgenstein, who was a severe critic of even his closest friends and who was, at best, unsuited for the role of collaborator, had been less than enthusiastic about Engelmann's earlier commissions for the Wittgenstein family.[6] Moreover, Wittgenstein had become antagonistic toward Engelmann's mentor, Loos. In a postwar pamphlet called *Directions for a Ministry of Art* (*Richtlinien für ein Kunstamt*), Loos declared that in the new Austrian Republic there must be government support for the arts, that "It was through the artist that Providence—the 'Holy Ghost'—realized civilization as a cultural flowering in man" (LWA 35). Wittgenstein wrote to Engelmann:

A few days ago I looked up Loos. I was horrified and nauseated. He has become infected with the most virulent bogus intellectualism [*bis zur Unmöglichkeit verschmockt*]! He gave me a pamphlet about a proposed "fine arts office," in which he speaks about a sin against the Holy Ghost. This surely is the limit! I was already a bit depressed when I went to Loos, but that was the last straw.[7]

Not surprisingly, then, as Engelmann was to put it in a 1953 letter to Friedrich von Hayek, from the moment that Wittgenstein signed on, "he was the actual architect, not I, and though the plans were ready when he joined the undertaking, I regard the result as his achievement, not mine" (LWA 54). This is politely put (to Hayek, who was Wittgenstein's second cousin), but Engelmann must have been quite disappointed. Indeed, although, as Wijdeveld tells us, Wittgenstein "did not change the overall conception of the ground floor plan and cubic arrangement of the building," and although he adhered to the "general asymmetric layout which seems partly descended from Loos's modernist programme" (LWA 159), he immediately set about "purifying" Engelmann's design. The house was stripped of all ornament and "reduced to an austere composition of lines, planes, and volumes" (LWA 104). If we compare one of the drawings in Engelmann's sketchbook (reproduced in Wijdeveld's book; see fig. 6) to the final appearance of the Kundmanngasse (see figs. 7 and 8), the difference is striking. For Wittgenstein, the key to architecture (as in the case of his evolving philosophy in these years) was the motto *Simplex sigillum veri* ("Simplicity is the hallmark of truth"). As Wijdeveld explains:

In contrast to Engelmann's design, wall-planes take priority over window-planes: the distance between the windows is consistently smaller than the distance between

6. Paul Engelmann, design for the Palais Stonborough, phase 10, southeast perspective (GC 78, 123 × 129 mm). Paul Engelmann, unpublished sketchbook. Courtesy Resource Collection of the Getty Center for the History of Art and the Humanities, Santa Monica, CA. Reproduced in *Ludwig Wittgenstein, Architect* (LWA), p. 93.

the windows and the edges of a wall plane, while the parapets of the roof terraces are extensions of the outer elevations—all this contributes to the impression of resolve. The windows are longer than they are wide, with vertical divisions only, and they diminish in height on successive levels to suggest height. The upward thrust which is thus implied is in turn tempered by the equally severe horizontals which mark the top of the wall planes; there are no roof gutters and the roof-edge has been pared down to the absolute minimum. (LWA 106)

Such "classical" modernism, Wijdeweld further explains, "is of a completely different order from Loos's" (LWA 165), whose 1927 counterpart

7. Ludwig Wittgenstein, *Kundmanngasse,* spring 1929. Photograph by Moritz Nähr, courtesy Michael Nedo, Cambridge. Courtesy The Pepin Press, Amsterdam. Reproduced in LWA 15.

to Kundmanngasse is the Villa Moller (see fig. 9). Here the street facade abandons the geometric purity favored by Wittgenstein in the interest of the residents' privacy and seclusion: the proportion of small window openings to large bare wall planes, an example of what Engelmann called "ornamenting with unornamented planes" (LWA 165), lacks what Wittgenstein considered essential qualities in architecture: logic and clarity.[8]

In planning the interior, Wittgenstein's concern for detail was to become legendary. His sister Hermine has remarked on his obsession with such secondary items as window locks and radiators; she recalls that during discussions with the engineering firm responsible for the high glass doors that Wittgenstein had designed, the engineer handling the negotiations broke down in tears, despairing of ever meeting Wittgenstein's stan-

8. Ludwig Wittgenstein, *Kundmanngasse*, south perspective, present situation. Photograph by Marghareta Krischanitz. Courtesy The Pepin Press, Amsterdam. Reproduced in LWA 107.

dards. "The strongest proof of Ludwig's relentlessness," writes Hermine, "when it came to getting proportions exactly right is perhaps the fact that he had the ceiling of a large room [the *Saal*] raised by three centimetres, just when it was almost time to start cleaning the completed house."[9]

It is this obsession with *getting it right,* this painful process of composition and revision, that may well have fascinated Kosuth, especially in light of the tension, everywhere visible in Wittgenstein's work, between the demand for beauty, perfection, and purification on the one hand, and, on

9. Alfred Loos, *Villa Moller,* 1927–28. Street
elevation (ALA 2445). Courtesy Graphische
Sammlung Albertina, Vienna. Reproduced in
LWA 165. © 1996 Artist Rights Society (ARS),
New York/VBK, Vienna.

the other, the recognition that the "Holy Ghost" of art can never be de-
fined or even described. Indeed, from the perspective of a post–World
War II conceptualist like Kosuth, the uncompromisingness and severity
of the Kundmanngasse design, as of the *Tractatus,* must be understood in
light of the "corrections" and revisions made in the *Investigations* and re-
lated writings, corrections that moved the later Wittgenstein to the recog-
nition that, after all, "Ordinary language is all right." Hence, *Letters from*

Wittgenstein, Abridged in Ghent may be looked at as a "play with the meaning system" (Kosuth's phrase) of Wittgenstein's own art. For Wittgenstein's erection of a beautiful, "perfect" house, Kosuth substitutes a series of demolition jobs. For the modernist "uniqueness" of the Kundmanngasse design, he substitutes a set of bland, impersonal photographs, chosen (but significantly not taken) by the artist to document the changing face of the contemporary city.[10]

In *Letters from Wittgenstein, Abridged in Ghent,* the "Kaiserliches und Königliches" Vienna of Wittgenstein's youth gives way to the Ghent of the 1990s—Ghent, once the great medieval art city of Flanders (one thinks immediately of Van Eyck's famous *Ghent Altarpiece*), now curiously refigured as just another site of urban sprawl and wrecking crews. Just as the Engelmann and Wittgenstein designs for Kundmanngasse can be paired as "before" and "after" views, just as the "English" translation on the right side of the page comes "after" the German original on the left, so Kosuth presents "views" of the same site—sometimes with something from the old site remaining, sometimes not—and forces us to contemplate the relation of the two. But "past" and "present" are complicated because, as in so many of the examples from the *Philosophical Investigations,* no context for the images we see has been provided. We don't even know how "past" the past is, only that the present is 1992. We can surmise, of course, the date a particular photograph was taken from the cars in front of a building or the graffiti on its walls, but such estimates can only be rough. At the same time, within the confines of the individual photograph, items are contextualized by their surroundings, just as, in a given Wittgenstein proposition, the meaning of words like "blue" and "pain" are specifiable within a given context.

"(The temptation to say 'I see it like *this,*' " we read in Part II of the *Investigations* in the section on the "duck vs. rabbit" conundrum, "point[s] to the same thing for 'it' and 'this'.) Always get rid of the idea of the private object in this way; assume that it constantly changes, but that you do not notice the change because your memory constantly deceives you" (PI p. 207). The conundrum of *seeing as* that Wittgenstein now goes on to describe is subtly refigured in Kosuth's photographs. The first set (figs. 10 and 11; see JKAG 4–5), for example, are pasted into a page where

[Feldpostkarte]   29.3.17
   Möchte Ihnen auch bald ausführlich schreiben. Ich
den

Fortlaan

10. *Fortlaan.*

[Field-postcard]   29.3.17
   I should also like to write to you soon and at length.
I think   ds.

Dear N   17
   I ha   t I
will tel   to
Olmüt   ed
today f   he
one wl   im
financi   he
favour   t's
just mu   to
me ou   e's
poems,   ns,
the El   ns[2]
(Recla   ish
I were   wo
things   I
often t   nd
the sec   he
time w   ur
mother   get
her eit   ne
to Zw

Please

Fortlaan (1992)

[2] IV. 2 and Appendix.
[3] The journal published by Karl Kraus in Vienna.
[4] II. 6.
[5] II. 4.

5

11. *Fortlaan* (1992).

[Karte aus der ital. Kriegsgefangenschaft.
Absender: Ludwig Wittgenstein, Sottotenente,
Cas   4.5.19
B   ür die
gün   ten in
mei   gen! –
Nu   sicher
und   schon
irge

Lie   5.8.19
V   h viel
mit   (näm-
lich   rüßen
Sie,   erge-
ben

Lie   2.9.19
V   ich in
der   n auf
die   h ein
biß   einen
Ber   u mir
kon   s. Ich
war entsetzt und angeekelt. Er ist bis zur Unmöglichkeit
verschmockt! Er gab mir eine Brochure über ein geplantes

Fortlaan

16

12. *Fortlaan.*

[Postcard from Italian prisoner-of-
war camp. Sender: Ludwig
Wittge
Prov. (.19
   Mar   the
favoura   en-
tally! I   nd
me, sa   *e.*[1]
You w   go
well w

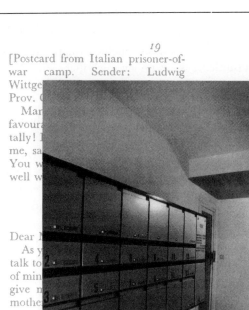

Dear   .19
   As y   t to
talk to   ate
of min   ase
give n   red
mothe

Dear   .19
   Mar   ütz
in the   reit
for 8–   an.
And a   er?
You ha   few
days a   ed.
                        Fortlaan (1992)
He ha   ̲gus
intellectualism! He gave me a pamphlet about a proposed

[1] *Grundgesetze der Arithmetik*, 1893–1903, now available in trans-
lation as *The Basic Laws of Arithmetic*.

c   17

13. *Fortlaan* (1992).

234 *C o d a*

Wittgenstein expresses his impatience at two novels the *Fackel* writer Albert Ehrenstein, whom he had once helped financially, had sent him at the front ("Ein Hundedreck; wenn ich mich nicht irre"; "a pile of dogshit if I'm not mistaken") and begs Engelmann to send him a copy of Goethe's poems instead.[11]

The photographs are labeled "Fortlaan," evidently a street in Ghent. On the left, we see an ugly striped pseudo-Venetian Renaissance building bearing a sign that says, "Residence Ulysse, Te Koop Luxe Appartementen." Underneath this sign, someone has written "Schande" ("shame," "disgrace"), and on the left of the doorway a graffito reads, "Help," to the right of a sign for "Scaldimo" ("heated") apartments, the "l" changed to "n" beneath to produce "Scandino" (either the noun for "hot-water bottle" or the participle for "scanned," which is nonsensical here). On the right-hand page is upward-looking close-up of a modern luxury building, perhaps the new Residence Ulysse, that has replaced the old structure. But it may also be a building next door and it remains unclear what the "Schande" is: that the old house is to be torn down, that someone still lives in it, that it itself has been converted into luxury co-op apartments, that it is perhaps a flophouse? The pictures remain equivocal: why, for that matter, are the graffiti and signs in different languages—English, German, French, Italian, Flemish? And since the car parked in front of the old building is of fairly recent vintage—a Renault sedan perhaps—the time sequence of A to B is unclear.

The dreary scenes are, in any case, a far cry from the Loos–Engelmann–Wittgenstein demand for a modernist architecture based on geometric balance and harmony, an architecture of purity and transcendence. But then, Wittgenstein was himself highly ambivalent about these notions: indeed, a few pages before the photographs in question are tipped into the text, he makes the scathing commentary on Ehrenstein, "Nur kein transzendentales Geschwätz" ("Only let's cut out the transcendental bullshit").[12] And the very next set of photographs (figs. 12 and 13; see JKAG 16–17) are pasted into the pages where Wittgenstein complains about Loos's pamphlet, in which the architect reveals himself to be "bis zur Unmöglichkeit verschmockt!" The photo on the left shows the corner of a room that seems to be in the process of demolition. The walls are covered with nondescript inlaid tile, the floor covered with rubble. The edge of an old fireplace is distinguishable on the far right, a double doorway (or is it a mirror in which the doorway on the other side is reflected?) on the left. Is this the interior of the old building in the previous left-page photograph, the building that made way for the Residence Ulysse? The caption says, again, "Fortlaan." On the right-hand page, we see what may well be the same space, now streamlined and modernized. There is a set of forbiddingly stark steel lockers, safes, or file cabinets on the left, each bearing a number. Bare walls, bare floors, a glass door with the names of its personnel beyond the steel cabinets. Is the "after" image worse than the "before"? It all depends, as Wittgenstein would say, on what you want to do with them. To the lay viewer, neither is especially appealing, but then, it might be possible to conceive of a situation in which, say, the photo on the left would be meaningful, a reminder, perhaps, of one's childhood home. But if I were a business executive, I might well prefer the "after" picture, a publicity photograph, perhaps, which might help persuade clients that, in these steel lockers, at any rate, their files would be safe.

Nor does Kosuth stick to a consistent "before-after" sequence. The third set of photos (figs. 14 and 15; see JKAG 28–29) present us with two views of Koepoortkaai. On the left, we see a rather elegant old building with balustrades and pilasters, stone moldings and entablatures, which seems to be vacant. The undraped windows are charred, and a fireman is hosing out the downstairs interior, which may well have been gutted. The house is on a cobbled street. In the right-hand photograph, the old building has disappeared, but other similar houses (including what seems to be the adjoining one) may be seen at the left rear, while those on the right look like slum tenements. These buildings, in any case, now form a kind of back wall to a parking lot, to be entered from the front as the arrows indicate. Tickets are taken at the left. A sign on the right says, in both Flemish and French, "Attention" and "Pay at the exit." A stop sign is at the end of the roadway, and beyond it the asphalt and rubble look incredibly dreary.

We can read this set of photos in a variety of ways. Wittgenstein, we know, wanted to get rid of all architectural ornament, but here we surely

Russell um die Einleitung geschrieben. Noch habe ich
aber nichts gekriegt.

Soll ich schon vorher an Reklam schreiben oder erst
we...

P.S ... r noch
kei ... ...einen
des ... b und
Gu ...

L. ... 9.2.20
sch ... ...en zu
die ... aß ich
Wo ... ...inigen
mit ... ...eklam
Lus ... ...t die
wir ... ...g und
Ha ... jeder
Ki ... h den
ihn ... ...gefällt

L. ... 4.4.20
Koepoortkaai nichts
mehr gehört! Schreiben Sie mir doch wieder eine Zeile.
Mir ist es in der letzten Zeit sehr elend gegangen und auch
jetzt fürchte ich noch, es möchte mich eines Tages der
Teufel holen. Das ist kein Spaß!

28

14. *Koepoortkaai.*

script and to Russell for the introduction. So far, however, nothing has reached me.

Shall I write to Reclam in advance or only when I send o

May

Kin

P.S. I   no
manus   top
public   . he
has. C

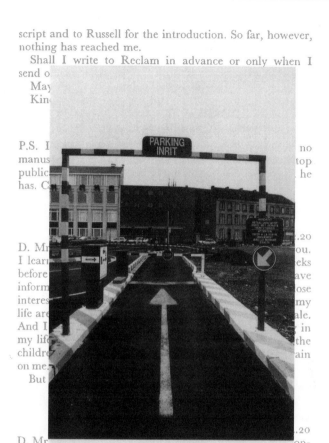

D. Mr   .20
I lear   ou.
before   eks
inform   ave
interes   ose
life are   my
And I   ale.
my lif   in
childr   the
on me.   ain
But

Koepoortkaai (1992)

D. Mr   .20 on-
able time? Do drop me a line again. I have had a very miserable time lately, and I am still afraid the devil will come and take me one day. I am not joking!

15. *Koepoortkaai* (1992).

by those who have not really understood what Kraus is really after (and that means the great majority, even of his regular readers and supporters). On the other hand

Veldstraat

words and phrases. As Kraus in his *literary* polemic takes an individual adversary at his word, and through him indirectly a whole era, so Wittgenstein in his *philosophical* polemic takes 'language' itself (i.e. the language of philo-

124

16. *Veldstraat.*

sophy) at its word. The crucial circumstance that, unlike Kant, he chooses to make not 'reason' but language the subject of his critique, is proof that he takes language at its
word po-
sition: on-
trast t nds
on it.
He or
that b tes
what no
matter led
frontie ion
he get had
persist ver
– thou the
questi to
answe ro-
positio
I gu nd
aesthe er-
stood hed
that t ant
to say nd
aesthe aid
by the ed,
yet so hat
point. ing
to the med
to pos the
insight tics
(logic asic
elemer

Veldstraat (1992)

Kraus was (after Weininger) the first to raise an earnest voice of warning, reminding an epoch given to judging life as well as art by one-sided aesthetic canons that the

[1] Pears & McGuinness: 'one and the same'.

17. *Veldstraat* (1992).

prefer the ornament on the left to the signs and arrows and the hideous asphalt roadway on the right. Indeed, even in the left-hand photograph, the "modern" fire hoses brandished by present-day firemen seem to intrude upon the charm of what we call a "nice old building." And on the right, the large vertical arrow, silhouetted against the black background, has the *trompe l'oeil* effect of being a vertical sign, even as the striped tubular gate bearing the sign "Parking Inrit" looks like an entrance to a jail. Yet, as different as this entrance is from the elegant arched doorway in the left-hand photograph, it itself has a curiously pictorial function, providing a frame for the "vertical" arrow, whose head is squarely in the center of the composition. The rules for "seeing" objects "as" X or Y are suspended, and the fascination of the photographs' visual language is that, like the grammar of the *Investigations,* it denies the possibility of assigning a fixed meaning. Wreckage, rubble, houses and bridges torn down, parking lots and new bridges, derricks, scaffolding—and everywhere cars—how are we to read this series of images?

On the Veldstraat (figs. 16 and 17; see JKAG 124–25), the old Majestic theatre, where *Chariots of Fire* is playing, is replaced by a new, upscale movie house—or is it a department store or office?—seen from slightly farther away. In the text, on the page in question, Engelmann is expatiating on Loos's view that "truly modern form [must] emerge *spontaneously,"* that "The path is this: God created the artist, the artist creates his age, the age creates the artisan, the artisan creates the button." "This," Engelmann explains, "is Loos's basic insight into the connection between the crafts and art" (PE 127). For the postmodern artist, Kosuth suggests, such "modernist" theorems have become merely absurd. Ghent now displays no more than a contrast (or comparison?) between the ugly and the uglier, between crumbling facades of nineteenth-century design and modernist—deprecatingly called "modren"—kitsch. But whose eyes see things this way? The paired pictures, as I noted above, are, after all, not taken by the same photographer. What would happen if their shots were reversed? Would the "new" buildings be bathed in a more romantic glow? Couldn't their representations—witness the framing device of the Koepoortkaai image in figure 15—be given a special aura? And how do we locate the sites photographed vis-à-vis the tourist Ghent of churches, museums, and old squares?

These are questions, Wittgenstein himself would say, that cannot be answered satisfactorily. The name *Ghent* has no fixed value. Rather, Kosuth suggests, street names like Veldstraat and Fortlaan cast an ironic light on Wittgenstein's own Kundmanngasse; they frame Wittgenstein's beautiful architectural design by confronting that design, and the verbal texts that surround it, with the "ordinary language" Wittgenstein himself came to find so worthy of study. In "The Play of the Unsayable," Kosuth talks of the "indirect double reflection on the nature of language, through art, to culture itself" (AAP 247). It is just such "indirect double reflection" that characterizes *Abridged in Ghent.* For the pleasure of Kosuth's art text is that it shows (without ever making a point about it), that the visual equivalent of Wittgenstein's vehement rejection of the "transcendental bullshit" of intellectual/artistic life, as he knew it in Vienna and Cambridge, could only be the "ugly" ordinariness of everyday life depicted in the photographs of Ghent that "overlay" the verbal text. And there is the further "double reflection" that Wittgenstein himself would have scoffed at such a notion, that he probably would have dismissed Kosuth's "abridgement" of his letters as so much "Hundedreck."

In a notebook entry for *Zettel,* Wittgenstein ponders the role of memory:

650. Memory: "I see us still, sitting at that table."—But have I really the same visual image—or one of those that I had then? Do I also certainly see the table and my friend from the same point of view as then, and so not see myself?—My memory-image is not evidence for that past situation, like a photograph which was taken then and convinces me now that this was how things were then. The memory-image and the memory-words stand on the *same* level.

But then, of course, the photograph, as Kosuth's "abridgement" suggests, is not reliable either: no more than the "memory-image" can it "convince" us that "this was how things were then." Memory "does *not* show us the past. Any more than our senses show us the present" (Z #663). For "memory" is itself conditioned by the specificity of context. And it is thus that the language game initiated by a sentence like "I see us still, sitting at that table" is charged with possibilities—possibilities for "philosophy" as a "form of poetic composition." Why does the person speaking remember just that particular table? Where was it located? Who are the "us" still seen in the mind's eye?

"Aesthetics," remarked Wittgenstein in a Cambridge lecture of 1932, "is descriptive. What it does is to *draw one's attention* to certain features, to place things side by side so as to exhibit these features. . . . Our attention is drawn to a certain feature, and from that point forward we see that feature" (LEC2 38–39). If this sounds insufficiently theorized, as it no doubt will to those of us conditioned to depend on the metalanguage of "theory" as explanatory model, we should bear in mind that our artists have perhaps been more acute, have understood, as Kosuth puts it in "The Play of the Unsayable," that "philosophy, *as a process to be shown,* resists the reification of the direct philosophical assertion."

In the case of *Abridged at Ghent,* the seemingly simple device of the photograph, placed on the page as a screen that occludes the actual words beneath it, is used, paradoxically, to bring out those words' latent meanings. It is a language game Wittgenstein himself would have found tantalizing, demonstrating, as it does, the intricate relationship of "family resemblance" to difference. "The problems," as he put it in the *Investigations,* "are solved, not by giving new information, but by arranging what we have always known" (PI #109).

Arranging what we have always known: here is the legacy Wittgenstein has given to artists and poets. Kosuth doesn't say it in so many words, but clearly one important lesson of his particular conceptualism is that "Ethics and aesthetics are one."

Introduction

1. Z #160; CV 24. Anscombe's translation of the German sentence is "Philosophy ought really to be written only as a *poetic composition*"; I have sought to render it more idiomatically.

When the propositions are numbered, as they are in the *Tractatus, Zettel,* and Part I of the *Philosophical Investigations,* the number cited, preceded by the symbol #, is that of the proposition rather than the page. When there is ambiguity, the page is indicated by p.

2. Norman Malcolm, *Ludwig Wittgenstein: A Memoir and a Biographical Sketch by G. H. von Wright,* 2d ed., with *Wittgenstein's Letters to Malcolm* (Oxford and New York: Oxford University Press, 1984), pp. 30, 35; the letter itself (dated 16.11.44) appears on p. 93. Subsequently cited in the text as NM.

3. *Notes on Logic,* dictated in Birmingham shortly before Wittgenstein went to Norway in the summer of 1913, is published as Appendix I to the *Notebooks* 1914–1916 (NBK). See p. 106.

4. Wittgenstein, "A Lecture on Ethics" (1929), PO 40.

5. Vernon Shetley, *After the Death of Poetry: Poet and Audience in Contemporary America* (Durham, NC: Duke University Press, 1993); Dana Gioia, *Can Poetry Matter? Essays on Poetry and American Culture* (Saint Paul, MN: Greywolf Press, 1993), pp. 1, 3. Shetley's poetic predilections are quite different from Gioia's "New Formalist" ones, but, like Gioia, he assumes that the "once-vital poetic enterprise" of poetry has been marginalized by contemporary culture.

6. Theodor W. Adorno, "Cultural Criticism and Society," in *Prisms,* trans. Samuel and Shierry Weber (1967; Cambridge, MA: MIT Press, 1981), p. 34.

7. *Wittgenstein: The Terry Eagleton Script, the Derek Jarman Film* (London: British Film Institute, 1933), p. 5. Subsequently cited in the text as WTE. For a slightly different version of this essay, see "My Wittgenstein," *Common Knowledge* 3, no. 1 (spring 1994): 152–57. The Jarman filmscript turned out to be so different from the original Eagleton screenplay that both are reproduced here; in his introduction Eagleton comments on the differences, as does Colin McCabe in his brief preface.

8. Wittgenstein did in fact rent a cottage on the Galway coast in 1948, after he had resigned his chair at Cambridge. But he lived there alone until the life became too strenuous for him and he moved, in the autumn of 1948, to a hotel in Dublin.

In "My Wittgenstein," Eagleton points out that Nikolai Bakhtin's own work "bears a remarkable resemblance to his younger brother's, even though the two had lost touch with each other in the aftermath of Soviet revolutionary turbulence, and Nikolai had no knowledge even that Mikhail had survived until he stumbled by chance on a copy of his book on Dostoevsky in a Paris bookshop" (p. 154).

9. Terry Eagleton, *Saints and Scholars* (London: Verso, 1987), pp. 112–13.

10. Guy Davenport, "The Aeroplanes at Brescia," in *Tatlin!* (Baltimore and London: The Johns Hopkins University Press, 1974), p. 64. Subsequently cited in the text as GDAB.

11. See Ray Monk, *Ludwig Wittgenstein: The Duty of Genius* (New York: The Free Press, 1990), pp. 28–29. Monk's definitive biography, to which I owe a great deal in the pages that follow, is subsequently cited in the text as RM.

12. See Paul Wijdeveld, *Ludwig Wittgenstein, Architect* (Cambridge: MIT Press, 1994). In his introduction, Wijdeveld writes: "Unlike most philosophers Wittgenstein never developed a systematic theory of aesthetics and wrote only a little on the subject. Moreover, the house was not built on his own initiative and was not meant to be a representation or illustration of his philosophical ideas, though its austere atmosphere inescapably reminds one of the rigor of his thinking. What made him an architect at that particular moment in his life was the situation in which he found himself . . . " (p. 11).

13. See John Fletcher, *The Novels of Samuel Beckett* (New York: Barnes and Noble, 1964), p. 144.

14. In *Self and Sensibility in Contemporary American Poetry* (Cambridge and New York: Cambridge University Press, 1984), Charles Altieri defines the "scenic mode" as the concern for "modest, highly crafted narrative structures producing moments of sudden illumination and [the] desire to correlate sincerity with rhetorical self-consciousness" (p. 5). In the "scenic" poem, "the craft must remain subtle and unobtrusive. . . . The central aim . . . is not to interpret experience but to extend language to its limits in order to establish poignant awareness of what lies beyond words. There is virtually never any sustained act of formal, dialectical thinking or any elaborate, artificial construction that cannot be imagined as taking place in, or at least extended from, settings in naturally conceived scenes" (pp. 10–11). Altieri's exemplary scenic poets include William Stafford, Richard Hugo, David Young, and Stanley Plumley.

15. Guy Davenport, "Wittgenstein," in *The Geography of the Imagination: Forty Essays* (San Francisco: North Point Press, 1981), p. 335. Subsequently cited in the text as DGI.

16. F. R. Leavis, "Memories of Wittgenstein" (1973; reprinted in *Recollections of Wittgenstein,* ed. Rush Rhees [Oxford: Oxford University Press, 1984]), p. 66. Subsequently cited in the text as RR.

17. Cyril Barrett, "Wittgenstein, Leavis, and Literature," *New Literary History* 19, no. 2 (winter 1988): 385–401.

18. RM 256. A further irony is that the homosexual Wittgenstein had absolutely no use for the homosexual subculture of Bloomsbury, with its emphasis on self-fulfillment and individual expression.

19. Theodor W. Adorno, *Against Epistemology,* trans. Willis Domingo (1971; Cambridge, MA: MIT Press, 1982), p. 42.

20. Theodor W. Adorno, *Hegel: Three Studies,* trans. Shierry W. Nicholson (1971; Cambridge, MA: MIT Press, 1993), pp. 101–2. Cf. Adorno, *Aesthetische Theorie, Gesammelte Schriften,* vol. 7 (Frankfurt: Suhrkamp, 1970), p. 305, where Benjamin is criticized for advocating "die Elimination des Unsagbaren" ["the elimination of the unsayable"] in the spirit of the (unknown to Benjamin) *Philosophical Investigations.* The latter's "almost masochistic reduction of speech to the humble and common" is submitted to a devastating critique by Adorno's colleague Herbert Marcuse. In *One Dimensional Man* (Boston: Beacon Press, 1964), Marcuse writes: "Wittgenstein devotes much acumen and space to the analysis of 'My broom is in the corner.'" Such sentences "might also occur in Hegel's *Logic,* but there they would be revealed as inappropriate or even false examples. They would only be rejects, to be surpassed by a discourse which, in its concepts, style, and syntax, is of a different order—a discourse for which it is by no means clear that every sentence in our language 'is in order as it is'" (pp. 175–77).

21. The most comprehensive effort to link the two is Henry Staten's *Wittgenstein and Derrida* (Lincoln and London: University of Nebraska Press, 1984). Staten makes his case primarily on the grounds that both Wittgenstein and Derrida reject the transcendental determination of being and the notion that there is anything outside language, the Derridean "Il n'y a pas d'*hors texte.*" But there are also irreconcilable differences, for instance on the speech/writing question as well as on the issue of the "ontological base" of the "forms of life"; see Charles Altieri, "Wittgenstein on Consciousness and Language: A Challenge to Derridean Literary Theory," *Modern Language Notes* 91, no. 6 (December 1976): 1397–1423. On the relation of Wittgenstein to deconstruction, see Susan B. Brill, *Wittgenstein and Critical Theory: Beyond Postmodernism and Toward Descriptive Investigations* (Athens: Ohio University Press, 1995), pp. 93–116.

Stanley Cavell, a key figure in Wittgenstein studies of whom more below, has been reluctant to take on Derrida, but in his most recent book, *A Pitch of Philosophy, Autobiographical Exercises* (Cambridge and London: Harvard University Press, 1994), he has spoken out quite sharply. The text in question is Derrida's "Signature Event Context," with its attack on J. L. Austin. Cavell writes: "Underlying the opposition to the metaphysical voice that I say Austin and Wittgenstein share with Derrida, there is all the difference between the worlds of the Anglo-American and the Continental traditions of philosophy, differences between their conceptions of and relations to science, to art, to culture, to religion, to education, to reading, to the ordinary. . . . While Derrida and Wittgenstein see metaphysics and the ordinary as locked in contrast, in Derrida, as differently in Nietzsche and in Plato, philosophy retains a given reality, an autonomous cultural, intellectual, institutional life, that in Wittgenstein is gone" (p. 63).

22. Jean-François Lyotard, *The Differend,* trans. Georges Van Den Abbeele (1983; Minneapolis: University of Minnesota Press, 1988), p. xi. Subsequently cited in the text as DIF.

23. Fredric Jameson, *The Prison-House of Language: A Critical Account of Structuralism and Russian Formalism* (Princeton: Princeton University Press, 1972), pp. 43, 207. In his more recent work, Jameson seems to be moving away from this need for a description of "language in the absolute"; in his *Political Unconscious: Narrative as Socially Symbolic Act* (Ithaca: Cornell University Press, 1981), he remarks that Wittgenstein needn't be "numbered among the ideologues of the Symbolic," but rather as one of its critics; see pp. 63–64. But in his next major study, *Postmodernism and the Cultural Logic of Late Capitalism* (Durham, NC: Duke University Press, 1991), Wittgenstein is not so much as listed in the index. Cf. Raymond Williams's *The Politics of Modernism: Against the New Conformists,* ed. Tony Pinkney (London: Verso, 1989), and David Harvey, *The Condition of Postmodernity* (Oxford: Basil Blackwell, 1989). The latter has a single mention of Wittgenstein, as part of a discussion of Lyotard's use of the term "language games" (p. 46).

There is no mention at all of Wittgenstein in the following: Jonathan Arac, ed., *Postmodernism and Politics* (Minneapolis: University of Minnesota Press, 1987); Hal Foster, ed., *The Anti-Aesthetic* (Port Townsend, WA: Bay Press, 1983), and Foster, ed., *Recodings: Art, Spectacle, Cultural Politics* (Port Townsend, WA: Bay Press, 1985); Arthur Kroker and David Cook, *The Postmodern Scene: Excremental Culture and Hyper-Aesthetics* (New York: St. Martin's, 1986); Andreas Huyssen, *After the Great Divide: Modernism, Mass Culture, Postmodernism* (Bloomington: Indiana University Press, 1986).

24. "Fieldwork in Philosophy," interview with A. Honneth, H. Kocyba, and B. Scwibs, Paris 1985, in Pierre Bourdieu, *In Other Words: Essays towards a Reflexive Sociology* (Stanford: Stanford University Press, 1990), p. 9; my emphasis. Subsequently cited in the text as PBOW.

25. Jacques Bouveresse, *Herméneutique et linguistique,* followed by *Wittgenstein et la philosophie du langage* (Paris: Editions de l'Eclat, 1991), p. 11; my translation. Bouveresse's other important Wittgenstein studies are found in *Wittgenstein: La Rime et la raison* (Paris: Editions de Minuit, 1973), *Le Mythe de l'intériorité* (1976; nouvelle édition, Editions de Minuit, 1987), and *La force de la règle. Wittgenstein et l'invention de la nécessité* (Paris: Editions de Minuit, 1984). Unfortunately, none of these has yet been translated into English.

26. Stanley Cavell, *This New Yet Unapproachable America: Lectures after Emerson after Wittgenstein* (Albuquerque, NM: Living Batch Press, 1989), pp. 29–75. Subsequently cited in the text as SCUA.

27. See Stanley Cavell, *Must We Mean What We Say?* (1969; Cambridge and New York: Cambridge University Press, 1976); *The Claims of Reason: Wittgenstein, Skepticism, Morality, and Tragedy* (Cambridge: Harvard University Press, 1979); *In Quest of the Ordinary: Lines of Skepicism and Romanticism* (Chicago: University of Chicago Press, 1988), pp. 153–78.

28. Guy Davenport, "Narrative Tone and Form," in DGI 311.

29. Gertrude Stein, *An Exercise in Analysis,* in *Last Operas and Plays,* ed. Carl Van Vechten (New York: Random House, 1975), p. 138.

30. LEC1 75. In this connection, Monk tells the following story. G. E. Moore, who attended these lectures, insisted that Wittgenstein was using the word "grammar" in an odd sense, arguing that "the sentence: 'Three men was working' is incontrovertibly a misuse of grammar, but it is not clear that 'Different colours cannot be in the same place in a visual field at the same time' commits a similar transgression. If this latter is also called a misuse of grammar, then 'grammar' must mean something different in each case."

Wittgenstein responded that "Grammatical rules are all of the same kind, but it is not the same mistake if a man breaks one as if he breaks another. If he uses 'was' instead of 'were' it causes no confusion; but in the other example the analogy with physical space . . . does cause confusion. . . . It is misleading to use the word 'can't' because it suggests a wrong analogy. We should say, 'It has no sense to say . . .' " (RM 322–23). The quotation from Wittgenstein comes from RR 123.

31. Gertrude Stein, "Arthur a Grammar," in *How to Write,* ed. Patricia Meyerowitz (1931; New York: Dover, 1975), p. 63. Subsequently cited in the text as HTW.

32. See Emmanuel Hocquard, "Conversation [with Claude Royet-Journoud] du 8 Fevrier 1982," in *Un Privé à Tanger* (Paris: P.O.L., 1987), p. 156. My translation.

Chapter One

1. Bertrand Russell, *Portraits from Memory and Other Essays* (London: Allen & Unwin, 1956), p. 31. Subsequently cited in the text as PM.

2. Bertrand Russell, "To the Editor of 'The Nation' " (15 August 1914), in *The Collected Papers of Bertrand Russell,* vol. 13: *Prophecy and Dissent,* ed. Richard A. Rempel et al. (London: Unwin Hyman, 1988), p. 7. This volume is subsequently cited in the text as CPBR.

3. CPBR xxxiii. Russell's letters to Lady Ottoline Morrell make clear that Wittgenstein had begun to make serious criticisms of his work by the summer of 1912, when Wittgenstein attacked Russell's article "The Essence of Religion" as a

betrayal of his former "exactness." By the spring of 1913, Wittgenstein was regularly on the offensive, with Russell, for the most part, agreeing with his objections and worrying how to obviate them. See *The Selected Letters of Bertrand Russell*, vol. 1: *The Private Years (1884–1914)*, ed. Nicholas Griffin (London: Penguin Books, 1992), pp. 437–38, 459–61, 462–64, 479–81.

4. This entry of 25 October 1914 is found in the "secret" portion of Wittgenstein's war diaries, written in code; see *Geheime Tagebücher 1914–1916*, ed. Wilhelm Baum (Wien: Turia & Kant, 1991): "Fühle darum . . . mehr als je die furchtbare Traurigkeit unserer—der deutschen Rasse—Lage! Denn dass wir gegen England nicht aufkommen können, scheint mir so gut wie gewiss. Die Engländer—die beste Rasse der Welt—*können* nicht verlieren! Wir aber können und werden verlieren, wenn nicht in diesem Jahr, so im nächsten! Der Gedanke, dass unsere Rasse geschlagen werden soll, deprimiert mich furchtbar, denn ich bin ganz und gar deutsch!" (p. 33). This edition is subsequently cited in the text as GT. All translations from this text are mine. See also RM 113–14; Brian McGuinness, *Wittgenstein: A Life*, vol. 1: *Young Ludwig 1889–1921* (Berkeley and London: University of California Press, 1988), p. 211; subsequently cited in the text as BMG.

5. On 16 August 1914, Wittgenstein notes in his secret diary, "Auf der 'Goplana.' Nochmals: die Dummheit, Frechheit und Bosheit dieser Menschen kennt keine Grenzen"; GT 17. On 25 August, he remarks, "Es ist nicht ein einziger anständiger Kerl in der ganzen Mannschaft" (There is not a single decent guy in the entire group; GT 18). Wittgenstein spent the early months of the war on board the *Goplana* on the Vistula River. The ship was making its way back toward Cracow, with the Russians in pursuit.

6. See, on this point, RM 111–16; Hermine Wittgenstein, "My Brother Ludwig," in RR 16–17.

7. Georg H. von Wright, in "A Biographical Sketch" (1955; reprinted in NM 8), gives a dramatic version of this "discovery": "Wittgenstein was reading in a magazine about a law suit in Paris concerning an automobile accident. At the trial a miniature model of the accident was presented before the court. The model here served as a proposition; that is, a description of a possible state of affairs. It had this function owing to a correspondence between the parts of the model (the miniature houses, cars, people) and things (houses, cars, people) in reality. It now occurred to Wittgenstein that one might reverse the analogy and say that a *proposition* serves as a model or *picture*, by virtue of a similar correspondence between *its* parts and the world. The way in which the parts of the proposition are combined—the *structure* of the proposition—depicts a possible combination of elements in reality, a possible state of affairs." But, as various commentators have shown, the picture theory evolved more slowly and tentatively than this anecdote suggests, although it is true that its working out begins in the *Notebooks* of August 1914. See David Pears, *The*

False Prison: A Study of the Development of Wittgenstein's Philosophy, vol. 1 (Oxford: The Clarendon Press, 1987), pp. 74–76, 117–52. Ironically, the picture theory of language, which Wittgenstein himself was to reject, remained the aspect of Wittgenstein's philosophy most palatable to Bertrand Russell. See Russell, *My Philosophical Development* (1959; London: Routledge, 1993), pp. 84–85.

8. See Ludwig Wittgenstein, *Briefwechsel mit B. Russell, G. E. Moore, J. M. Keynes, F. P. Ramsay, W. Eccles, P. Engelmann und L. von Ficker,* ed. B. F. McGuinness and G. H. von Wright (Frankfurt: Suhrkamp, 1980), p. 74; subsequently cited in the text as BRI. The letter is cited in English in RM 134.

9. Wittgenstein was taken prisoner on 29 October 1918, transferred to a camp in Cassino in January 1919, and not released until the following July or August, after the war. See RM 157–59.

10. For an amusing account of Wittgenstein's invitation to join and then resignation from the exclusive Cambridge conversation society, which counted among its former members Russell, Moore, and Alfred North Whitehead, and, among Wittgenstein's contemporaries, Rupert Brooke, John Maynard Keynes, and Lytton Strachey, see RM 44–47, 66–69; and BMG 146–49.

11. BRI 100–101. This letter has not been published in its original English, although there are references to it in RM 182–83 and in BMG 290–91. The retranslation into English is mine.

12. The complex publishing history, beginning with the German edition in the *Annalen der Naturphilosophie,* ed. William Ostwald (1921), an edition Wittgenstein dismissed as quite simply "pirated," "full of errors," is succinctly recounted by Brian McGuinness: see BMG 296–99.

13. On 8 May 1920, Wittgenstein wrote his friend Paul Engelmann: "My book will probably not be printed, as I could not bring myself to have it published with Russell's introduction, which looks even more impossible in translation than it does in the original." See Paul Engelmann, *Letters from Ludwig Wittgenstein with a Memoir* (Oxford: Basil Blackwell, 1967), pp. 30–31 (German and English on facing pages). Subsequently cited in the text as PE.

Wittgenstein had reason to be irritated. The introduction contains a number of backhanded compliments and disclaimers, for example: "The totalities concerning which Mr. Wittgenstein holds that it is impossible to speak logically are nevertheless thought by him to exist, and are the subject-matter of his mysticism" (T 23). Russell's tone is condescending and Wittgenstein knew it. But he was later persuaded to accept Russell's introduction; see BMG 296–99.

14. NM 95; in the "Memoir," Norman Malcolm recalls that "When Wittgenstein and I later talked about his own service in the First World War he said emphatically that he had never been bored, and I believe that he even said he did not dislike his army service. He related how he kept a notebook in his rucksack

and whenever he had a chance wrote in it the thoughts that composed his first book, the *Tractatus Logico-Philosophicus*" (NM 37).

15. "Wittgenstein an Ficker," October or November 1919, in BRI 96–97. I cite the English translation in RM 178. Ficker, of course, owed Wittgenstein a great deal, since the latter had made the very generous gift of 100,000 kronen to a group of poets of Ficker's choice in the pre-war summer of 1914. After the war, however, Ficker had neither the money nor the understanding of philosophy to publish the *Tractatus,* and the project came to nothing. See RM 106–10, 131–32.

16. Ronald W. Clark, *The Life of Bertrand Russell* (1975; New York: Penguin Books, 1978), p. 291.

17. Paul Fussell, *The Great War and Modern Memory* (Oxford and New York: Oxford University Press, 1975), pp. 23–24. Subsequently cited in the text as PF.

18. Leonard Woolf, *Beginning Again: An Autobiography of the Years 1911 to 1918* (New York: Harcourt, Brace & World, 1964), p. 20. Subsequently cited in the text as BA. The original Bloomsbury circle, then in its formative stages, consisted, according to Woolf, of thirteen persons: "three women [Virginia and Vanessa Stephen, Desmond McCarthy's wife Molly] and ten men; of the ten men [McCarthy, Adrian Stephen, Clive Bell, Duncan Grant, John Maynard Keynes, E. M. Forster, Lytton Strachey, Roger Fry, Saxon Sidney-Turner, and himself], nine had been at Cambridge, and all of us except Roger had been more or less contemporaries at Trinity and King's" (pp. 22–23). Further, seven of the ten had been Apostles, thus overlapping with Russell and Moore, and almost with Wittgenstein. Keynes, who acted as Wittgenstein's sponsor, was the link to Bloomsbury, but Wittgenstein kept his distance from the group.

19. BA 147. Woolf himself had strong pacifist leanings and was sympathetic to Russell's views, but other Apostles, for example Rupert Brooke, who had read Classics at King's, was violently anti-German and hence eager to fight for the English cause; see Paul Delaney, *The Neo-Pagans: Rupert Brooke and the Ordeal of Youth* (New York: Macmillan, 1987).

20. Allan Janik and Stephen Toulmin, *Wittgenstein's Vienna* (New York: Simon and Schuster, 1973), p. 242. Ray Monk's biography, although less specifically concerned with Viennese cultural and artistic life, takes the same position, emphasizing, for example, the important role of Weininger in Wittgenstein's development (RM 19–25).

21. Modris Eksteins, *Rites of Spring: The Great War and the Birth of the Modern Age* (Boston: Houghton Mifflin, 1989), pp. 72–73; see chapter 2, "Berlin," passim. Subsequently cited in the text as ME.

22. Marjorie Perloff, *The Futurist Moment: Avant-Garde, Avant Guerre, and the Language of Rupture* (Chicago: University of Chicago Press, 1986), chapter 1 passim. By 1916, when the realities of trench warfare had become apparent, the mood

changed to one of bitter disillusionment and even pacifism. But ironically, the "anti-war" Cabaret Voltaire, founded in 1916 by German poets and artists escaping the war as well as by exiles from Eastern Europe like Tristan Tzara, adopted a rhetoric of violence and revolutionary change not unlike the rhetoric they found so distasteful when it was implicated in actual politics.

23. PE 73. It should be pointed out, however, that even in Wittgenstein's immediate circle the outlook on war was by no means uniform. Engelmann himself, for instance, was wholly opposed to the war, even though he did not go so far as to become a pacifist, believing that it was incumbent on himself to find "an alternative to combatant war service in some other equally serious activity" (PE 70–72).

24. The often illogical numbering in the *Tractatus* was first suggested to me by David Antin in his unpublished 1984 lecture "The Poetry of Ideas and the Idea of Poetry," presented at the West Coast Humanities Institute at Berkeley.

25. I am grateful to Daniel Herwitz for elucidating this proposition for me.

26. Ray Monk links the later sections of the *Tractatus,* especially the discussion on will, to *The World as Will and Representation,* a book Wittgenstein knew well. But Monk admits, "What distinguishes Wittgenstein's statement of the doctrine [the dichotomy between "world as idea" and "world as will"] from Schopenhauer's is that in Wittgenstein's case it is accompanied by the proviso that, when put into words, the doctrine is, strictly speaking, nonsense" (RM 143–44).

27. M. O'C. Drury, "Conversations with Wittgenstein," in RR 127–28.

28. See, on this point, LEC1 26: "What we find out in philosophy is trivial: it does not teach us new facts, only science does that. But the proper synopsis of these trivialities is enormously difficult, and has immense importance. Philosophy is in fact the synopsis of trivialities."

29. GT 70: "Rührenden Brief von David. Er schreibt, sein Bruder sei in Frankreich gefallen. Schrecklich! Dieser liebe freundliche Brief öffnet mir die Augen darüber, wie ich hier in der *Verbannung* lebe. Es mag eine heilsame Verbannung sein, aber ich fühle sie jetzt als Verbannung" (26.7.16). "Wurde gestern beschossen. War verzagt. Ich hatte Angst vor dem Tode. Solch einen Wunsch habe ich jetzt, zu leben! Und es ist schwer, auf das Leben zu verzichten, wenn man es einmal gern hat" (29.7.16).

Chapter Two

1. "O Zvukax stixotovornogo jazyka" (1916), trans. I. R. Titunik; cited by Boris Eichenbaum in "The Theory of the Formal Method" (1927), in *Readings in Russian Poetics: Formalist and Structuralist Views,* ed. Ladislav Matejka and Krystyna Pomorska (Cambridge and London: MIT Press, 1971), p. 9. This book is subsequently cited in the text as RRP.

2. "What Is Poetry?" (1933–34), in Roman Jakobson, *Language in Literature,*

ed. Krystyna Pomorska and Stephen Rudy (Cambridge and London: Harvard University Press, 1987), p. 378. Jakobson had coined the term *literaturnost* as early as 1917 in his study of Velimir Khlebnikov, *The Newest Russian Poetry* (Prague, 1921); see Eichenbaum in RRP 8. Jakobson's notion of *literariness* has had impressive staying power. As late as the early 1970s, in the special issue of *New Literary History* called "What Is Literature?" Henryk Markiewicz writes, "the poetic function is manifested when an utterance is ordered additionally in a way which cannot be justified by the usual requirements of linguistic communication" ("The Limits of Literature," IV [1972]: 8). And in the same issue Manuel Duran writes, "An essential condition of poetic language is therefore its lack of naiveté, its constant self-consciousness. When we speak in everyday life about trivial matters, we do so with a minimum of respect for language" ("Inside the Glass Cage: Poetry and 'Normal' Language," 67).

   3. See Richards, *Principles of Literary Criticism* (1924); *Practical Criticism* (1929). In 1923, when Wittgenstein was teaching elementary school in Trattenbach, C. K. Ogden sent him a copy of *The Meaning of Meaning,* written jointly with Richards. According to Ray Monk, "Ogden regarded the book as providing a causal solution to the problem of meaning addressed by Wittgenstein in the *Tractatus,*" but Wittgenstein dismissed it as irrelevant" (RM 214). Later, when Wittgenstein returned to Cambridge and began to lecture, Richards, who heard him, wrote a poem about his lecture style called "The Strayed Poet." It begins:

> Your voice and his I heard in those Non-Lectures—
> Hammock chairs sprawled skew-wise all about;
> Moore in the armchair bent on writing it all out—
> Each soul agog for any word of yours.
>
> Few could long withstand your haggard beauty,
> Disdainful lips, wide eyes bright-lit with scorn,
> Furrowed brow, square smile, sorrow-born
> World-abandoning devotion to your duty. . . . (Cited in RM 290)

The irony here is that Richards, the advocate of poetic speech as noncognitive, figural, connotative, etc., is writing a perfectly straightforward "informational" prose whose only "poeticity" is its verse form.

   4. Viktor Shklovsky, "Art as Technique," in Lee T. Lemon and Marion J. Reis, eds. and trans., *Russian Formalist Criticism: Four Essays* (Lincoln, NE: Bison Books, 1965), pp. 3–41. For an assessment of this essay, see Victor Erlich, *Russian Formalism: History—Doctrine,* 4th ed. (The Hague: Mouton, 1980), pp. 175–80; Peter Steiner, *Russian Formalism: A Metapoetics* (Ithaca and London: Cornell University Press, 1987), pp. 48–67.

   5. Pierre Bourdieu, "The Historical Genesis of a Pure Aesthetic," in *The Field*

of Cultural Production, ed. Randal Johnson (New York: Columbia University Press, 1993), p. 254. Subsequently cited in the text as FCP. Bourdieu cites Arthur Danto's critique of the distinction "between works of art and simple, ordinary things," noting that although, in the case of art, theorists seem to be able to see that "the principle of this ontological difference must be sought in an institution," in the case of philosophy the institutional constraint is simply ignored.

6. Jacques Derrida, *Of Grammatology,* trans. Gayatri Chakravorty Spivak (Baltimore and London: The Johns Hopkins University Press, 1976), pp. 69, 86.

7. Fredric Jameson, *The Prison-House of Language* (Princeton: Princeton University Press, 1972), pp. 173–74. For a contrary view, see Henry Staten, *Wittgenstein and Derrida* (Lincoln and London: University of Nebraska Press, 1984). Staten begins with Deconstruction and then tries to accommodate Wittgenstein to it. He writes, for example, "Wittgenstein in fact presents 'ordinary language' in a double aspect, as Penelope and as Circe, as the home to which language has to be returned and as the seduction of the play of surfaces" (p. 77). But "play of surfaces" is a Derridean, not a Wittgensteinian, locution, in that the latter made no claim for a "depth" beneath the surface. Or again, when Staten paraphrases Wittgenstein to say, "When I use language normally, according to custom, I use it without thinking: and it is just this that makes it possible for the philosophical illusions to arise. *Normality is the necessary background against which it would be possible to think the essence*" (p. 79), he is, I think, misreading Wittgenstein, who never makes the distinction between background and foreground.

8. Stanley Fish, "How Ordinary Is Ordinary Language?" *New Literary History* 5 (1973), special issue "What Is Literature?": 41–54; reprinted in *Is There a Text in This Class? The Authority of Interpretive Communities* (Cambridge and London: Harvard University Press, 1980), pp. 97–111; see p. 97. Since a number of changes were made for the book version, I refer to the book, subsequently cited in the text as ITT.

9. See also Stanley Fish, "Change," in *Doing What Comes Naturally: Change, Rhetoric and the Practice of Theory in Literary and Legal Studies* (Durham and London: Duke University Press, 1989), pp. 141–60.

10. See Gary A. Olson, "Fish Tales: A Conversation with 'The Contemporary Sophist' " (1992), printed as appendix to *There's No Such Thing as Free Speech and It's a Good Thing Too* (New York: Oxford University Press, 1994), pp. 292–93. See also Reed Way Dasenbrock, "Accounting for the Changing Certainties of Interpreting Communities," *MLN* 101, no. 5 (December 1986): 1022–41. Dasenbrock argues that Fish derived more from Wittgenstein than he has perhaps recognized but that his version of Wittgensteinian thought is reductive.

11. On the influence of Piero Sraffa, who was a close friend of Antonio Gramsci's, see RM 260–62. In the preface to PI, Wittgenstein says that he is indebted to Sraffa "for the most consequential ideas of this book" (PI vi).

12. Pierre Bourdieu, "Postscript: Toward a 'Vulgar' Critique of 'Pure Critiques,' " *Distinction: A Social Critique of the Judgement of Taste,* trans. R. Nice (Cambridge and London: Harvard University Press, 1984), pp. 494–98.

13. For a good general discussion of the language game, see Austin Quigley, "Wittgenstein's Philosophizing," *New Literary History* 19, no. 2 (winter 1988): 209–37. Quigley's is the lead piece in a whole issue devoted to "Wittgenstein and Literary Theory." See especially Henry Staten, "Wittgenstein and the Intricate Evasions of 'Is,' " and Jules David Law's "Uncertain Grounds: Wittgenstein's *On Certainty* and the New Literary Pragmatism." All these essays are clarifications of philosophical intent rather than, as in my own case, studies of Wittgenstein as someone who is "writing poetically."

14. BB 17, my emphasis. It should be noted, as is clear from other contexts, that "primitive" for Wittgenstein does not refer to "primitive" societies but to our earliest childhood experience or first exposure to something that is later taken for granted.

15. Wittgenstein's *Remarks* date from 1931, when he and his friend M. O'C. Drury read sections of Frazer's monumental work and discussed them. Part II was added later: according to Rush Rhees, "not earlier than 1936 and probably after 1948." The *Remarks* were first published in 1967 in the journal *Synthese* and later in book form; they have recently been reprinted in a bilingual edition in PO 118–55.

16. PO 137. See James George Frazer, *The Golden Bough, A Study in Magic and Religion,* 3d ed., 12 vols. (London: Macmillan, 1917), 2:2, cited in PO 136.

17. PO 146–47. The Klagge-Nordmann translation, "The *surroundings* of a way of acting," seems unnecessarily awkward.

18. Herman Rapaport, letter to the author, 10 March 1995.

19. Wittgenstein wrote paragraphs 1–188 of the present *Philosophical Investigations* in Norway in 1936. The typescript of Part I was completed by the summer of 1938 and Wittgenstein asked Rush Rhees to translate it. But he was not satisfied with the translation and then the war intervened. Wittgenstein then began to revise and add: paragraphs 189–421 were done by 1944, 421–693 by 1946. Part II is really a separate manuscript, based on Wittgenstein's lectures of the summer term of 1947 and left in a transitory state in 1949. Hence, the *Investigations* is only nominally a separate or single book. See RM 327–405.

20. NM 71. In his *Companion to Wittgenstein's "Philosophical Investigations"* (Ithaca and London: Cornell University Press, 1977), Garth Hallett points out that Augustine's view is not essentially different from Plato's or, for that matter, from Bertrand Russell's (GH 73). For an excellent treatment of the "naming" theory of language, see Gordon P. Baker and Peter M. S. Hacker, *Language, Sense and Nonsense, A Critical Investigation into Modern Theories of Language* (Oxford: Basil Blackwell, 1984), pp. 14–46 and passim.

21. Hazard Adams and LeRoy Searle, eds., *Critical Theory since 1965* (Tallahassee, FL: Florida State University Press, 1986), pp. 767–88.

22. Emphasis mine. The chess example first appears in a lecture of 1932 (LEC2 1), where it is stated more baldly: "Words and chess pieces are analogous; knowing how to use a word is like knowing how to move a chess piece. Now how do the rules enter into playing the game?" When Wittgenstein reworks this passage (as he does in a number of places), he inverts it and begins with the questions, thus taking the game one step at a time.

23. This statement appears in an early version (manuscript 110, 1930–31) of the PI and is cited in GH 204. Cf. PI #410: " 'I' is not the name of a person, nor 'here' of a place, and 'this' is not a name. But they are connected with names." Many similar passages appear in the "Notes for Lectures on 'Private Experience' and 'Sense Data' " (c. 1934–36), recorded by Rush Rhees; see PO 202–88. For example, "The word 'I' does not designate a person" (228); "There is not difference, for me, between *I* and *this;* and for me the word 'I' is not a signal calling attention to a place or a person" (269).

24. WTE 10. It is only fair to point out that this interpretation is hotly contested by the more traditional Wittgensteinians. In a review of *Wittgenstein: The Terry Eagleton Script* along with the newly edited *Philosophical Occasions,* Colin McGinn, citing Eagleton's statement above, protests: "Wittgenstein was not concerned with such issues. The social intrudes on his thinking only as the requirement that rules of language should be open to public correction, that they not be 'private.' This has nothing to do with whether one's personality is a product of social determinants. It is a risible distortion to read Wittgenstein's later work as some kind of anticipation of Foucault and company. . . . [Wittgenstein] was not a literary or political theorist. He was a pure philosopher" (*New Republic,* 20 June 1994, p. 39). But how, Wittgenstein might have countered, is "personality" created except through language? And how can one separate the linguistic from the social?

25. The most eloquent spokesperson for this position is probably Cary Nelson; see *Repression and Recovery: Modern American Poetry and the Politics of Cultural Memory 1910–1945* (Madison: University of Wisconsin Press, 1989).

26. Pierre Bourdieu, *In Other Words: Essays towards a Reflexive Society* (Stanford: Stanford University Press, 1990), p. 9. "Action," says Bourdieu, "is not the mere carrying out of a rule or obedience to a rule. Social agents in archaic societies as well as in ours, are not automata regulated like clocks in accordance with laws which they do not understand. In the most complex games, matrimonial exchange for instance, or ritual practices, they put into action the incorporated principles of a generative habitus" (p. 9).

27. See, for example, CV 18–22. On Wittgenstein's anti-Semitic statements in the early thirties, see RM 313–17.

Chapter Three

1. Gertrude Stein, "Arthur a Grammar," in HTW 57, 59. My chapter title "Grammar in Use" is found in the same essay on p. 54.

2. The first sentence comes from *Tender Buttons* (1913–14), the second from *What Happened, A Five Act Play* (1913), the third and fourth from *Pink Melon Joy* (1915). The original edition of *Tender Buttons* (Paris: Claire Marie, 1914), subsequently cited in the text as TB, has been reprinted by Sun & Moon Press (Los Angeles: Sun & Moon Press, n.d.); for *What Happened* and *Pink Melon Joy,* both first published in *Geography and Plays* (1922; reprint, Madison: University of Wisconsin Press, 1993), see Ulla E. Dydo, ed., *A Stein Reader, Gertrude Stein* (Evanston, IL: Northwestern University Press, 1993). The *Reader,* subsequently cited in the text as UD, provides us with the most authoritative texts available for each Stein piece selected, as well as with Dydo's excellent headnotes; it is the single most important book anyone interested in Stein should consult. On "Roast potatoes for" and related "Tender Buttons," see the excellent analysis of grammatical form and language in Peter Quartermain, *Disjunctive Poetics: From Gertrude Stein and Louis Zukofsky to Susan Howe* (Cambridge and New York: Cambridge University Press, 1992), pp. 21–43.

3. Anon., review of *Tender Buttons,* in *Louisville Courier-Journal,* 6 July 1914; cited in Ray Lewis White, *Gertrude Stein and Alice B. Toklas, A Reference Guide* (Boston: G. K. Hall & Co., 1984), p. 9. Subsequently cited in the text as RLW.

4. As the poet Lyn Hejinian puts it in a fascinating essay called "Two Stein Talks," *Temblor* 3 (1986): 128–39: "The incorrectness of the dangling preposition attracts one's attention." Subsequently cited in the text as LH.

5. Bettina L. Knapp, *Gertrude Stein* (New York: Continuum, 1990), pp. 127–28.

6. The most convincing work on the sexual coding in Stein's work is that of Catharine R. Stimpson: see "Gertrude Stein and the Transposition of Gender," in *The Poetics of Gender,* ed. Nancy K. Miller (New York: Columbia University Press, 1986), pp. 1–18; "The Somagrams of Gertrude Stein," *Poetics Today* 6, nos. 1–2: 67–80; "The Mind, the Body, and Gertrude Stein," *Critical Inquiry* 3, no. 3 (spring 1977): 489–506. See also Pamela Hadas, "Spreading the Difference: One Way to Read Gertrude Stein's *Tender Buttons,*" *Twentieth-Century Literature* 24 (1978): 57–75; Elizabeth Fifer, "Is Flesh Advisable: The Interior Theater of Gertrude Stein," *Signs* 4 (1979): 472–83.

In *A Different Language: Gertrude Stein's Experimental Writing* (Madison: University of Wisconsin Press, 1983), Marianne DeKoven follows Julia Kristeva's psychoanalytic model, distinguishing Stein's *écriture féminine* from patriarchal writing: "Conventional language is patriarchal not because it *is* male, but because it exaggerates, hypostasizes, exclusively valorizes male modes of signification, silencing the female presymbolic, pluridimensional modes articulated by experimental writing.

These modes are female only because they are pre-Oedipal" (p. xix); such "pre-Oedipal" modes "attack the cultural hegemony of sense, order, linearity, unitary coherence" (p. 7). Subsequently cited in the text as MDK. A related case is made by Harriet Chessman, whose *The Public Is Invited to Dance: Representation, the Body and Dialogue in Gertrude Stein* (Stanford: Stanford University Press, 1989) discusses the ways "difference" may subvert the authoritarian identity of the Lacanian Father.

The most elaborate treatment of the larger gender issue in Stein's work to date is Lisa Ruddick's *Reading Stein: Body, Text, Gnosis* (Ithaca and London: Cornell University Press, 1990). Ruddick reads pre–World War I Stein (whom she takes to be *the* significant Stein) as a case of "feminine gnosticism." *Tender Buttons,* for example, "represents Stein's fully developed vision of the making and unmaking of patriarchy," where patriarchy is defined as "sacrifice," "crucifixion," or "live burial." "Once one sees male dominance as dependent on sacrifice, one is in a position to undo sacrifice and to transcend patriarchal thinking" (p. 191).

7. Stein never met Wittgenstein. She might, of course, have known him (or known of him) through Alfred North Whitehead, one of Stein's "three geniuses" (see *The Autobiography of Alice B. Toklas*), whom she and Alice B. Toklas met during their trip to England in July 1914. When war broke out between England and Russia on August 1, Evelyn Whitehead insisted the two ladies stay with them at their country house in Wiltshire until they were out of danger. The visit lasted for six weeks, during which Stein took frequent walks with Whitehead and discussed philosophy. Later, Evelyn Whitehead visited Stein at the rue de Fleurus.

Wittgenstein had been a visitor to Whitehead's Wiltshire cottage exactly a year earlier, in August 1913. But despite Bertrand Russell's advocacy of Wittgenstein in this period, Whitehead kept his distance. As Whitehead's biographer Victor Lowe explains it, Whitehead disliked what he took to be the Austrian philosopher's absolutism, his insistence that one *must* not ask certain questions, and he felt that Wittgenstein drove science and philosophy, the two disciplines he himself had tried to reconcile, further apart by making philosophy a very special kind of linguistic activity; see Victor Lowe, *Alfred North Whitehead, The Man and His Work*, vol. 2, *1910–1947*, ed. J. B. Schneewind (Baltimore and London: Johns Hopkins University Press, 1990), pp. 29–31, 277–78. The dislike was mutual: Wittgenstein never took Whitehead seriously.

After Stein's death, when Toklas was asked by Allegra Stewart whether Stein had ever read Wittgenstein, Toklas insisted that she hadn't. Santayana, James, Whitehead—these, she said, were Stein's masters. But Wittgenstein was an entirely unknown quantity.

8. Note, incidentally, that the usual explanation that, as a lesbian, Stein left the repressive U.S. for the "freedom" of France is only a partial one. Wittgenstein's Vienna was probably less straitlaced than the England of the years 1910–19, yet Cam-

bridge was an easier place for him to have a private life. It is more a case of going *away,* of living far from one's family where one can be anonymous, than a case of leaving a repressive society for a free one. In Wittgenstein's case, the reasons for leaving Vienna were, of course, less consciously articulated than Stein's; on the other hand, he never felt "at home" in Cambridge as she felt at home in Paris.

9. Françoise Collin, "L'Ecriture sans rature," in *Gertrude Stein, encore* (Amiens: Trois Cailloux: In 'hui, 1983), pp. 107–8. My translation. This important collection of translations and essays is subsequently cited in the text as GSE.

10. Gertrude Stein, "Poetry and Grammar," in *Lectures in America* (1935; reprint, Boston: Beacon Press, 1985), pp. 209–10. Subsequently cited in the text as LIA.

11. F. T. Marinetti, "Technical Manifesto of Futurist Literature" (11 May 1912), in *Let's Murder the Moonshine: Selected Writings,* ed. R. W. Flint, trans. R. W. Flint and Arthur A. Coppotelli (Los Angeles: Sun & Moon Press, 1991), pp. 92–93. This volume is subsequently cited in the text as LMM; "Manifesto technico della letteratura futurista," in *Opere di F. T. Marinetti: Teoria e invenzione futurista,* ed. Luciano De Maria (Rome: Mondadori, 1968), pp. 41–42. Subsequently cited in the text as TIF. In *The Futurist Moment: Avant-Garde, Avant Guerre, and the Language of Rupture* (Chicago and London: University of Chicago Press, 1986), I argue that the English Vorticists, including Ezra Pound, derived much of their aesthetic from *parole in libertà.*

12. F. T. Marinetti, "Destruction of Syntax—Imagination without Strings—Words in Freedom 1913," in *Futurist Manifestos,* ed. Umbro Apollonio, trans. Robert Brain et al. (New York: Viking Press, 1973), pp. 95–106; see especially pp. 104–5. Subsequently cited in the text as UA. "Distruzione della sintassi, Immaginazione senza fili, Parole in libertà," in TIF 57–70.

13. LLM 92; cf. "Destruction of Syntax," in UA 103: "Everywhere we tend to suppress the qualifying adjective because it presupposes an arrest in intuition, too minute a definition of the noun."

14. See, for example, Richard Bridgman, *Gertrude Stein in Pieces* (New York: Oxford, 1970), pp. 255–56: "The lectures [*Lectures in America*] were Gertrude Stein's earnest effort to explain and justify the perplexing sprawl of her literary evolution." Stein's efforts to find "a way of naming things . . . without naming them," "sounded surprisingly like automatic writing. . . . Her desire to escape from staleness was commendable. . . . But the actual creation was arbitrary and really only approximate."

15. See Stimpson, "The Mind, the Body, and Gertrude Stein," *Critical Inquiry* 3, no. 3 (spring 1977): 499–503.

16. *The Variorum Edition of the Poems of W. B. Yeats,* ed. Peter Allt and Russell K. Alspach (New York: Macmillan, 1957), p. 515.

17. See UD 2; cf. Terry Castle, review of Ulla E. Dydo, *A Stein Reader,* in *Times Literary Supplement,* 18 February 1994, p. 4. The remarkable thing about Stein's descriptive language, says Castle, is that it is "grounded in actuality": "the perplexing *non sequiturs* must all be read as revivifying gestures, as ways of forcing the reader to 'begin again,' to see the world in a new and more immediate way."

18. Gertrude Stein, "A Transatlantic Interview," in Robert Bartlett Haas, ed., *A Primer for the Gradual Understanding of Gertrude Stein* (Santa Barbara, CA: Black Sparrow Press, 1976), p. 25. Subsequently cited in the text as PGU.

19. See *The Flowers of Friendship: Letters Written to Gertrude Stein,* ed. Donald Gallup (New York: Alfred A. Knopf, 1953), p. 50. Stein had sent James a copy of *Three Lives* when it was published in 1909 and had asked her former teacher what he thought. James responded: "You know how hard it is for me to read novels. Well, I read 30 or 40 pages, and said 'this is a fine new kind of realism—Gertrude Stein is great!' I will go at it carefully when just the right mood comes." Since James died the next year, he did not comment further.

20. Gertrude Stein, *The Autobiography of Alice B. Toklas* (1933), in *Selected Writings of Gertrude Stein,* ed. Carl Van Vechten (New York: Vintage, 1990), p. 223. Subsequently cited in the text as ABT.

21. In "Arthur a Grammar," Stein leaves off the acute accent on the second "e" of "René" for the same reason that she does not use question marks and exclamation points. Structurally, she argues, such punctuation marks are unnecessary, for the sentence should carry its own intonation contour without such props.

22. Johanna Drucker, *The Visible Word: Experimental Typography and Modern Art, 1909–1923* (Chicago and London: University of Chicago Press, 1994), pp. 105–40. Drucker's excellent study is the fullest treatment to date of the semiotic of Marinetti's typography.

23. First published in 1955 in *Painted Lace and Other Pieces (1914–1937),* vol. 5 of the 8-vol. *Yale Edition of the Unpublished Writings of Gertrude Stein,* the 1917 text is reprinted in a corrected version in UD 308–13. In the Yale Edition, the subtitle is printed as the first line of the text. All further references are to Dydo's text, abbreviated as MN.

24. In *Gertrude Stein in Pieces,* Richard Bridgman writes, "Gertrude Stein played upon the name of the leader of the Futurists, Filippo Marinetti, although she made no other reference to him in the portrait" (p. 154). This view is echoed by Ulla E. Dydo, who says in her headnote, "The Italian futurist Marinetti is not the subject of *Marry Nettie.* Rather, the name offered Stein the pun. In this piece done in Mallorca, there is no futurism and no serial composition" (UD 308).

25. Dydo supplies another reason for the reference to "series." "In late March 1916 Carl Van Vechten wrote that if Stein came to America she would be received like Jenny Lind, the famous Swedish soprano. On 18 April Stein answered she was

making 'so much absorbing literature with such attractive titles and even if I could be as popular as Jenny Lind where oh where is the man to publish me in series' (*The Letters of Gertrude Stein and Carl Van Vechten,* 53). She wanted a publisher to take her on and print her seriatim" (UD 308).

26. See "Poetry as Word-System: The Art of Gertrude Stein," in *The Poetics of Indeterminacy: Rimbaud to Cage* (1981; Evanston, IL: Northwestern University Press, 1993), pp. 67–108; *The Dance of the Intellect: Studies in the Poetry of the Pound Tradition* (Cambridge: Cambridge University Press, 1985), pp. 190–93; " 'A Fine New Kind of Realism': Six Stein Styles in Search of a Reader," in *Poetic License: Essays in Modernist and Postmodernist Lyric* (Evanston, IL: Northwestern University Press, 1990), pp. 145–59; "Ninety-Percent Rotarian: Gertrude Stein's Hemingway," *American Literature* 62, no. 4 (December 1990): 668–83.

Chapter Four

1. Samuel Beckett, *Watt* (1953; London: John Calder, 1976), p. 83. Subsequently cited in the text as W.

2. For the publishing history of the *Philosophical Investigations,* see RM, 465–70, 478–84; and the Editors' Note to PI, p. iv.

3. See Carlton Lake, *No Symbols Where None Intended: A Catalogue of Books, Manuscripts and Other Materials Relating to Samuel Beckett in the Collections of the Humanities Research Center* (Austin: University of Texas Humanities Research Center, 1984), p. 75. Subsequently cited in the text as CL. Lake points out that Routledge, for example, dismissed *Watt* as "wild and unintelligible."

4. For the publishing history of *Watt,* see Richard W. Seaver, "Beckett and Merlin," in *Samuel Beckett: I Can't Go On, I'll Go On* (New York: Grove Press, 1976), pp. x–xxv; reprinted in slightly abridged form in S. E. Gontarski, ed., *On Beckett: Essays and Criticism* (New York: Grove Press, 1986), pp. 19–28. For the chronology of the manuscripts and editions, see CL 75–79. Lake comments on the irony that *Watt* was an "eminently respectable, almost chaste" novel (p. 75).

5. Georges Bataille, review of *Molloy* in *Critique* (15 May 1951); reprinted in Lawrence Graver and Raymond Federman, eds., *Samuel Beckett: The Critical Heritage* (London and Boston: Routledge & Kegan Paul, 1979), pp. 50–63; see p. 57. This volume is subsequently cited in the text as LG.

Cf. Maurice Nadeau, review of *Molloy* in *Combat,* 12 April 1951 (reprinted in LG 50–54): "Language . . . dissolves into nothingness (annihilates itself) as soon as it is established, erases, instantly its faintest traces," p. 53; and Bernard Pingaud in *Esprit,* September 1951 (reprinted in LG 67–70). " 'Molloy,' " writes Pingaud, "appears like a monstrous and disturbing myth, mysterious in its origins. . . . this excessively human and, despite its arbitrariness, so deeply credible picture of degradation is not without seduction. We live in a time of despair, where wrecks are everywhere, and Molloy is a wreck, hardly a man, an absence of a man" (pp. 67–68).

6. Maurice Blanchot, review of *L'Innommable* in *Nouvelle Revue Française,* October 1953; reprinted in LG 116–21; see p. 119.

7. Theodor W. Adorno, "Trying to Understand *Endgame*" (1958), in *Notes to Literature,* vol. 1, trans. Shierry Weber Nicholson (New York: Columbia University Press, 1991), p. 251.

8. See Michael Robinson, *The Long Sonata of the Dead* (New York: Grove Press, 1969), p. 125. Subsequently cited in the text as LSD.

9. See Lawrence Harvey, *Samuel Beckett, Poet and Critic* (Princeton: Princeton University Press, 1973), pp. 354, 359. Subsequently cited in the text as LH.

10. Thomas J. Cousineau, *"Watt:* Language as Interdiction and Consolation," *Journal of Beckett Studies,* 1979; reprinted in S. E. Gontarski, ed., *The Beckett Studies Reader* (Gainesville: University Presses of Florida, 1993), p. 64. Cf. Gottfried Büttner's full-length study *Samuel Beckett's Novel "Watt"* (Philadelphia: University of Pennsylvania Press, 1984). One of *Watt's* "central themes," declares Büttner (p. 125), is "that all existence is misery, and birth, which ushers in a life of inevitable suffering, is itself a lamentable event."

11. See introduction, note 6.

12. Samuel Beckett, *Murphy* (1938; New York: Grove Press, 1957), p. 26.

13. Samuel Beckett, *Disjecta: Miscellaneous Writings and a Dramatic Fragment,* ed. Ruby Cohn (New York: Grove Press, 1984), pp. 171–72. Subsequently cited in the text as DMW. The letter, originally written in German, is reproduced on pp. 51–54; the translation cited above is by Martin Esslin.

14. Peggy Guggenheim, *Out of This Century: The Informal Memoirs of Peggy Guggenheim* (New York: Dial Press, 1946), p. 197. Guggenheim is detailing her affair with Beckett in late 1937–38.

15. Beckett's movements during the war years are known in broad outline, but little attention has been paid to the role the war played in Beckett's work. For the facts themselves, I am indebted to Deirdre Bair, *Samuel Beckett* (New York: Harcourt Brace Jovanovich, 1978), chapters 13 and 14 passim. Subsequently cited in the text as DB. On p. 331, Bair points out that "Immediate comparisons spring to mind between Beckett and Watt, Mr. Knott's house and World War II, the asylum [where Watt is confined] and Roussillon." But she does not take the question any further.

One critic who does is Hugh Kenner, who notes in *The Reader's Guide to Samuel Beckett* (New York: Farrar Straus, 1973) that the relaying of information in *Watt* recalls Beckett's actual situation in his Resistance cell, the constant fear of possible leaks and betrayals leading to a sense that communication, far from being a natural give and take, is something *extorted* (see pp. 72–75).

16. See CL 75–76. Notebook 5 also has the first drafts, dated "Novembre-Janvier 46/48," of a novel called *L'Absent,* which was to be *Malone meurt.* Page 99 has the note "End of continuation of Watt. Conclusion in Notebook VI." Lake ex-

plains: "Although in Notebook I, Beckett placed the completion of *Watt* in 1945, he concludes the sixth notebook with "Dec. 28th 1944 / End." In that case, *Watt* was essentially completed while Beckett was in Roussillon.

17. See DB 311–12; Enoch Brater, *Why Beckett* (London: Thames and Hudson, 1989), pp. 42–43.

18. M. R. D. Foot, *SOE in France: An Account of the Work of the British Special Operations Executive in France 1940–1944* (London: Her Majesty's Stationery Office, 1966), p. 94. Subsequently cited in the text as SOE.

19. See DB, chapter 14 passim.

20. Vladimir tells Estragon, "Nous avons fait les vendanges, tiens, un nommé Bonnelly, à Roussillon." In the English version, Beckett dropped this line.

21. See, respectively, Richard Coe, *Samuel Beckett* (New York: Grove Press, 1968), p. 38; Michael Robinson, LSD 121; Ruby Cohn, *Back to Beckett* (Princeton: Princeton University Press, 1973), p. 42. Cohn compares Watt's entrance into Mr. Knott's house to the knight's entrance into the Chapel Perilous; p. 52. All three critics also refer to the Christ references in *Watt,* the protagonist undergoing a kind of Passion.

22. See, for example, Jennie Skerl, "Fritz Mauthner's 'Critique of Language' in Samuel Beckett's *Watt,*" *Contemporary Literature* 15, no. 4 (autumn 1974): 474–87. Skerl writes, "Samuel Beckett's *Watt* is the story of modern man's confrontation with the basic irrationality of existence and his inability to comprehend or communicate this ultimate reality. As a modern rationalist and descendant of Descartes, the novel's protagonist attempts to understand his experience in terms of twentieth-century rationalist and empiricist philosophies" (p. 474). Subsequently cited in the text as JSK. Cf. Michael Robinson, LSD 121–30; Edouard Morot-Sir, "Samuel Beckett and Cartesian Emblems," in *Samuel Beckett: The Art of Rhetoric,* North Carolina Studies in the Romance Languages and Literatures Symposia, no. 5, ed. Edouard Morot-Sir, Howard Harper, and Douglas McMillan III (Chapel Hill: University of North Carolina Press, 1976), pp. 25–104; Hugh Kenner, *Samuel Beckett: A Critical Study* (Berkeley and Los Angeles: University of California Press, 1968), pp. 117–32. Subsequently cited in the text as HKSB.

23. See Michel Beausang, "*Watt:* Logique, démence, aphasie," in *Beckett avant Beckett, Essais sur le jeune Beckett (1930–1945),* rassemblés par Jean-Michel Rabaté (Paris: P.E.N.S., 1984), pp. 168–72.

24. The word does not appear in the OED or in the various scientific dictionaries. It is evidently a coinage—*raven* (black, predatory) + *astron* (astronomer)—hence a rare form of raven or perhaps a black astronomical instrument similar to a telescope. How is it that Watt is able to identify this object?

25. Tom Driver, interview with Samuel Beckett, *Columbia University Forum,* summer 1961, pp. 21–25; reprinted in LG 217–23; see p. 218.

26. Jacqueline Hoefer, "*Watt,*" *Perspective* 101, no. 3 (autumn 1959); reprinted

in Martin Esslin, ed., *Samuel Beckett, A Collection of Critical Essays* (Englewood Cliffs, NJ: Prentice-Hall, 1965), pp. 62–76. Subsequently cited in the text as JH. Ruby Cohn, in an essay reprinted in the same volume, "Philosophical Fragments in the Works of Samuel Beckett" (*Criticism* 6, no. 1 [1964], pp. 169–77), expands on Hoefer's argument, suggesting that Louis in *Murphy* is French for "Ludwig" and is another allusion to Wittgenstein (see p. 174). "In Beckett's *Watt*," says Cohn, "the hero acts like Wittgenstein's prize student—using his senses, logic, and language with maddening meticulousness." And further: the solipsistic circle of Beckett's heroes derives from Wittgenstein (p. 175). See also Raymond Federman, *Journey to Chaos: Samuel Beckett's Early Fiction* (Berkeley: University of California Press, 1965), pp. 120–22; Michael Robinson, LSD 122.

27. John Fletcher, *The Novels of Samuel Beckett* (New York: Barnes and Noble, 1964), pp. 58–59. Cf. Linda Ben-Zvi, "Samuel Beckett, Fritz Mauthner, and the Limits of Language," *PMLA* 95 (March 1980): 183–200.

28. The claim that Wittgenstein was a logical positivist is repeated by critics throughout the fifties and sixties; even Hugh Kenner calls Wittgenstein "the father of Logical Positivism" (HKSB 58). For a definitive critique of this reading of Wittgenstein, see Jacques Bouveresse (introduction, note 25).

29. E. M. Cioran, "Encounters with Beckett," trans. Raymond Federman, *Partisan Review* 43, no. 2 (1976): 280–85; reprinted in LG 334–39; see p. 338.

30. In the original German, the two words are *O B E N/N E B O*. The proposition in question has provided the inspiration for Steve McCaffery's *Evoba: The Investigation Meditations, 1976–78* (Toronto: Coach House Press, 1987).

Chapter Five

1. For an overview of the relationship between the two writers, see Martin Esslin, "Beckett and Bernhard: A Comparison," *Modern Austrian Literature* 18, no. 2 (1985): 67–78.

2. For an excellent discussion of the range of meanings of T #5.6, in relation to its sources in Kant and Schopenhauer, see David Pears, *The False Prison: A Study of the Development of Wittgenstein's Philosophy,* vol. 1 (Oxford: Clarendon Press, 1987), pp. 152–90. Subsequently cited in the text as DP.

3. The case of Peter Handke is somewhat different. Handke is perhaps the most overtly Wittgensteinian of Austrian writers; he has repeatedly insisted that "It is not properly understood that literature is made with words, not with the things described by words. . . . it is words that constitute the reality of literature" (*Ich bin ein Bewohner des Elfenbeinturms* [Frankfurt: Suhrkamp, 1972], p. 29, my translation). In keeping with such statements and Handke's direct allusions to the *Tractatus* and *Philosophical Investigations,* plays like the 1968 *Kaspar* have been called Wittgensteinian, but Handke's interest in the power of language to manipulate, and

especially in the ways specific technological discourses control and police individuals, is more properly Foucaultian than Wittgensteinian.

This is not surprising when one bears in mind that Handke, born in 1942 during the war, represents the ethos of a later generation than Bernhard's or Bachmann's. See Gunther Sergooris, *Peter Handke und die Sprache* (Bonn: Bouvier Verlag Herbert Grundmann, 1979); Werner Thuswaldner, *Sprach- Und Gattungsexperiment Bei Peter Handke: Praxis und Theorie* (Salzburg: Verlag Alfred Winter, 1976).

One of Handke's most genuinely Wittgensteinian works (written after the above monographs appeared) is his 1992 *The Hour We Knew Nothing of Each Other,* which dispenses with language altogether in favor of tableau and pantomime. The inability of verbal or, in this case, visual elements to name and to refer is powerfully dramatized.

4. Born in 1926, Bachmann was an impressionable teenager during the war. In an interview of 24 December 1971, she remembers: "There was a specific moment which destroyed my childhood. The entry of Hitler's troops into Klagenfurt. It was something so terrible, that my memory begins with that day: with that early sorrow, whose intensity was perhaps never to be repeated. Naturally, I didn't understand all this at the time, in the way an adult would understand it. But this enormous brutality, which could be sensed, this screaming, singing and marching—the origin of my fear of death. A whole army intruded on our quiet peaceful Carinthia." See Bachmann, *Wir Müssen wahre Sätze finden: Gespräche und Interviews* (Munich: R. Pier & Co., 1991), p. 111. Subsequently cited in the text as IBGI. Translations here and elsewhere, unless otherwise noted, are my own.

For Bernhard's assessment of his childhood, see *Gathering Evidence: A Memoir,* trans. David McLintock (New York: Alfred A. Knopf, 1985). In Chapter 1, Bernhard gives a moving account of his mother's "disgrace," escape to Holland, and subsequent bitterness.

5. "In Vienna," Bachmann explained to an interviewer, "we were always waging a fierce fight against German metaphysics" (IBGI 136).

6. The near-riots produced by the performance of *Heldenplatz* at the Burgtheater in 1988 is the subject of a fascinating article called "Thomas Bernhard" by Gitta Honegger, in *Partisan Review* 58, no. 3. (Summer 1991): 493–505.

7. Ingeborg Bachmann, *Werke,* ed. Christine Koschel, Inge von Weidenbaum, and Clemens Münster, 4 vols. (Munich: Suhrkamp, 1978); vol. 1: *Gedichte, Hörspiele, Libretti, Übersetzungen,* p. 56. This edition is subsequently cited in the text as IBW. Mark Anderson's *In the Storm of Roses: Selected Poems,* trans. and ed. Mark Anderson (Princeton: Princeton University Press, 1986), is subsequently cited in the text as ISR. Peter Filkins's more recent translation, *Songs in Flight: The Collected Poems of Ingeborg Bachmann* (New York: Marsilio, 1994, subsequently cited in the text as PF), has the advantage of including all of Bachmann's extant lyric, but Fil-

kins's translations are often quite unreliable; for example, he translates *Die Gestundete Zeit* as *Borrowed Time* and loses the complexity of the "mortgage" metaphor in the title poem. When neither Anderson nor Filkins is cited, the translation is my own.

8. In his *Ingeborg Bachmann* (Munich: Beck, 1988), Peter Beicken cites, as possible sources, Klopstock's "Die frühen Gräber," Goethe's "Anakreons Grab," Höltys's "Die Mainacht," Hölderlin's "Abendphantasie," C. F. Meyer's "Wetterleuchten," Trakl's "Das Gewitter," and Rilke's Rose Poems (p. 94). In English, an interesting analogue is the dream-like sequence in Chapter 1 of D. H. Lawrence's *Sons and Lovers,* in which the pregnant Mrs. Morel, pushed out the door by her husband after a late-night quarrel, is pursued (and then comforted by) the seemingly gigantic flowers in her garden.

9. Mark Anderson translates "fremden" as "foreign," which is, I think, more restrictive than "alien." It should be noted that "fremden" carries the broader meaning of "strange." A stranger, foreign or otherwise, is "ein Fremder" in German.

10. Paul Celan, *Poems,* a Bilingual Edition, trans. Michael Hamburger (New York: Persea Books, 1980), pp. 180–81. Line 7 may be literally translated: "With everything, what has room inside it."

11. Peter Filkins, who also poses this question in his introduction, argues that her turn to prose is not quite the departure it is often taken to be because the "major strategy of the poetry is its use of 'fragments' welded into mosaic patterns by the silence they seek to break. In the prose fiction and drama, the same strategy occurs, so that the question of genre is largely irrelevant" (PF xxviii). This explanation, I think, skirts the gender issue as well as the relation of lyric, as Bachmann inherited it, to ideology.

12. ISR 43, my italics. Mark Anderson notes that the references to the loved one as female here and elsewhere in Bachmann's poetry have given rise to speculation that hers is a lesbian poetics. He argues, rightly I think, that such speculation is unwarranted, the gender transposition being too obvious and conventional to suggest the homoerotic (ISR 8). But it is true that in some of Bachmann's short stories (e.g., "A Step toward Gomorrah") and certainly in *Malina,* gender identity becomes a vexed issue.

13. Paul Celan, "Antwort auf eine Umfrage der Librairie Flinker, Paris" (1958), in Celan, *Gesammelte Werke,* III (Frankfurt: Suhrkamp Verlag, 1983), p. 167.

14. Thomas Bernhard, *Gesammelte Gedichte,* ed. Volker Bohn (Frankfurt: Suhrkamp, 1991), p. 55. Subsequently cited in the text as GG.

15. Ogden renders "vorstellende" as "presenting"; Pears renders the sentence, "There is no such thing as the subject that thinks or entertains ideas." I find both inadequate. "Vorstellende" means, roughly, "conceptualizing," but "imagining" would also be adequate.

16. Thomas Bernhard, letter to Hilde Spiel (1971), in *Ver Sacrum: Neue Hefte*

für Kunst und Literatur (Wien-München, 1971), p. 47; cited in Albrecht Weber, "Wittgenstein's Gestalt und Theorie und ihre Wirkung im Werk Thomas Bernhards," *Oesterreich in Geschichte und Literatur* 25, no. 2 (1981): 86–104; see p. 99.

17. *Correction* (*Korrektur* [Frankfurt: Suhrkamp, 1975]), trans. Sophie Wilkins (Chicago and London: University of Chicago Press, 1990), is the story of an Austrian scientist named Roithamer (the Wittgenstein double), born to a wealthy family in the Aurach Valley, who lives and works in Cambridge, England, but cannot escape his love-hate obsession with his native Altensam. Like Wittgenstein, Roithamer renounces his family fortune and dedicates himself to constructing a geometrically pure house for his sister—in this case a cone, set in the isolated forest where they spent their childhood. Roithamer's obsessive love for his sister is displaced by a similar obsession to design the perfect house; when finished, the Cone is so fully "corrected" that his sister cannot bear it and kills herself, a suicide that triggers Roithamer's own. The narrator who tells this story is in turn obsessed by Roithamer, undertakes to edit his papers after his death, and "corrects" his friend's work to the extent of entering into it and almost succumbing to Roithamer's fate. The third character is the more normal Hoeller, like Roithamer a taxidermist, but one who functions in the everyday world of marriage and children. Hoeller's attic is where Roithamer has produced his work on Altensam and where the narrator comes to live as he re-creates his friend's life.

The play *Ritter, Dene, Voss* (Frankfurt: Suhrkamp, 1984), reprinted in *Histrionics: Three Plays,* trans. Peter Jansen and Kenneth Northcott (Chicago and London: University of Chicago Press, 1990), received its title from the names of three famous German actors: Ilse Ritter, Kirsten Dene, and Gert Voss. In the dark, sardonic play, the actress-sisters Ritter and Dene bring home their brother Voss (an amalgam of Ludwig and Paul Wittgenstein) from the mental hospital where he has spent many years, and he proceeds to turn the tables on them, calling into question their every "good" motive and debunking the bourgeois household in which he was raised. In the course of the play, there are repeated allusions to Wittgenstein's aphorisms and propositions.

But Bernhard also uses a good bit of poetic license. In both *Korrektur* and *Ritter, Dene, Voss,* Wittgenstein is depicted as motivated at least in part by an incestuous feeling for his sister, which is not at all documented, and his "madness" and hatred of bourgeois values are in great excess of anything we find in Wittgenstein's biography.

18. Thomas Bernhard, *Wittgenstein's Nephew: A Friendship,* trans. David McLintock (Chicago: University of Chicago Press, 1988), p. 3. Subsequently cited in the text as WN. The German original is *Wittgensteins Neffe: Eine Freundschaft* (Frankfurt: Suhrkamp, 1982), subsequently cited in the text as WNEF.

19. In the original this distribution is similar, although the count is not exactly the same. If anything, in German the repetitions are even more emphatic: "Der **Pav-**

illon Ludwig war im Augenblick *seine Residenz.* Und ich zögerte auf einmal, ob es ratsam sei, von mir aus, also vom **Pavillon Hermann** aus, eine Verbindung zum **Pavillon Ludwig** herzustellen, ob es uns beiden nicht eher Schaden als Nutzen bringe. Denn wer weiß, in was für Zustand der Paul sich wirklich befindet, möglicherweise in einem, der mir nur schädlich sein kann und es daher besser ist, ich melde mich vorläufig gar nicht, ich stelle keine Verbindung zwischen dem **Pavillon Hermann** und dem **Pavillion Ludwig** her. Umgekehrt, dachte ich, könnte ja mein Auftreten im **Pavillon Ludwig,** noch dazu ein überraschendes, für meinen Freund auch eine verheerende Wirkung haben. Tatsächlich fürchtete ich jetzt auf einmal ein Zusammentreffen und ich dachte, unsere Freundin Irina entscheiden zu lassen, ob eine Kontaktaufnahme zwischen dem **Pavillon Hermann** und dem **Pavillon Ludwig** angebracht sei oder nicht" (WNEF 52–53).

20. At least Bernhard interprets the smoking "accident" as a suicide: see his "Auslöschung" (1986), in Andrea Stoll, ed., *Ingeborg Bachmann's "Malina"* (Frankfurt: Suhrkamp, 1992), pp. 29–43. This collection is subsequently cited in the text as AS.

21. Ingeborg Bachmann, *Malina* (1971; Frankfurt: Suhrkamp, 1991), pp. 7–8; subsequently cited in the text as MA. For an English translation, see *Malina,* trans. Philip Boehm (New York and London: Holmes & Meier, 1990), pp. 1–2; subsequently cited in the text as M. Since the Boehm translation is a very free one, I have preferred to give my own translations of most of the citations, especially of the dialogue passages, where word order and repetition are very important.

22. A number of the novel's original reviewers dismissed it as kitsch; see, for example, Helmut Heißenbüttel, "Im Namen der Liebe. Ingeborg Bachmann weicht ins 19. Jahrhundert zurück," *Christ und Welt,* 4 September 1971; reprinted in AS 119–21. For an overview of the novel's reception, see Andrea Stoll, "Kontroverse und Polarisierung: Die 'Malina'-Rezeption als Schlüssel der Bachmann-Forschung," in AS 149–67.

23. In the early fifties, the *Tractatus* was barely known in Wittgenstein's native city. As for the *Philosophical Investigations,* published by Macmillan (London) in 1953 in a bilingual edition, the Suhrkamp edition did not appear until 1960 and even then, Bachmann recalls, she had to persuade the publisher to bring it and the *Tractatus* out in an accessible paperback reprint; see ISR 12; cf. interview with Harald Grass, 1 May 1965, IBGI 58; interview with Karol Sauerland, May 1973, IBGI 135–36.

24. Ingeborg Bachmann, "Ludwig Wittgenstein—zu einem Kapitel der jüngsten Philosophiegeschichte," *Frankfurter Hefte: Zeitschrift für Kultur und Politik,* July 1953; reprinted in IBW, vol. 4, pp. 12–23.

25. IBGI 84. This important interview with Ekkehart Rudolph (23 March 1971, IBGI 81–92) is also reprinted in AS 129–33.

26. MA 40. The German punning is on "Tücken"/"Mücken" ("Das Telefon hat eben seine Tücken / Wie? Es redet dauert jemand hinein. Mücken, wieso"). "Tics"/ "sticks," which I take from Boehm, captures the general sense of the passage.

27. I have followed Boehm in translating "glücklich" as "happy" here, but "glücklich" is more emphatic than "happy," closer to "overjoyed," "delighted," "ecstatic," and so on.

28. Ezra Pound, "A Retrospect" (1918), in *Literary Essays of Ezra Pound,* ed. T. S. Eliot (London: Faber and Faber, 1954), pp. 4–5.

Chapter Six

1. Jean-François Lyotard, "Wittgenstein 'After' " (1983), in Lyotard, *Political Writings,* trans. Bill Redings and Paul German (Minneapolis: University of Minnesota Press, 1993), pp. 21–22.

2. Ian Hacking, "Wittgenstein the Psychologist," *New York Review of Books,* 1 April 1982, p. 42.

3. M. M. Bakhtin, *The Dialogic Imagination: Four Essays,* ed. Michael Holquist, trans. Caryl Emerson and Michael Holquist (Austin and London: University of Texas Press, 1981), pp. 285, 287. Subsequently cited in the text as DI.

4. For a good short discussion of Bakhtin's distinction between "monologic" lyric and the "dialogic" novel, a novel "whose language is still 'warm' from its daily use," see Gary Saul Morson and Caryl Emerson, "Introduction: Rethinking Bakhtin," in *Rethinking Bakhtin: Extensions and Challenges,* ed. Gary Saul Morson and Caryl Emerson (Evanston, IL: Northwestern University Press, 1989), pp. 52–55. Cf., in the same volume, Paul de Man, "Dialogue and Dialogism," pp. 105–14, and Matthew Roberts, "Poetics Hermeneutics Dialogics: Bakhtin and Paul de Man," pp. 115–34.

Morson's discussion of Bakhtin's ethical assumptions, here and elsewhere, shows that there is a definite affinity between Bakhtin and Wittgenstein, although the latter's name does not come up. In "Bakhtin and the Present Moment," *The American Scholar,* spring 1991, pp. 201–22, for example, Morson discusses Bakhtin's rejection of "theoretism" and notes, "Bakhtin repeatedly stressed that, although norms and rules are often helpful, ultimately ethics is a matter of sensitivity to particular cases" (p. 207). An oddly Wittgensteinian note!

5. In *Self and Sensibility in Contemporary American Poetry* (Cambridge and New York: Cambridge University Press, 1984), Charles Altieri describes this "scenic mode" as "the concern for modest, highly crafted narrative structures producing moments of sudden illumination and [the] desire to correlate sincerity with rhetorical self-consciousness" (p. 5). Its "central aim . . . is not to interpret experience but to extend language to its limits in order to establish poignant awareness of what lies beyond words" (p. 10). Subsequently cited in the text as S & S.

6. Andreas Huyssen, *After the Great Divide: Modernism, Mass Culture, Postmodernism* (Bloomington: Indiana University Press, 1988), passim.

7. Henri Lefebvre, *Critique of Everyday Life,* 2d ed., vol. 1, trans. John Moore (1958; London and New York: Verso, 1991), pp. 12–13.

8. See GH 204; cf. PI #410, PO 228, 269. The sentence and its correlatives are discussed more fully in chapter 2.

9. Guy Davenport, "Narrative Tone and Form," in *The Geography of the Imagination: Forty Essays* (San Francisco: North Point, 1981), p. 311.

10. I have translated "kochen" as "cooking" rather than the rarer (and exclusively British) word "cookery" and have made a few other slight changes so as to render Wittgenstein's idiomatic German more accurately.

11. Charles Bernstein, *A Poetics* (Cambridge and London: Harvard University Press, 1992), p. 117. Bernstein goes on to argue that there is "no longer one imperial standard for all the English-speaking people of England, with its dozens of dialects, much less for all of Britain and Ireland. By *imperial* I mean a single, imposed standard for correctness of speaking or writing or thinking or knowing; I mean a unitary cultural canon, an artifice denying its artificiality" (p. 117).

12. Consider, for example, the CBS-Los Angeles program "Eyewitness News at Noon," currently monitored by Tricia Toyota, Linda Alvarez, and Maclovio Perez. Despite the racial and gender diversity of these newscasters (one Japanese-American, one Chicana, one Chicano), their tele-idiom is nearly identical.

13. Robert Creeley, *Away,* illustrations by Bobbie Creeley (Santa Barbara: Black Sparrow Press, 1976), p. 11. Subsequently cited in the text as A. The whole book, minus the illustrations, is reprinted in *The Collected Poems of Robert Creeley, 1945–1975* (Berkeley and Los Angeles: University of California Press, 1982), pp. 583–630. Subsequently cited in the text as RCCP.

14. The notation used here is standard in linguistics textbooks: ($'$) primary stress, ($`$) secondary stress, ($//$) caesura, ($/$) plus juncture or breath stop.

15. Robert Pinsky, *The Situation of Poetry: Contemporary Poetry and Its Traditions* (Princeton: Princeton University Press, 1976), pp. 10–11.

16. John Perreault, "Holding Back and Letting Go," *New York Times Book Review,* 19 November 1967, p. 97; cited by John Thompson in "An Alphabet of Poets," *New York Review of Books,* 1 August 1968, p. 35; reprinted in John Wilson, ed., *Robert Creeley's Life and Work: A Sense of Increment* (Ann Arbor: University of Michigan Press, 1987), pp. 153–74; see pp. 172–74. This collection is subsequently cited in the text as JWRC. See also Reed Whittemore, review of *Pieces, New Republic,* 11 October 1969, pp. 25–26; reprinted in JWRC, pp. 236–38. For the *Times Literary Supplement* review, see John Wilson, introduction to JWRC, p. 1, p. 19, n. 1, which refers the reader to John Berryman's poem "In & Out," in *Love & Fame* (New York: Farrar Straus & Giroux, 1970), p. 24. The stanzas in question, using the Berryman persona Henry, go like this:

'Dear Mr. Creeley, A Reviewer in *The Times*
considering 200 poems of yours

> produced over a period of fifteen years
> adjudged them 'crushingly dull'; my view too,
>
> though you won't suppose of course I read them all.
> Sir, you are trivial.
> Pray do not write to me again. Pitch defileth.
> Yours faithfully, Henry.'

17. Harold Bloom, *The Western Canon: The Book and School of the Ages* (San Diego: Harcourt Brace Jovanovich, 1994), appendix. There are, of course, significant exceptions: see the long essays by Charles Altieri, *Enlarging the Temple: New Directions in American Poetry during the 1960s* (Lewisburg, PA: Bucknell University Press, 1979), pp. 170–93, and S & S 103–31; Robert von Hallberg, *American Poetry and Culture, 1945–1980* (Cambridge: Harvard University Press, 1985), pp. 36–53; and Sherman Paul, *The Lost America of Love: Rereading Robert Creeley, Edward Dorn, and Robert Duncan* (Baton Rouge: Louisiana State University Press, 1981), pp. 3–73. There are many excellent essays in the *boundary 2:* Robert Creeley issue (6, nos. 2 and 3 [spring/fall 1978]), as well as in Carroll F. Terrell's collection, *Robert Creeley: The Poet's Workshop* (Orono, ME: National Poetry Foundation, 1984).

But even Charles Altieri has expressed substantive reservations about the minimalism of the late work. "When the self becomes only a set of abstract relations," he says in S & S, "the expanded field of play becomes a flexible cage" (p. 127). And again, "The poet threatens to appear only as someone who suffers and needs, and the space he creates for motion seems often to close in on itself with terrifying repetitiveness" (p. 129). Cf. Lynn Keller, *Re-Making It New: Contemporary American Poetry and the Modernist Tradition* (Cambridge and New York: Cambridge University Press, 1987): "Having lost interest in the modernist's careful selection of fresh images and particular formulations, Creeley does not intend to provide a dramatic or imagistic focus for the reader's feelings. Yet his language games, unlike Ashbery's or Bishop's explorations of the possibilities of worn and ordinary speech, fail to provide a rich enough substitute to sustain the reader's imaginative or emotional engagement in the poet's discoveries" (p. 182).

18. Robert Creeley, "The Creative," in *Was That a Real Poem and Other Essays,* ed. Donald Allen, with a chronology by Mary Novik (Bolinas, CA: Four Seasons, 1979), pp. 33–34. This collection is subsequently cited in the text as WRP.

19. In a letter to me (30 August 1994), Creeley explains that he first came across Wittgenstein in Louis Zukofsky's *Bottom: On Shakespeare,* part II of which he published in the *Black Mountain Review* in 1955. *Bottom* (1963; reprint, Berkeley and London: University of California Press, 1987) contains dozens of passages from Wittgenstein, almost all from the *Tractatus*—passages that Zukofsky relates to the Shakespeare extracts, especially from *Midsummer Night's Dream, Romeo and Juliet,*

and *Hamlet,* that he is discussing in this extraordinary Commonplace Book. See pp. 46–47, where *Tractatus* #2.0121, 2.0123, and 2.0131 are read against *Hamlet,* III, iv, 125: "A tone must have *a* pitch, the object of the / the sense of touch *a* hardness."

Cf. Creeley, "On the Road: Notes on Artists and Poets 1950–1965" (1974), in WRP 84; Creeley, "Some Senses of the Commonplace" (lecture at New College of California, 1991), reprinted in Tom Clark, *Robert Creeley and the Genius of the American Common Place* (New York: New Directions, 1993), pp. 81–116. The Wittgenstein sentence is cited on p. 106. This whole essay is very important for an understanding of Creeley's approach to the "commonplace."

20. Hugh Kenner, review of *The Collected Poems of Robert Creeley,* in *New York Times Book Review,* 7 August 1983; reprinted in JWRC 410–14; see p. 412. See also Russell Banks, "Notes on Creeley's *Pieces,*" in JWRC 248–52; Linda W. Wagner, "Creeley's Late Poems: Contexts," *boundary 2:* Creeley issue: 301–8. Wagner was one of the first to see the connection between the later poems and Wittgenstein, particularly *Zettel.* See also Peter Quartermain, *Disjunctive Poetics: From Gertrude Stein and Louis Zukofsky to Susan Howe* (Cambridge and London: Cambridge University Press, 1992), pp. 155–60.

21. Robert Creeley, "A Note," *Nomad,* winter-spring 1960; reprinted in *A Quick Graph* (San Francisco: Four Seasons Foundation, 1970), pp. 32–33. Subsequently cited in the text as QG.

22. On the last page, Creeley gives us the signature *"San Cristobal, N. M., May 29, 1974,"* but the text itself is evasive as to setting.

23. Ron Silliman, "The New Sentence," in *The New Sentence* (New York: Roof Books, 1987), pp. 89–91. Subsequently cited in the text as NS.

24. Ron Silliman, "The Chinese Notebook," in *The Age of Huts* (New York: Roof Books, 1986), pp. 43–66. Subsequently cited in the text as AH.

25. Alan Davies, "?S to .S," *The Difficulties:* Ron Silliman Issue, ed. Tom Beckett, special issue of *The Difficulties* 2.2 (1985): 77. In this version, Silliman's entries are printed in italics, Davies's responses follow them in roman. This issue of *The Difficulties* is subsequently cited in the text as DRS.

26. Alan Davies, *Signage* (New York: Roof Books, 1987), pp. 109–10.

27. Edward Foster, "An Interview with Rosmarie Waldrop," *Talisman* 6 (spring 1991): 31, 38–39.

28. Rosmarie Waldrop, *The Reproduction of Profiles* (New York: New Directions, 1987). Subsequently cited in the text as RP.

29. Here Waldrop may be alluding playfully to the great scene in Thomas Mann's *Magic Mountain,* in which the mysterious Claudia Chauchat appears at Hans Castorp's door and reminds him (in French) not to forget to return her pencil.

30. W. B. Yeats, "The Wild Swans at Coole," in *The Collected Works of W. B. Yeats,* vol. 1, *The Poems,* ed. Richard J. Finneran (New York: Macmillan, 1989), pp. 131–32.

31. Lyn Hejinian, "The Composition of the Cell," in *The Cold of Poetry* (Los Angeles: Sun & Moon Press, 1994), pp. 111–24; see p. 111. Subsequently cited in the text as CPO.

32. Lyn Hejinian, *The Cell* (Los Angeles: Sun & Moon Press, 1992), p. 7. Subsequently cited in the text as CELL. Note that the indented portion above counts as part of the same line, new lines beginning always at the left margin.

33. Lyn Hejinian, "The Rejection of Closure," *Poetics Journal* 4: Women and Language Issue (May 1984): 134–36. Subsequently cited in the text as RC.

34. "The Person" appears in CPO 143–81.

35. Lyn Hejinian, "The Person and Description," in symposium on "The Poetics of Everyday Life," *Poetics Journal* 9 (1991): 166. Subsequently cited in the text as PEL.

36. T #5.631. I have retranslated this passage because it seems to me misleading to refer to "Glieder" as "members" and to translate "nicht die Rede sein" as "mention could *not* be made."

Coda

1. Joseph Kosuth, "The Play of the Unsayable: A Preface and Ten Remarks on Art and Wittgenstein," first published as the preface to the catalogue *Das Spiel des Unsagbaren: Ludwig Wittgenstein und die Kunst des 20. Jahrhunderts* (Vienna: Wiener Secession, 1989), reprinted in Kosuth, *Art after Philosophy and After: Collected Writings, 1966–1990,* ed. Gabriele Guercio (Cambridge and London: MIT Press, 1991), p. 249. Subsequently cited in the text as AAP.

2. Joseph Kosuth, *Letters from Wittgenstein, Abridged in Ghent* (Uitgevers: Imschoot, 1992). Subsequently cited in the text as JKAG. Kosuth reproduces *Letters from Ludwig Wittgenstein with a Memoir* by Paul Engelmann, ed. B. F. McGuinness, trans. L. Furtmüller (Oxford: Basil Blackwell, 1967); subsequently cited in the text as PE. The page numbers in the two are identical.

3. In the later twenties, Engelmann became a Zionist; he emigrated to Tel Aviv in 1934 and remained there until his death in 1963; see RM 228–29 and cf. Joseph Schächter, preface to PE ix–x.

4. See PE 58–59. This letter concerns the mysterious "Confession" Wittgenstein had drafted at Cambridge in 1936 and distributed to some of his friends, including Engelmann; see RM 367–68.

5. See RM 235–38. "[Wittgenstein's] role in the design of the house," writes Monk, "was concerned chiefly with the design of the windows, doors, window-locks and radiators" (p. 236). But the Engelmann and Wittgenstein sketchbooks (see below) indicate that his role was much broader.

6. See Paul Wijdeveld, *Ludwig Wittgenstein, Architect* (Cambridge, MA: MIT Press, 1994), pp. 51–55. Subsequently cited in the text as LWA.

When, for example, Engelmann, who had become Loos's first assistant after the war, renovated the interior of Neuwaldegg, the Wittgenstein family's house in the Viennese suburb by that name, Wittgenstein's oral criticisms prompted Engelmann to reply, "I regret very much that you do not like my work for Neuwaldegg, as appears from the letter of your *Fraülein* sister; although I did the best I could and though nothing false can be found in the plans, I am not sure whether I succeeded" (20 December 1917; cited in LWA 51).

7. PE 17–18. Cited in LWA 24. The German phrase "bis zur Unmöglichkeit verschmockt" is more properly translated as "impossibly kitschified" or "hopelessly phony."

In his memoir, Engelmann has a chapter called "Kraus, Loos, and Wittgenstein," which argues for the close conjunction of the three, glossing over what are very real differences; see PE 122–32.

8. Indeed, whereas Wittgenstein's facade cannot be "read" as anything else, Loos's window and plane arrangement looks like a human face with two "eyes" above the "mouth" area.

9. See Hermine Wittgenstein, "My Brother Ludwig," in *Recollections of Wittgenstein,* ed. Rush Rhees (Oxford: Blackwell's, 1984), pp. 6–8, and citation in LWA 168–69.

10. The photos in figure 10–17 are from Joseph Kosuth, *Letters from Wittgenstein* and are used with the permission of Mr. Kosuth. According to the photo credits on the book's final page, Kosuth found these pictures in the Photoarchive De Gentenaar. Almost all the pictures on the left-hand pages are taken by Michiel Hendryckx, the ones on the right-hand pages by Wouter Rawoens.

11. JKAG 5. L. Furtmüller translates "Hundedreck" as "just muck," which is hardly accurate.

12. PE 10. Furtmüller translates "Geschwätz" as "twaddle"; chapter 1 above, p. 31.

Boldface numbers indicate pages on which main treatments of subjects can be found; italic numbers refer to pages with illustrations.